THE JUMPS

and Training

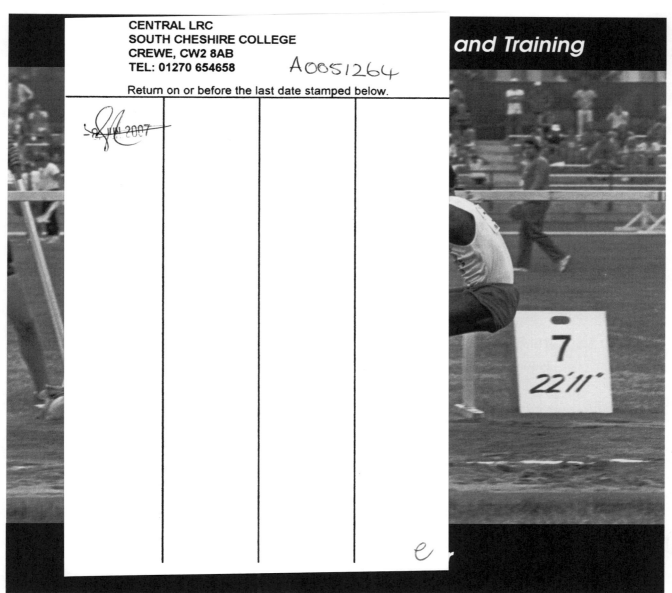

Fifth Edition

TAFNEWS PRESS
Book Division of Track & field News

First published in 2000 by Tafnews Press,
Book Division of Track & Field News,
2570 El Camino Real, Suite 606,
Mountain View, CA 94040 USA.

Copyright © by Tafnews Press
All rights reserved.

Publishing history:
First edition printed in 1972
Second edition printed in 1981
Third edition printed in 1988
Fourth edition printed in 1994
Fifth edition printed in 2000

Each edition is a unique compilation of articles.

Standard Book Number 0-911521-57-7
Printed in the United States of America

Cover design and production: Teresa Tam

CONTENTS

CHAPTER I: SOME GENERAL ASPECTS

CHAPTER II: THE HIGH JUMP

CHAPTER III: THE POLE VAULT

CHAPTER IV: THE LONG JUMP

CHAPTER V: THE TRIPLE JUMP

PHOTO CREDITS

Page	Subject	Photographer
Cover	Robert Kennedy, 1999 California state HS long jump champion	Don Gosney
1	Carl Lewis	Jeff Johnson/Geek Media
9	Lawrence Johnson	John Giustina
25	Ashia Hansen, Great Britain	Chai von der Laage/The Sporting Image
45	Charles Austin	Victor Sailer/Photo Run
59	Stefka Kostadinova, Bulgaria	Victor Sailer/Photo Run
63	Amy Acuff	Chai von der Laage/The Sporting Image
65	Javier Sotomayor, Cuba	Rhein-Ruhr-Foto/Gustav Schröder
67	Jeff Hartwig	Chai von der Laage/The Sporting Image
75	Stacy Dragila	Greg Armstrong
87	Jean Galfione	Chai von der Laage/The Sporting Image
89	Pat Manson	Chai von der Laage/The Sporting Image
92	Sergey Bubka, Ukraine	Chai von der Laage/The Sporting Image
93	Sergey Bubka, Ukraine	Victor Sailer/Photo Run
94	Sergey Bubka, Ukraine	ALLSPORT/Gray Mortimore
97	Fiona May, Italy	Chai von der Laage/The Sporting Image
101	Carl Lewis	Jeff Johnson/Geek Media
106	Erick Walder	Victor Sailer/Photo Run
109	Iván Pedroso, Cuba	Chai von der Laage/The Sporting Image
118	Mike Powell	ALLSPORT/Mike Powell
123	Paraskevi Tsiamita, Greece	Chai von der Laage/The Sporting Image
128	Kenny Harrison	Chai von der Laage/The Sporting Image
131	Inessa Kravets, Ukraine	Chai von der Laage/The Sporting Image
138	Jonathan Edwards, Great Britain	Chai von der Laage/The Sporting Image
138	Mike Conley	Victor Sailer/Photo Run
143	Willie Banks	Don Gosney
Back cover	Hollis Conway	John Giustina

ACKNOWLEDGEMENTS

The publishers with to thank the following publications for their cooperation and permission to reprint articles that originally appeared in their pages:

COACHING CONGRESS 1999 REPORT, Published by Australian Track and Field Coaches Association, Office 1.10, Sports House, Castlemain Street, Milton, Queensland 4064, Australia.

DIE LEHRE DER LEICHTATHLETIK, Helmar Hommel, Editor. Published as part of LEICHTATHLETIK (see below)

FITNESS AND SPORT REVIEW INTERNATIONAL, Michael Yessis Ph.D., Editor. Published by Sports Training Inc. 403 E 17th Avenue, Escondido, California 92025, USA.

GRUNDLAGEN DER LEICHTATHLETIK, Karl-Heinz Bauersfeld and Gerd Schröter, Editors. Published by Sportverlag Berlin, former German Democratic Republic.

LEGKAYA ATLETIKA, 10321 Moscow K-31, Rodjeatvensk Bulvar 10/6, Russia.

LEICHTATHLETIK, Klaus Sigl, Editor. Published by Deutscher Sportverlag Kurt Stroof GMBH, Eintrachtstrasse 110-118, 50668 Köln, Germany.

MODERN ATHLETE AND COACH, Jess Jarver, Editor. Published by Australian Track and Field Coaches Association, 1 Fox Avenue, Athelstone, S.A. 5076, Australia.

NEW STUDIES IN ATHLETICS, Pasquale Bellotti, Helmar Hommel, Elio Locatelli, Bjorn Wangemann, Executive Editors. Published by IAAF Publications Department, BP 359, MC98007, Monaco Cedex.

POLE VAULT STANDARD, Bob Fraley, Editor. 4860 N. Woodrow, #105, Fresno, CA 93726, USA.

SCIENTIFIC PROCEEDING: XVII INTERNATIONAL SYMPOSIUM OF BIOMECHANICS IN SPORT, RH Sanders and BJ Gibson, Editors. Published by Edith Cowan University, Perth, WA, Australia.

TRACK COACH, Russ Ebbets, Editor. Published by Track & Field News, 2570 El Camino Real, Suite 606, Mountain View, California 94040, USA.

TRACK & FIELD COACHES REVIEW, Dave Milliman, Editor. Published by United States Track Coaches Association, 1408 N.W. 6th Street, Gainesville, Florida 32601, USA.

Chapter I:
General Aspects

Running Training In Jumping Events

By L.S. Homenkova, Russia

The approach run is a critical performance factor in most jumping events. The following text takes a look at the basic principles applied to the development of a fast and accurate runup and presents ways and means to improve runup speed with a controlled stride length and stride frequency.

OBJECTIVES

The objective of running training in all jumping events is to improve running speed and to develop speed endurance in order to establish a fast, confident and stable approach run. It is essential for a jumper to learn to run at maximal speed, perhaps even faster than a sprinter over the last four to six strides of the approach run. To achieve this the main functional and technical training means include:

- A variety of sprinting drills and exercises over 40-60m distances.
- Different accelerations—steady increase of tempo to the maximum, shifting of tempo (5 to 6 strides fast followed by 5 to 6 strides free running, etc.), emphasis on stride length, emphasis on stride frequency. Pole vaulters should also perform with a regular pole and with a heavier-than-regular pole.
- Sprinting segments (30 to 300m) from a crouch start on the flat, changing to uphill or downhill stretches and back on the flat. High jumpers should perform the same using a banked curve.

During their running training jumpers must constantly monitor and improve the prime components of running speed—stride length and stride frequency. Stride length can be developed by using 20 to 40m accelerations and sprints from a flying start, attempting to reduce the number of strides needed to cover the distance. It also is important in an attempt to acquire a longer stride to develop the hip extensor muscles.

Stride frequency is developed by using down-hill sprints (2.5° decline), towing and running with a tail wind. In all these exercises it should be kept in mind that the length of segments in the development of pure running speed should not exceed 80m.

It is recommended that the coach employ different combinations of segments in the running training for jumpers. For example: 20 + 40 + 60 + 80m, or 30 + 50 + 80 + 50 + 30m, or 10 x 20m + 6 x 30m, or 6 x 40m + 3 x 50m + 6 x 40m, or 6 x 30m + 4 x 60m + 2 x 50m. Pole vaulters should perform one half to one third of the runs while carrying a pole.

All the above segments should be performed at a gradually increased speed, using the same principles as applied to the development of speed endurance. The coach should regularly time the runs and inform the athlete about his/her performance in order to assist in the development of a "sense" for running speed. It is extremely important for a jumper to control speed, effort and freedom of action in the execution of the approach run.

Jumpers require specific speed endurance to be able to maintain maximal speed for multiple repetitions of speed development sprints, repetitions of approach runs and jumping from full runups. The most effective way to develop speed endurance is systematic runs over distances in the 150 to 300m ranges. The volume and speed of repetitions are planned according to the athlete's best 100m time. The recovery intervals can be adjusted by the athlete's heart rates. Any combination can be used. For example: 6 x 150m, 5 x 200m, 3 x 300m, 100 + 200 + 300 + 200 + 100m etc.

The intensity of a jumper's running training can be objectively evaluated and calculated from the mean running speed for various training distances, while the volume of a training session is based on the total distance covered in the workout. If running form breaks down toward the end of a particular training distance, it is best to shorten the segments. Speed should be reduced if stress or technical deviations become obvious.

IMPROVING THE RUNUP

Improving the runup is an essential part of a jumper's training. One of its aim is to determine the length of the runup, as athletes frequently employ approach runs that are too short or too long. When a jumper's runup is too long, he/she reaches top speed before the start of the takeoff and consequently loses velocity during the final strides. This can result in up to 50cm losses in triple jump distances.

When the runup is too short, the athlete fails to exploit his/her speed potential and reaches the takeoff well below maximal velocity. This naturally leads to performance losses, keeping mind that a 0.1m/sec. increase in the pre-takeoff runup speed can add 1 to 2% to the distance jumped in horizontal events.

The choice of a specific runup length could be calculated from the jumper's potential speed, based on 40m and 100m times. As a guideline for male long jumpers, triple jumpers and pole vaulters a best 40m time of 5.2 sec. and 100m time of 11.3 sec. should equate with a runup of 16 strides. Times of 5.0 sec. and 11.0 sec. correspond to 18 strides, 4.8 sec. and 10.8 sec. to 20 strides and 4.6 sec. and 10.4 sec. to 22 strides.

Female jumpers with best 40m times of 5.3 to 5.4 sec. and best 100m times of 12.0 to 12.4 sec. should use a 17 to 18 strides runup, which corresponds to approximately 32 to 36m. As a general rule, women who run similar times to the above-noted male jumpers, should add two strides to the male approach runs.

As an athlete's ability to accelerate develops and his times over the 40m and 100m improve, the jumper should lengthen his runup by one or two strides. Further skill increases and faster running speeds, reaching 100m times of 10.2 to 10.4 sec. (11.3 to 11.5 sec. for women), lead to a further lengthening of the runup. The approach run will now be composed of 22 to 24 strides (20 to 21 strides for women) and corresponds to an approximate distance of 43 to 46m (38 to 40m for women). Elite triple jumpers usually employ a 20 to 21-stride approach run, pole vaulters use 18 to 20 strides and high jumpers around 12 strides.

When marking off a partial approach run in training it is common to use a conversion ratio of one running stride to two walking strides. Approach runs of up to eight strides in horizontal jumps and the pole vault (three to five strides in the high jump) are considered short. Medium runups are in the 16 to 20 strides (8 to 12 in the high jump) range. Naturally, when a full approach run is used in competition or training, the distance is measured precisely by using a tape.

HOW TO INCREASE RUNUP SPEED

How can one's approach run speed be increased? Despite the fact that the runup plays a decisive role in the horizontal jumps and the pole vault, many athletes exhibit serious flaws in this phase of the jump. For this reason coaches should constantly strive to increase the jumper's running speed and tempo without overlooking the need for an even distribution of power throughout the approach.

To develop the rhythm of the runup athletes should practice full 22 to 24 stride repetitions, using a gradual and smooth increase in tempo, stride length and running speed. While it is important to distribute power evenly in the approach, it also is important to learn how to increase speed. This should take place with an active running technique, while maintaining a "sense" of contact with the track in order to support the transition to an active takeoff.

Athletes employ a variety of exercises to develop and improve their approach runs. These include, besides sprint drills, gradually extended maximal speed approach runs, running with the wind in an approach run rhythm, running down a 1- to 2-degree decline followed by 4 to 6 strides on the flat.

High jumpers also perform curve running and pole vaulters execute at least half of their runs carrying a pole. Other recommended exercises include 20- to 24-stride runs from a crouch start, running over low hurdles, running over markers placed 1.5 to 2.0m apart to develop stride frequency and performing speed-strength development exercises, such as bounding.

When full-speed runups are performed in training it is helpful to compare their stride pattern with runups used in actual jumping. This allows us to note differences and to identify reasons why they occur. Chalk marks can be helpful on synthetic tracks. In all these exercises it is important to observe that the approach to the takeoff board is always performed actively.

The aim of the runup should be to reach maximal speed just beyond the takeoff board (the takeoff point in the high jump and the pole vault).

HOW TO IMPROVE RUNUP ACCURACY

Perfecting a fast and accurate runup is the key to successful jumping. The following factors increase the accuracy and stability of the approach run:

• The use of a consistent starting position.
• A preliminary mental adjustment to the task prior to the start of the runup.
• Remembering the muscular sensations that occur in the performance of the runup. These include the effort and rhythm, the distance and duration, and the length of individual strides in the approach.
• The use of check marks and regular monitoring of the last six runup strides.
• Paying attention to external conditions to make allowances for the wind, track surface and personal sense of well-being.
• A prompt modification of the length of the runup to fit the conditions.

The skill of self-analysis and the jumper's motor memory is a critical factor in the development of runup accuracy. The key to producing record jumps is having confidence in one's approach run. This can be improved by regularly recording the duration and length of the entire runup, as well as that of the last six strides, to objectively assess the average speed and rhythm.

IN CONCLUSION

The development of runup speed in jumping events is based on the understanding that athletes reach their highest speed just before the takeoff. This speed is slightly reduced in active preparation for the takeoff. The reduction is relatively smaller in the long jump in comparison to the pole vault and the triple jump. Hence triple jumpers and pole vaulters should use long jump competitions in order to improve their approach runs. All jumpers are well advised to compete in sprinting events.

Every jumper has an individual ratio and range within which he can vary his stride length and stride frequency without fear of losing speed. An athlete can reach a speed of 10m/sec. while using a stride length of 200cm, as well as a stride length of 250cm. However, in using a stride length of 200cm the stride frequency is 5 strides/sec.; for a stride length of 250cm the frequency corresponds to 4 strides/sec.

The above examples represent extreme values. The optimal relationship ranges between a stride length of 230 to 235cm and a stride frequency of 4.3 to 4.4 strides/sec. This corresponds to 1.36 to 1.40 sec. speed for the last six strides. Violating the allowable range, that is, running with overlong strides or an overfast stride frequency, usually is responsible for velocity losses, particularly in the last six strides prior to the takeoff.

It is most important for a jumper to know the range of stride length and stride frequency that develops maximal speed. The most accurate indicator here is the distance and duration of the last six strides in one's best attempts. Even experienced jumpers often artificially extend or shorten their approach run strides when approaching the takeoff point, forgetting that they are depriving themselves of the chance to reach maximal speed.

Constructing An Optimal Runup In The Horizontal Jumps

By Vladimir Popov, Russia

A close look into the length, velocity and precision of the runup in the horizontal jumps with recommendations for the optimal development of the extremely important approach run.

The runup is a decisive component in the horizontal jumping events. It is characterized by the perception of acceleration, an elastic contact with the track, a bold approach to the takeoff.

How should a fast and precise runup be constructed and developed? The following text attempts to give some advice on how it can be achieved.

LENGTH OF THE RUNUP

Athletes often employ unjustifiably long or short runups. In the first case, maximal speed is reached well before takeoff, with velocity losses in the last strides. In the second case, athletes simply fail to reach their top speed prior to takeoff. It should be kept in mind here that a runup velocity improvement by 0.1 m/sec. prior to the takeoff adds up to 2% to the distance.

The length of the runup depends on an athlete's physique, level of preparation and, above all, on his/her acceleration capacity. This capacity can be evaluated with reasonable objectivity in the comparison of individual 40m and 100m performances. The following can be used as a rough guide:

Times of 5.7 and 13.0 sec. correspond to a runup length of 12 strides, 5.4 and 12.5 sec. to 14 strides, 5.2 and 12.0 sec. to 16 strides, 5.0 and 11.3 sec. to 18 strides, 4.8 and 10.9 sec. to 20 strides, and 4.6 and 10.4 sec. to 22 strides. Female jumpers should on average add two strides to the corresponding times.

It follows therefore that athletes who clock 5.1-5.2 sec. in the 40m sprint and 11.3 -11.6 in the 100m (women 5.3-5.4 sec. and 12.0-12.4 sec.) are advised to employ runups of 17 to 18 strides, about 32 to 36m in length. Shorter and fast-striding athletes will have slightly shorter approach runs. The runup can be increased by a stride or two as the performance level of an athlete improves and reaches 22 to 24 strides among elite jumpers, corresponding to a distance of 43 to 46m.

The length of the runup changes within a season according to the athlete's form, track conditions and wind direction. Generally a head wind requires a shortening of the runups by 30 to 50cm, while a tail wind adds 20 to 40cm to its length. It is important that the runup in competition and in training jumps from a full runup is always measured exactly with a tape.

A typical example of how the runup changes during a long jumper's career is outlined in Table 1.

SPEED OF THE RUNUP

Although the runup plays a leading role in horizontal jump performance, many shortcomings in this phase can be observed, even in important competitions. Obviously athletes and coaches should pay more attention to the development of runup speed, rhythm and precision in training.

The development of runup rhythm usually takes place in repetition runs with a gradually increased tempo and stride length. It is important to perform these runs with a correctly distributed effort and with active last strides that resemble the

Table 1: An actual example of the development of a long jump runup.
Phase 1 = 15 to 17 yrs. (youth competition); Phase 2 = 18 to 19 yrs. (junior competition);
Phase 3 = 20 - 22 yrs. (senior competition); Phase 4 = elite senior competition.

PHASE	RESULTS			RUNUP	
	30m (sec)	100m (sec)	LONG JUMP (m)	STRIDES (No.)	LENGTH (m)
1. 1947 - 1948	4.8 - 4.4	14.0 - 12.3	4.50 - 5.55	12 - 14	18 - 23
2. 1950 - 1951	4.3 - 4.2	12.0 - 11.7	5.62 - 6.46	16	25 - 27
3. 1952 - 1954	4.2 - 4.1	11.5 - 11.1	6.94 - 7.16	18	32 - 34
4. 1954 - 1959	4.0 - 3.8	11.0 - 10.8	7.29 - 7.69	20	37 - 41

actual preparation for the takeoff. Other common drills to develop an optimal runup include the following:
- Repetition runups in correct rhythm with two to four strides added to the normal runup.
- Wind-assisted runups in correct rhythm.
- Runups on a declined track (1° to 2°) with the last four to six strides executed on a flat surface.
- Sprints from a crouch start using 18 to 24 strides.
- Runs over low hurdles in a 3- or 5-stride rhythm.

The most effective speed-strength exercises in the development of runup speed include the following examples:
- Standing imitation arm action with a gradually increased tempo up to the maximal.
- Standing, wall supported, imitation sprint leg action with a gradually increased tempo up to the maximal.
- A variety of jumping exercises, including bounding, with emphasis on ankle extension, fast jumps on one leg, fast repetition jumps into a wide split position etc.

- Walking and running with a load on the shoulders, followed by a swift unloaded action to exploit the sudden relief.

It's important in the performance of full length runups to provide constant evaluation and intelligent correction of any deviations from the desired optimal execution. This can be facilitated by placing check marks for the sixth stride from the start of the runup and six strides before the takeoff. As a fast runup is decisive in reaching optimal distances, it is particularly important to execute an active approach to the board, indicating that the athlete aims to reach maximal velocity at the take-off.

PRECISION ON THE RUNUP

The development of a precise, stable and reliable runup can be assisted by:
- Using a simple unchanged position for the start of the runup.

Table 2: Sample diary recordings of the changes in the runup during a competition.

	START OF THE RUNUP (m)	DEVIATION (cm)	ACTUAL LENGTH (m)	DISTANCE (m)	LENGTH OF LAST 6 STRIDES (m)
Trial Runups					
First	39.80	+5	39.85	-	13.75
Second	39.90	-	39.90	-	13.80
Competition Jumps					
First	40.00	-5	39.95	7.34	13.80
Second	40.00	+5	40.05	7.60	13.90
Third	40.10	-10	40.00	7.26	13.85
Final Jumps					
First	40.00	+2	40.02	7.65	14.00
Second	40.10	-5	40.05	7.50	13.85
Third	40.10	-12	39.98	7.69	13.95

Table 3: The relationship between runup velocity and the stride length and stride frequency over the last six strides.

TIME OF LAST SIX STRIDES (SEC)		1.50	1.40	1.36	1.33	1.30	1.20
STRIDE FREQUENCY (ST/SEC)		4.0	4.3	4.4	4.5	4.6	5.0
AVERAGE STRIDE LENGTH (M)	LAST SIX STRIDES (M)	AVERAGE RUNUP VELOCITY (M/SEC)					
1.85	11.10	7.4	7.95	8.14	8.32	8.51	9.25
1.90	11.40	7,6	8.17	8.36	8.55	8.74	9.50
1.95	11.70	7.8	8.38	8.58	8.77	8.97	9.75
2.00	12.00	8.0	8.60	8.80	9.00	9.20	10.00
2.10	12.60	8.4	9.03	9.24	9.45	9.66	10.50
2.20	13.20	8.8	9.46	9.68	9.90	10.12	11.00
2.30	13.80	9.2	9.89	10.12	10.35	10.58	11.50
2.40	14.40	9.7	10.32	10.56	10.80	11.04	12.00
2.50	15.00	10.0	10.75	11.00	11.25	11.50	12.50

- Using a check mark and regularly controlling the length of the last six strides.
- Paying attention to external factors to make the necessary changes according to the direction and strength of the wind and the condition of the track surface.
- Attempting to concentrate thoroughly not only during competition but also in full length runups in training.
- Using mental imagery to rehearse the distribution of effort and the rhythm of the runup before the start of a competition and before each jump.

Experience, movement memory, self-confidence and attention to external conditions help to adjust the length of the runup during the precompetition trials. Nevertheless, it is essential to check the exact takeoff point and whether the check mark was hit after each jump to make the necessary adjustments. It is also advisable to improve confidence by shortening the runup about 10 to 15cm for the first competition attempt.

The same applies to the appearance of first signs of fatigue in prolonged competitions. All these adjustments are naturally individual and depend on an athlete's experiences, which can be helped by keeping a diary of competition and training jumps as shown in Table 2.

An analysis of the diary recordings (Table 2) is helpful in the establishment of a fast, stable and reliable runup. Further improvement is possible by finding an individual optimal relationship between the length and frequency of the last six runup strides. As can be seen in Table 3, it is possible to reach a runup velocity of 10m/sec. with a stride length of 2.00 or 2.50m. However, this requires in the first case a stride frequency of 5 strides/sec., in the second case only 4 strides/sec.

We have included in Table 3 unrealistic border values and believe that a possible optimal relationship is in a 2.30 to 2.35m stride length and 4.4 to 4.3 strides/sec. stride frequency range. In this case the time for the last six strides would be between 1.36 and 1.40 sec. Obviously any deviations from the individual's optimum leads to velocity losses in the last six or even the last two strides.

The Cognitive Management Of Approach Speed In Horizontal Jumping

By Alberto Madella, Italy

Observations have shown that horizontal jumpers make adjustments to stride length and stride frequency in the final phase of the approach run. These modifications take place through visual, cognitive and proprioceptive information. This confirms that the approach run is not a "closed skill" and requires special attention in training.

1. INTRODUCTION

The speed developed in the approach phase is considered to be a principal precondition of effective performance in the horizontal jumps. Many of the training methodologies for jumpers are based largely on this premise. The same can be said for talent selection procedures. Consequently, a substantial part of the training load undertaken by long jumpers of all ages and levels is aimed at increasing horizontal speed and motor abilities (fast strength, muscle elasticity) that contribute to this specific pre-condition, using, where appropriate, nonspecific means.

Practical field experiments and the results of some limited scientific research into gait regulation (Lee, Lishman and Thompson 1982; Laurent, et al. 1985; Hay and Koh 1988), would lead us to conclude, however, that the relation between horizontal speed and jumping performance does not in itself provide the best, or at any rate the most discriminating, variable for a satisfactory prediction of the actual final length of the jump.

This is confirmed by the frequent use made by those working in this field of the expression "maximum controlled or controllable speed." This concept is, in fact, said by coaches and the authors of the principal technical texts to be the true determinant of performance in this discipline, given the

necessity at the moment of takeoff and during flight to merge a series of complex voluntary actions with a very high horizontal speed.

Although this opinion is widely shared, attention has not always been focused closely enough on this problem, either in the research or with regard to the implications for teaching and for the training of the coaches themselves.

The coefficients of correlation, reported in the literature, between the actual length of the jump and the horizontal speed recorded in the final phase of the approach (in general measured during the last 5-6 meters) tend to have very high values, especially if we consider the individual athlete's best performance and include athletes of different levels in the population analyzed in the calculation.

On the other hand, the values of the correlations decrease considerably—as might seem predictable—when several jumps by the same athlete are analyzed, groups with a similar performance level and horizontal speed are studied, and more sophisticated and appropriate statistical techniques are used, as we hope will be the case in this study.

That varying performance levels exist in the same subject is stating the obvious. This is a concept, however, which has not been analyzed in sufficient depth in field research, which usually devotes more attention to differences between athletes or performance levels than to those producing variations in the results obtained by the same athlete.

Coaches and, in many cases, researchers too have attributed these differences to factors such as flight technique, takeoff angle, or landing efficiency (to which Hay, for example, in his model of the 3-phase jump, attributed about 12% of the total length of jump, 1985).

Even more frequently, these differences have been attributed, in the scientific literature, to the reduction or loss of horizontal speed which occurs at the moment of contact with the board. This has been explained by the way in which the takeoff is conditioned by the properties or characteristics of those elements of the athlete's musculature that are specifically involved in the takeoff action.

It would, in any case, be difficult to assert that these muscle properties can undergo substantial changes in the course of one competition or of competitions taking place over a short time scale.

Furthermore, this assertion does not take into due consideration the data already published by some researchers and confirmed, as we shall see, in this study, which often show marked reductions and variations in horizontal speed and in time and length of flight in the last 4-5 touchdowns of the approach, rather than, as some authors claim, only from the second last to the last.

In some cases this has been attributed to excessive fatigue or an over-long approach, but this explanation does not appear at all convincing, when compared with other hypotheses which lay the emphasis on factors of a cognitive nature and, particularly, on the treatment of visual information (processed in sequence with proprioceptive information), while the athlete is moving at very high speed along the approach.

The hypothesis sustained in this study is that variables such as muscle properties and simple final horizontal velocity, while they obviously have an influence on the ultimate outcome of the jump, are not enough in themselves to account for such differences in performance. These must, therefore, also be traced back to information-related phenomena and to how, and how well, the athlete is able to process this information cognitively during the runup to the takeoff board.

This also ties in with what every coach has noted, when trying to correct an athlete who has performed a no-jump or taken off before reaching the takeoff board. In such cases, it is not sufficient to move the starting point of the approach mechanically by a distance equal to the difference between the athlete's disallowed takeoff and the end of the board, to be sure of obtaining a surer or more precise "launch." Indeed, in some cases, not necessarily restricted to inexperienced jumpers, this makes it more difficult for the athlete to "manage" the approach.

It can thus be hypothesized that, although the approach in the long jump has in the past been defined principally as a closed motor skill, and many coaches continue to insist that it be carried out in a uniform manner, what actually happens is that, during some of its phases, an intense cognitive processing of perceptive parameters, mainly visual, occurs.

Through training and competition, this cognitive treatment can be said to be structured into an approach management strategy. This cognitive strategy was described some years ago by Lee, Lishman and Thompson (1982). On the basis of a truly innovative, systematic study of three athletes, they affirmed that, after an initial phase based essentially on preprogrammed, automatic control, in the final part of the approach the jumpers utilize visual information to regulate the length of their stride. This hypothesis fits some of the claims advanced as part of the ecological paradigm of gait regulation (Gibson 1979).

Maraj and others later went on to analyze the triple jump from a similar point of view (1993), but many aspects, linked, for example, to speed control and frequency of movement, still remain to be explored.

The particular hypothesis posited by Lee, Lishman and Thompson is that only the first part of the approach is pre-programmed (and therefore stereotyped and corresponding to the closed skills profile) and that the final part, as the athlete approaches the takeoff board, is subject to cognitive processing and adjustment.

As a consequence, according to these authors, the approach actually consists of a phase in which visual control is limited and an adjustment phase, in which it plays a considerable part. Pursuing this line of investigation, Hay affirmed that the beginning of this phase of cognitive treatment of the approach corresponds to the fifth-last touchdown (1988), albeit with variations, which can be identified using specific analysis and data-gathering techniques.

The objective of this project, then, is to provide further evidence of these cognitive approach management methods and of their practical implications for the teaching of the long jump, with particular emphasis on the linkage between approach and takeoff. The practical implications are of undoubted significance: particularly during competitions, most of the corrections suggested by coaches in this discipline are focused on their athletes' methods of approach. It follows from this that a greater understanding of the phenomena involved in this phase will greatly increase the effectiveness of such corrections.

2. METHODOLOGY

Two different methods of investigation were used in this project:

A) as a preliminary, a further analysis of data already gathered by other researchers (over 150 athletes of each sex for a total of about 470 long and triple jumps);

B) a new, descriptive field analysis of the behavior during the approach of 16 athletes of both sexes and varying performance levels, who were studied using film analysis and specific markers. The characteristics of the group analyzed are shown in Table 1.

Table 1: Characteristics of the athletes in Study B

Variables	Minimum	Maximum
Age	17	24
Performance long jump	5.74m	7.08m
Performance triple jump	12.94m	16.04m
Years of activity	4	17

The jumps were analyzed in relation to parameters which included management of approach speed and length of stride, frequency of the different jumps, the relation between horizontal speed and length of stride, and the variations in width and length of the approach in the various trial runs, during the competition itself and the practices preceding it. Only part of the data and subsequent processing procedures is, however, reported in this paper.

With reference to the methodological choices on which this project is based, and the possibility that doubts might be raised regarding the small number of athletes studied, it is probably a good idea to advance some considerations of a methodological character.

Research in sport has generally concentrated on large sample populations and a small number of variables, analyzed and processed, by preference, using correlational and multivariate techniques. We believe, however, that, to make real progress and provide sport-oriented research with

more scope for dialogue and with a greater practical impact on coaches, it is better to work on large quantities of data and variables, gathered over time from just a few athletes (or even just one), using appropriate statistical techniques (e.g., time series analysis).

3. RESULTS

3.1 Study A

The first step was to analyze the wide range of existing scientific literature dealing with the variability recorded in some performance parameters in the long jump. These data were gathered from a wide variety of sources during major international competitions, such as the Olympic Games and World Championships.

The range of sources may give rise to some doubts about the specific methods used to gather the data, through film analysis or by direct measurement of kinematic parameters. A total of 470 jumps, performed by 165 athletes, were, in any case, analyzed, with reference to the relationship between horizontal speed and length of jump. The coefficient of correlation between horizontal speed and jump measurement was $r=0.90$, calculated on the group as a whole and, therefore, excluding considerations of sex or performance level.

If, however, we consider only the higher-level athletes (for example, over 16 meters in the male triple jump, over 7.80 in the male long jump and over 6 meters in the women's long jump), the correlation coefficients fall considerably, to between $r=0.58$ in the male triple and $r=0.62$ in the male long. This is in keeping with Hay's findings in 1985, in which a coefficient of correlation between speed at takeoff and the result of the valid jump was calculated at $r=0.49$ in top-level female jumpers.

This means that, in this analysis model, 25-30% of the final performance of the jump can be said to result from horizontal speed, if we consider athletes of a similar performance level. For them, an increase in horizontal speed does not translate automatically into an increase in performance.

The results become even more interesting, if we consider the analysis of the variations in different jumps by the same athlete. In this paper we will focus only on the results of athletes performing a sufficiently high number of jumps for the correlations to be calculated: for Mike Conley, for example, the coefficient of correlation between takeoff speed and length of jump in the triple jump is equal to r = -0.75—in other words, a negative correlation, which would seem to imply that, at least in the jumps under consideration, the greater the speed the shorter the jump.

It should be said that Conley's speed at takeoff is on average 10.45m/sec (d.s.=0.20), ranging from a minimum of 10.10m/sec to a maximum of 10.78m/sec, with a variation coefficient equal to 1.92%. The coefficients of variation for all the athletes with a sufficiently high number of jumps showed a considerable degree of variation.

The correlation coefficients were generally higher for women than for men, albeit with a considerable range of variation (e.g., Sakirkin r=0.39, Vokuhl r= 0.42). Overall, about 32% of the coefficients calculated had a negative value, and 54% had values which were not relevant for predictive purposes.

The value of the correlation between length of jump, distance lost and speed of jump, which in the triple jump was evaluated as r= -0.44, is also of interest. It is clear that very few coaches consider competition performance to be purely a result of horizontal speed developed during the approach, but these data seem to support the idea that the role of the control and regulation mechanisms are of particular importance to successful jumping. This leads us on to more detailed and specific analyses of single individuals, like those in Study B.

3.2 Study B

Since the data published in the literature does not provide a wide enough range of parameters to enable the starting hypothesis to be evaluated more accurately, an original study of horizontal jumpers was carried out. For this purpose, an analysis was made of the jumps of 16 male and female athletes, some of good national level and others of regional class. This variability did not reduce the value of the study, which was meant to be not so much a fully representative analysis as a means of gaining a better understanding of intra-individual variability.

Two cameras, with a speed of 72 frames a second, were used to film 3 to 6 jumps, after which some parameters relating to the approach in both the penultimate and final phases were analyzed. In all, the individual behavior of the 16 athletes was analyzed in great detail, although only some of these (six for the long jump and 4 for the triple) will be analyzed in this project.

For each athlete we recorded the total lengths of the approach and of the jump, as well as the disparities with respect to a marker placed 15 meters from the takeoff board and, of course, the distance lost in centimeters with respect to the takeoff board.

The long jump group included both men and women. The latter were of a higher standard, since the results under consideration were obtained by athletes with personal records ranging from 5.71 to 6.23 and jumps with effective lengths of 5.51 to 6.12, including no-jumps, the actual length of which was also measured.

For the female athletes, it is interesting to note that speed in the last four touchdowns of the approach does not appear to be stable and that individual behavior varies greatly. On average, in the sample we analyzed, it seems that maximum horizontal speed emerges three or four touchdowns before takeoff, with the average and variability values given in Table 2.

Table 2: Values of variability in the final touchdowns of the approach for the athletes in Study B.

Touchdown	Average speed [m/sec]	Standard deviation	Coefficient of variation
fourth-last	8.5	0.47	5.6%
third-last	8.55	0.48	5.6%
second-last	8.44	0.29	3.5%
last	7.99	0.5	7.2%

It is interesting to note that a considerable degree of variability in speed values was found at the moment of takeoff and at the third- and fourth-last touchdowns, while the values for the second-last touchdowns appear to be more homogeneous, as can be seen from an analysis of Figure 1, where they are shown in graph form.

Overall, variability between the athletes in the study is fairly high and it is interesting to note that a higher correlation was found between actual length of jump and the speed of the third last touchdown (r=0.76), which would also appear to be statistically significant (p<0.01). This leads us to surmise that, in keeping with the initial hypothesis, the last two or three touchdowns are directed essentially at the preparation for the takeoff and that this produces considerable reduction in speed, amounting in some cases to 12.2%.

The data relating to variations in length of stride and flight were also analyzed. These were calculated using the horizontal coordinates of the barycenter at takeoff and the coordinates of the barycenter at the moment of impact.

Table 3: Length of stride in the approach to the long jump [cm].

Subject	5th last	4th last	3rd last	2nd last	last	Length of jump	Mean	Std dev	Cv
a	210	227	222	211	223	698	218.6	7.6	3.5%
b	212	223	219	220	220	691	218.8	4.1	1.9%
c	198	207	200	225	208	610	207.6	10,6	5.1%
d	211	217	203	208	218	708	211.4	6.3	3.0%
e	202	183	206	194	218	574	200.6	13.1	6.5%
f	174	203	197	205	223	584	200.4	17.7	8.8%
Minimum	174	183	197	194	208	574	200.4	4.1	1.9%
Maximum	212	227	222	225	223	708	218.8	17.7	8.8%
Mean	201.7	210.0	207.8	210.5	218.3	644.2	209.6	9.9	4.8%
Standard dev.	14.4	16.1	10.3	11.0	5.5	61.4	8.2	5.0	2.6%
Cv	7.17%	7.66%	4.96%	5.25%	2.54%	9.54%	3.93%		

Table 4: Length of flight in approach strides—long jump [cm].

Subject	5th last	4th last	3rd last	2nd last	last	Length of jump	Mean	Std dev	Cv
a	85	113	123	113	86	698	104.0	17.4	16.7%
b	97	114	101	94	95	691	100.2	6.2	8.2%
c	83	103	104	134	83	610	101.4	20.9	20.6%
d	95	97	94	97	93	708	95.2	1.8	1.9%
e	105	85	113	86	92	574	96.2	12.3	12.8%
f	76	101	92	87	107	584	92.6	12.1	13.11.
Minimum	76	85	92	86	83	574	92.6	1.8	1.9%
Maximum	105	114	123	134	107	708	104.0	20.9	20.6%
Mean	90.2	102.2	104.5	101.8	92.7	644.2	98.3	12.1	12.2%
Standard dev.	10.7	10.8	11.8	18.5	8.4	61.4	4.3	6.7	6.6%
Cv	11.8%	10.5%	11.3%	18.2%	9.0%	9.5%	4.4%		

These data are shown, for both the women and the men in the study, in Tables 3 and 4. These tables show clearly that there is less variability in the data relating to the last step, which, in this group of athletes, remains more homogeneous than the third- and fourth-last touchdowns, in which the greatest variability in length of step is recorded (cf. Figure 2). The frequency of stride data (not reported analytically here) show a slight reduction in the fourth- and third-last steps of the approach, while, in some subjects, the last step generally shows a considerable increase in frequency.

For the triple jump, a supplementary measurement was introduced: the stability of the touchdowns in the central and final parts of the approach, with particular reference to the hypothesis that the approach can be divided into a preprogrammed part and a final, visually processed, part.

Figure 2 shows the standard deviations of four athletes in the last six steps of the approach leading up to the takeoff. These show quite clearly how the variability of the approach reaches particularly high values in the sixth- and fifth-last touchdowns, and remains high afterwards.

Unfortunately, a lack of data for touchdowns preceding the sixth-last makes it difficult to evaluate the development of these strategic adjustment methods over the whole approach. On the basis of the available data, however, this adjustment seems quite obvious.

4. CONCLUSIONS

The results confirm that high intra-individual variability in performance exists at all levels of technical skill. This variability, however, manifests itself in very different forms from one subject to another and is associated with different methods of adjusting the approach run, in terms of length, speed management and stride frequency, corresponding to the inflow of different types of information through the sensory channels.

In particular, it would seem that the athletes with the best performances seem to begin their cognitive processing of approach speed earlier, although there is a considerable degree of intra-individual variability here, also (very high coefficients of variation in takeoff precision). Informa-

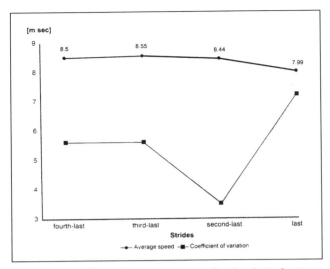

Figure 1: Variations in speed in the last four touch-downs—female long jumpers (horizontal jumpers). Athletes ranging from 5.71 to 6.23m.

tion of a proprioceptive as well as of a visual nature also seems relevant, given that the conditions of speed, strength, etc. in which athletes of different performance levels operate are very different.

It appears, in particular, that the cognitive treatment depends not so much on individual performance levels as on the athlete's own specific characteristics, which should be analyzed, using techniques and methodologies that focus more closely on inter-individual variations.

These results seem to confirm that the teaching of the approach as a rigid and stable rhythmic structure, on the assumption that it is a closed skill, is not founded on observed data, that the motor programs used throughout the approach are subject to strong parameterization and adjustment, and that the more highly skilled athletes are able to manage this perceptive aspect, based essentially on visual information, more

effectively.

This leads us to suppose that visual feedback, in keeping with the research carried out as part of the ecological and, in some cases, the proprioceptive approach, is absolutely vital in the management of speed. One possible consequence of this seems to be that the training of the approach speed should be closely targeted, as happens for example in situation sports, and that it should make use of suitable conditions of variability, to favor the most appropriate transition from approach to takeoff.

BIBLIOGRAPHY

Hay, J. (1988): Approach Strategies in the Long Jump. *International Journal of Sport Biomechanics*, 4, pp. 114-129.

Hay, J. G. and T.J. Koh (1988): Evaluating the Approach in the Horizontal Jumps. *International Journal of Sport Biomechanics*, 4, pp. 372-392.

Laurent, M. (1985): Aspects cinematiques et dynamiques de la course d'élan en saut en longueur. In: *Recherches en Activités Physiques et Sportives*, pp. 235-245.

Lee, D. N., Lishman, J. R. and J. A. Thomson (1982): Regulation of Gait in Long Jumping. In: *Journal of Experimental Psychology: Human Perception and Performance*, 8, pp.448-459.

Maraj, B. K., D. Elliot, T.D. Lee and B. J. Pollock (1993): Variance and Invariance in Expert and Novice Triple Jumpers, *Research Quarterly for Exercise and Sport*, 64, 4, pp. 404-412.

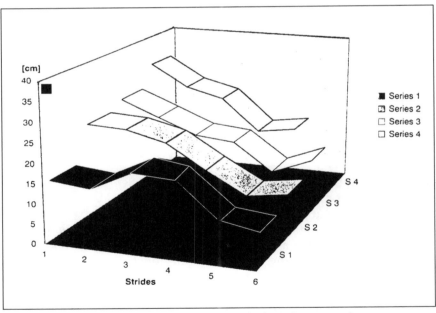

Figure 2: Variations in regularity of approach in the last six touchdowns.

Building Specific Strength For Horizontal Jumps

By Gary Bourne, Australia

While there is a need in the early stages of training to build up a solid foundation of general strength, mature and well conditioned horizontal jumpers have to change to a specific approach in their strength development. This can be achieved by developing "selective hypertrophy" in order to maintain an effective power-to-weight ratio.

Once a solid foundation of conditioning and skill development work has been completed and the horizontal jumper reaches the end of his/her major growth spurt, the coach can begin to develop performance-specific strength traits in the athlete.

This period of training will involve the coach in trying to mold the structural and functional aspects of the jumper's body, to allow it to meet all of the demands which are likely to be placed upon it in the achievement of elite-level horizontal jumping performances.

MUSCLE HYPERTROPHY

In the very early stages of training, and with younger athletes in particular, muscular work should be of a fairly general nature, the purpose being to build a solid foundation throughout the body. In later conditioning phases, where we are dealing with more mature and better conditioned athletes, this muscular work should be much more specific. The purpose here is to generate specific alterations to the structure of the muscles which will allow them to perform at the specific levels required in elite-level horizontal jumping performance.

Hakkinen, et al., (1981), indicated that there is an heirarchical order in which changes take place in a strength training program. The initial changes, in the first eight weeks of a weight training program, are essentially functional in nature, involv-

ing better programming and functioning of those aspects of the central nervous system which are involved in the coordination and operation of the targeted muscles. Further increases occurring after this period can be attributed to both hypertrophy and ongoing neural changes.

The initial improvement in neural pathways to the training muscle is an essential precondition to the hypertrophic changes which follow. The length of this period of adjustment is influenced by the complexity of the exercise being undertaken and the general coordination ability of the athlete. Once there has been some neural adaptation of the muscles, allowing better specific recruitment of antagonists and synergists and improved relaxation of antagonists, the process of muscle hypertrophy will follow.

This process involves increasing the number of myofibrils contained within each muscle fiber. These myofibrils are made up of action and myosin protein filaments. The laying down of additional protein filaments in the fibers occurs in response to progressive overloading and "work" done by the muscles.

The process of muscle hypertrophy also requires the presence of the male hormone testosterone, present in varying degrees in both males and females, but to a much greater degree in males. Males generally obtain much greater degrees of muscle hypertrophy than do females as a result of this hormonal difference.

Some structural changes also occur to the innervating nerves as hypertrophy is taking place.

These involve an increase in the size of the motor endplate area, thus allowing for better transmission of acetyl-choline into the muscle cell to induce muscle contraction.

Increases in the size of the supporting bones and ligaments, as well as the tendons which attach the muscles to the bones, occur at a slightly delayed rate. Increases in the size of bone seem to require a foundation period of training where the loadings are not too high if potential injuries are to be avoided.

This fact underlines the importance of a well planned, patient, long-term developmental training program, in successfully building the performance potential of horizontal jumpers, because many of the advanced training activities which these athletes must undertake in their programs place considerable stress on the bones, ligaments and tendons in their legs and feet.

It is important that the strength training program be developmental in nature and that the processes which will stimulate the major structural changes (i.e., weight training) should precede those training processes which will stimulate functional changes (i.e., plyometric training activities). The program must allow an appropriate period for structural adjustments within the body to tendons, ligaments and bones if the potential for injuries to these areas, in younger athletes in particular, is to be minimized.

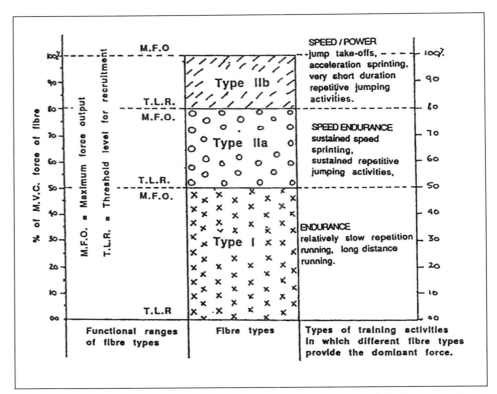

Figure 1: Maximum force outputs of the three different fiber types. It is important to observe in training threshold levels at which the different fiber types are recruited in significant number.

"SELECTIVE" HYPERTROPHY

There are three different types of muscle fibers. They are categorized according to their contractile properties as "slow-twitch" (a slow-twitch fiber with low-to-medium force output capabilities but with considerable endurance characteristics), "fast-twitch A" or fast-twitch oxidative-glycolytic (a fast-twitch fiber with medium-to-high force output characteristics and with some fatigue resistant characteristics), and "fast-twitch B" or fast-twitch glycolytic (a fast-twitch fiber with very high force output ability, but with minimal endurance capabilities).

Each fiber type has a different "threshold level for recruitment" (stimulus or effort required to get it to contract). From a practical training viewpoint these levels may be expressed as a proportion of the one-repetition maximum contraction capacity of the muscle (the maximum weight the individual can complete one full repetition of an exercise). The threshold levels for recruitment of the different fiber types can be seen in Figure 1.

While we are all born with different numbers of each fiber type, training methods can produce "selective development" of one particular fiber type by specifically targeting them through the utilization of appropriate training loads and recoveries.

This process of "selective development" is a basic principle of training, falling under the category of "specificity." Selective development means that the percent area of a muscle occupied by a particular fiber type is increased through training. As a result, the overall performance characteristics

British triple jumper Ashia Hansen.

Therefore the greater the area of the muscle made up of these fibers, the greater will be the force production potential of that muscle.

From a horizontal jumping performance perspective, the muscle-hypertrophying aspects of the training program must lead to selective hypertrophy of the fast-twitch "B" fibers. We must be careful not to induce too much hypertrophy in the remaining two groups of fiber types. The reason being that in horizontal jumping, from a muscular training viewpoint, we are principally concerned with the power-to-weight ratio in the athlete.

We must therefore be guided by the overriding rule that the overall training efforts must be directed toward increasing this power-to-weight ratio. Any muscle bulk which does not cause an increase in the absolute power-to-weight ratio, either directly or indirectly, is an unnecessary burden on the athlete and must be detrimental to performance. The idiom "train your body and not your ego" can be a timely remark when made to some horizontal jumpers who may appear to become obsessed with the mirrors in the weights gym, or their performances at the disco.

A jumper carrying an excess of 4-5 kilograms or more of hypertrophied fast-twitch type "A" and slow-twitch muscle fiber across a range of muscles is effectively reducing their absolute power-to-weight ratio. This unneeded hypertrophy will reduce the jumper's performance potential in the same way that excessive body fat levels.

ACHIEVING SELECTIVE HYPERTROPHY

The coach can avoid unwanted hypertrophy of certain fiber types while achieving hypertrophy of the selected fibers by manipulating the variables of load (as a percentage of 1RM), the number of repetitions (which are essentially limited by loads anyway), and the number of sets of each exercise.

Weight training provides the road to meaningful changes in the hypertrophy of muscle fibers. It is now well recognized that plyometric training activities, while producing functional changes which contribute positively to muscle performance output, do not lead to muscle hypertrophy.

For guidance in the selection of weight training loads, we need to refer to the graph in Figure 1. This indicates that the targeted fiber group are not recruited at loads up to 80% of the individual's one-repetition maximum of an exercise. It would seem reasonable to assume that these fibers will

of individual muscles may be altered to better meet the performance demands of the event.

Muscles targeted for selective development may acquire the potential to exert greater speed and force (selective development of fast-twitch type "B" fibers), greater speed endurance, (selective development of fast-twitch type "A" fibers), or greater endurance (selective development of slow-twitch fibers), according to the training routine implemented.

The limiting factor in performance of the horizontal jumps in terms of the structure and makeup of the muscles involved, is the area of the muscle occupied by fast-twitch type "B" fibers. This is because these "pure" fast-twitch fibers are responsible for the maximum force output of the muscle.

not be recruited in substantial numbers until the training load exceeds 90% of 1RM.

At this load, it could be assumed that most, if not all fast-twitch oxidative-glycolytic and slow-twitch fibers, will also be recruited. Hypertrophy of these fibers will be limited however, because the number of repetitions (amount of "work") done at this load does not provide sufficient stress to induce big changes in them.

Fast-twitch "A" fibers require a repetition range above 6 and up to 15 to induce large amounts of hypertrophy (the repetition range usually prescribed is between 8 and 12). The higher the percentage of 1RM used (and therefore the less repetitions used in an exercise), the less these fibers will be induced to hypertrophy.

After the obligatory period of general weight training conditioning, horizontal jumpers need to be provided with loads in the 90% to 100% range of their 1RM. To ensure that an optimal amount of "work" is done by the fast-twitch "B" fibers, the best recipe for loading appears to be a weight which will allow a maximum of between 3 and 5 repetitions per set.

These loads and repetitions set limitations on the amount of work which can be done in each set. With the extent of hypertrophy being dependent upon the total amount of work imposed upon the selected fiber type, it would seem necessary to have the athletes complete a reasonable number of sets of each exercise.

If loads were chosen in the 4-to-5-repetition range, the number of sets needed would be between 2 and 4, whereas if loads permitting only 1 to 3 repetitions were chosen, the number of sets may be up to 4 or 5 during the major conditioning period. The number of sets prescribed here may not seem very high. Choosing a larger number of sets however leads to a drop-off in the quality of the lifts and compromises other equally or more important aspects of training. Prescribing larger numbers of sets or repetitions may also force this fiber type to develop greater endurance characteristics to the detriment of the fiber's ultimate capacity for force development.

Research (Staron, et al., 1989) has demonstrated that fast-twitch "B" fibers will take on the characteristics of fast-twitch "A" fibers as a consequence of a heavy weight training program.

With the potential loss in ultimate force development which may occur, it would appear to be wiser to err on the side of lower repetitions and sets, rather than place at risk the ultimate force potential of the muscle fibers primarily responsible for horizontal jumping performance. In the case of other muscle groups, decisions in this area would be less crucial, (not withstanding the comments made previously about unwanted muscle bulk).

Strength Training Program For Jumpers

By Ed Jacoby, USA

A comprehensive sample macrocycle program for all jumping events designed to achieve a peak performance during the indoor season and then an absolute peak during the major outdoor competitions.

The following information is a sample of a yearly training macrocycle program showing the components of a planned performance scheme for all jumpers.

Each specific phase is a cycle to be employed and completed over a designated period of time. The program includes:
• General Preparation (Four Weeks)
• Special Preparation (Six Weeks)
• Power Development (Three Weeks)
• Indoor Competition Preparation (Four Weeks)
• Power Development (Three Weeks)
• Outdoor Competition Preparation (Four Weeks)

This program is designed to achieve a peak performance indoors and then an absolute peak during the outdoor championships.

The left hand column for each phase shows activities and indicates the areas of emphasis during each mesocycle. To the right is the actual description, volume and duration of each activity. For strength training activity occurring after the General Prep Phase, all weights are determined by a maximum two-rep test at the end of each cycle. This is indicated by the "Test for Max."

As the athlete moves into the new mesocycle, all lifting activities are prescribed by a percentage figure. For example, during the Special Preparation Cycle an athlete completed a power clean lift of 250 pounds x 2 reps. He shows a max lift of 250 pounds.

During the Power Development Cycle, it is prescribed that power cleans be done at 70 percent. The athlete looks at Table 1 and sees that 70 per-cent of 250 pounds is 175 pounds. So as you see, all lifts are performed on the basis of a percentage of the previous cycle's max test (See Weight Training Percentage Table).

Planned performance training is the most effective means of achieving success at a particular time. It is important that the athlete achieve his/her best performance at a time of greatest importance. For example, the high school athlete's ultimate mark should occur during the State Championships, and the elite athlete during the World Championships or the Olympic Games.

Peaking as desired cannot be considered luck. It comes only through definite, planned preparation which entails a step-by-step physiological, psychological and competitive set of progressive activities.

For many years, athletes were trained at or near their maximum potential as long as toleration would allow. We now know that loads, duration and intensity must be mixed and matched. For example, when volume increases, intensity must decrease.

For any type of training, the body responds to stress by making an adaption. In fact, the adaption is a new compensation, better known as super-compensation. You will note that rest or recovery must precede supercompensation. That means sitting high on the list of peaking priority would be the interruption of all types of training with proper amounts of rest to allow the body to recover before assuming additional stress.

Terminology which has evolved out of recent research on planned performance denotes the differ-

Table 1: Weight Training Percentages (Rounded to Five Pounds).

Weight	40%	45%	50%	55%	60%	65%	70%	75%	80%	85%	90%	95%
50	20	25	25	30	30	35	35	40	40	45	45	45
60	25	30	30	35	35	40	40	45	50	55	55	55
70	30	35	35	40	40	50	50	55	55	60	60	65
80	30	40	45	50	50	55	60	65	70	70	75	
90	35	40	45	50	55	60	65	65	75	80	80	85
100	40	45	50	55	60	65	70	75	80	85	90	95
110	45	50	55	60	65	70	75	85	90	95	100	105
120	50	55	60	65	70	80	85	90	95	100	110	115
130	55	60	65	70	80	85	90	100	105	110	115	125
140	55	65	70	75	85	90	100	105	110	120	125	135
150	60	70	75	85	90	100	105	115	120	130	135	145
160	65	75	80	90	95	105	110	120	130	135	145	150
170	70	80	85	95	100	110	120	125	135	145	155	160
180	70	80	90	100	110	115	125	135	145	155	160	170
190	75	85	90	105	115	125	135	145	150	160	170	180
200	80	90	100	110	120	130	140	150	160	170	180	190
210	85	100	105	115	125	135	145	155	170	180	190	190
220	90	100	110	120	130	145	155	165	175	185	200	210
230	95	108	115	125	140	150	160	175	185	195	205	220
240	95	110	120	130	145	155	170	180	190	205	215	230
250	100	115	125	140	150	165	175	190	200	215	225	240
260	105	120	130	145	155	170	180	195	210	220	235	245
270	110	125	135	150	160	175	190	200	215	230	245	255
280	110	125	140	155	170	180	195	210	225	240	250	265
290	115	130	145	160	175	190	205	220	230	245	260	270
300	120	135	150	165	180	195	210	225	240	255	270	285
310	125	140	155	170	185	200	215	230	250	265	280	295
320	130	145	160	175	190	210	225	240	255	270	290	305
330	135	150	165	180	200	210	230	250	265	280	300	315
350	145	160	175	195	210	230	245	265	280	300	315	335
360	140	160	190	200	220	230	250	270	290	310	320	340
390	160	180	200	210	230	250	270	290	310	330	350	370
420	170	190	210	230	250	270	290	320	340	360	380	400
450	180	200	230	250	270	290	320	340	360	380	410	430
480	190	220	240	260	290	310	340	360	380	410	430	460
510	200	230	260	280	310	330	360	380	410	430	460	490
540	220	240	270	300	320	350	380	410	430	460	490	510
570	230	260	290	310	340	370	400	430	460	480	510	540
600	240	270	300	330	360	390	420	450	480	510	540	570

ent sequences which occur at a particular time or stage of the athlete's program.

Moving from the large and total program picture down to a daily training session, the terms would include:

1. Macrocycle

This refers to the largest unit and thus would include our long-range training program. It could be a five-year program, but it normally refers to a training plan for a year.

2. Mesocycle

In some cases, we would consider mesocycles as several weeks of time, a particular time where a definite set of goals are established. It could be a unit where aerobic activity is the major emphasis. It could be the unit where special activities are specified such as overload plyometrics. Each phase can be considered a mesocycle. Sometimes a coach might want to limit an activity to half a mesocycle. That means if a mesocycle is set for six weeks, then that activity may be emphasized for three weeks only.

3. Microcycle

This is a small unit of time—a week or 10 days usually.

4. Session

A session is generally one training unit. If the athlete trains one time per day, then that's one session. Sometimes a coach prescribes two sessions a day, and in extreme instances three sessions.

When the coach is ready to set the microcycle and the session units of the training plan, only the prescription of activities from the outline are used during that time of training.

Also, it is important to see that all items, even the less important activities, such as flexibility, coordination and aerobic running, are incorporated in that particular time phase.

On the bottom of each mesocycle outline is a legend of work-rest ratios. During each time unit, each athlete can tolerate different work loads. As mentioned, there must be set load levels which are always followed by some type of recovery. Some activities require more rest than others and some activities supplement others.

It is important, therefore, to learn the particular load levels of each athlete, or at least groups of athletes, and prescribe a sequence train-recover ratio to use during the different mesocycles. The "T" in the sequence means Train. Training indicates stress response training and usually represents at least a moderate work load, "A.R." indicates Active Rest. This certainly is activity of some type but usually not demanding as to physiological activity. "R" denotes Rest.

In the fall, for example, Saturday is listed as a rest day with Sunday being a strength training day. Later in the power development phase you will see "P.P." This is intense training and indicates Power Program. With the intensity of the power program, it can only occur two times per week and will be followed by Christmas vacation, which will incorporate a lengthy rest period. Finally, "C" indicates individual competitions which are generally preceded by a rest day. Any time skill is indicated a filming session or a simulated competition occurs. It too should be preceded by a rest day.

General Preparation is designed to move the athlete up to a moderate level of fitness. Primary importance is placed upon aerobic conditioning early and then later begin moving toward aerobic power. A general strength conditioning is initiated with all athletes using a standard low load with 10-12 repetitions.

Each athlete will be tested with a single-leg five-hop test; a standing long jump; standing triple jump; overhead shot put; lateral bench hop for 20 seconds; 30-meter sprint and a three-mile run.

The Special Preparation Mesocycle has an established goal for the identification of "special needs." It is used to establish aerobic power through tempo runs of 100m to 300m using the application of effective force while running, e.g., uphill running. In addition, much time is spent on the development of technique or form running.

In regard to strength, training loads have been moved up to 70-80 percent with a transition of volume from five repetitions up to 10. Specific body areas and lifts are identified and taught. Tuesday's strength training session is more jump-specific than the work on Thursday and Sunday, and expresses more specialization in loading and activity.

Strength-speed is an attempt to blend the power activities of plyometrics with the running activities. There is much emphasis on the technical aspects, as this is the period of time that major changes must be completed in the athlete's technique. In fact, major technique changes should never occur after this time.

The Power Development Phase is best described as a maximal volume and load cycle. If performed properly, it takes the athlete to his level of tolerance regarding fatigue. As you remember, fatigue must be followed by a rest/time unit. In this instance, two or three days will not allow sufficient recovery. Thus, we place this prior to Christmas vacation where all athletes are inclined to be far less active than normal.

The real emphasis of the cycle occurs on the Saturday and Thursday strength sessions. Not only do you see fairly high repetitions and percentages, but activities are intensified. Specifically, a half-squat exercise followed by another half-squat with greater intensity, which is followed by a more intense activity of bounding, and it doesn't stop here. The athlete immediately moves into a prone leg press repeated two times with more bounding to follow. All of these are accomplished before the program moves to upper body work. This is a very intense activity and is certainly not recommended for your young jumper. The program must be modified (eased) for the younger athlete.

GENERAL PREPARATION PHASE (FOUR WEEKS)

Activities:

RUNNING

A. 30 minute runs or Fartlek (1/2 mesocycle)
B. Extensive tempo-long intervals—med. rec. or short intervals. Very short recovery 35-70% (1/2 mesocycle)
C. Intensive aerobic power—80-89% (hills or flat)
D. Speed—80m—90-100%

STRENGTH
1. Muscle Balance
2. Develop Tendon Ends

A. Body weight circuits (1/2 mesocycle) (full squats).
B. Cleans (3 x 10), High Step-Ups (3 x 15), Quads (3 x 15)
Hamstrings (3 x 15 x 1-day wk/neg.), Incline Bench (3 x 15),
Dumbells (3 x 25). Test for maximum—last day of mesocycle. Goal range of movement.
10 reps for all or none 3 units/week (All). Only thing different, two sessions may be better than one.

STRENGTH-SPEED
1. Power Strength
2. Dynamic Balance Ends

Meso Endurance—1/2 Mesocycle
A. Lateral Bench Hops (2 x 20 sec.) To be completed during strength days.
B. Double-Leg 20-40m/set, Progress double to single.
C. RR-LL Single Flat and Stadium Stairs.
D. Backward Hopping (1/2 mesocycle)
    Meso Power 6-10 reps/set   Weighted Vest
        1. Depth Jumps
        2. Hurdle Hops
        3. Longer Jumps

MULTI-THROWS

Meso Endurance—1/2 Mesocycle—Light medicine ball for strength endurance
Meso Strength—1/2 Mesocycle
A. Heavy implement throwing and drills,
B. Heavy medicine ball work (All 2 sessions/week),

FLEXIBILITY

Static Testing—Static Stretching

COORDINATION

General   Games: Basketball, Badminton, Volleyball and Soccer
Specific   Standing Triple Jump, Lateral Bench Hops, Sprint, Hurdle Drills

PSYCHOLOGICAL

Educate   Skills, Power Lifting, Multi-Hops, Multi-Throws, Technique, Film Study, Motivate.

LEGEND OF WORK-REST RATIOS							
WEEK	Monday	Tuesday	Wednesday	Thursday	Friday	Saturday	Sunday
1	T	A.R.	T	A.R	T	R	T
2	T	T	R	T	A.R.	R	T
3	T	T	A.R.	T	R	R	T
4	T	T	R	T	T	R	T

T = Train; A.R. = Active Rest; R = Rest

It should be noted that after Christmas vacation the athlete will often return and exhibit the highest strength and explosive capabilities yet achieved in his career. This is due to the supercompensation principle.

The Indoor Preparation Phase should be considered the preparation phase for high school or non-indoor competitors. The outdoor preparation precludes strength activities for those college programs that provide both indoor and outdoor seasons.

Basically, the idea here is to reduce the volume of training and begin special speed activities. The purpose is not to provide a backing-off attitude toward training, but to temper or moderate activity, particularly strength training. You see that load

SPECIAL PREPARATION PHASE (SIX WEEKS)

Activities:

RUNNING
- A. Speed (Runways)
- B. Speed Endurance
- C. Aerobic Power 2/weeks
  Sprint Drills 2/weeks
- D. Power Speed (hills, stadium stairs) 1 /each 2/weeks

STRENGTH

A. **Thursday, Sunday**

Cleans	3 x 5,	1 x 10 @ 70%	
Half-Squats	3 x 5,	1 x 10 @ 70%	
Hamstrings	3 x 5,	1 x 10 @ 70%	
Dumbells		3 x 10 @ 80%	
(Arm Action)			
Incline P.	3 x 5,	1 x 10 @ 70%	

B. **Tuesday**

Clean & Jerk	2 x 3 @ 80%	2 x 2 @ 85%	1 x 3 @ 90%
Inverted Leg Press		3 x 8 @ 80%	
Hamstrings	3 x 8 @ 80%	(Single)	
Snatch	3 x 5 @ 70%		
Low Step-Ups	2 x 3 @ 80%	2 x 5 @ 80%	
Increase	0/0 x 2 5 each week		
Test for maximum.			

STRENGTH-SPEED

Meso Power—1/2 Mesocycle
- A. Standing—1 step—2 step Triple Jumps
- B. All 1/2 Approach—Full Approach Jumping
- C. Box Jumping
- D. Lateral Bench Hops
- E. Hurdle Hops
- F. Depth Jumps
- G. Depth to Hurdles (No Weight)

Meso Endurance—Longer Jumps 3-4 Sets (While Outdoors)—1/2 Mesocycle

TECHNICAL
- A. Full run approaches
- B. Drills specific for pole vault
- C. Jump for height (film evaluation)

MULTI-THROWS
- A. Medicine balls and varied implements—medium weight
- B. Decreasing volume—increased intensity

FLEXIBILITY
- A. Static
- B. Dynamic (i.e., Sprint—Hurdle Drills)

COORDINATION

Event-Specific drills.

PSYCHOLOGICAL

Dedication, Persistence, Concentration

LEGEND OF WORK-REST RATIOS							
WEEK	**Monday**	**Tuesday**	**Wednesday**	**Thursday**	**Friday**	**Saturday**	**Sunday**
I	T	T	T	A.R	T	T	R
2	T	T	T	A.R.	T	T	R
3	A.R.	T	A.R.	T	T	T	R
4	T	T	T	T	A.R.	R	R
5	T	T	R	T	R	T	R
6	T	T	R	T	T	A.R.	R

T = Train; A.R. = Active Rest; R = Rest

POWER DEVELOPMENT PHASE
(THREE WEEKS, TO BE USED PRIOR TO CHRISTMAS VACATION)

Emphasis is to be placed on maximum amount of weight which can be moved during a specific amount of time. This is the "optimal load" concept, used to produce faster movement response. Lifting is to be interspersed with plyometric work two sessions a week.

Activities

RUNNING

SPEED POWER	SPECIAL ENDURANCE	
A. Stadium Stairs	A. 200-300	80-90%
B. Hill Sprints	B. 150's	90-100%
C. Belt Sprints	C. 80's	90-100%
D. Sprint—Hurdle Drills (Daily)		

STRENGTH &
POWER JUMPS

First and Third Days

A. Half-Squats/set	x 6 reps	@ 80%	
B. Half-Squats/set	x 8 reps	@ 90%	
C. Single-Leg Hops to 40 each leg,			
D. Inverted-Leg Press/set	x 5	@ 100% of 1/2 squat.	
E. Inverted-Leg Press/set	x 4	@ 110% of 1/2 squat.	
F. 8 x Stair Hops Single-Leg each flight.			
G. Power Clean/set	x 8	@ 70%	
H. Power Clean/set	x 10	@ 60%	
I. Depth Jump over Hurdle	x 15		
J. Snatch/set	x 4	@ 90%	

Second Day

A. Cleans	3 x 5,	1x10	@ 70%
B. Half-Squats	3 x 4,	1x10	@ 70%
C. High Step-Ups		2x16	@ 85%
D. Hamstrings		3x5	@ 70%
		2x8	@ 75%
E. Low Step-Ups		1x8	@ 70%
& Downs		1x8	@ 75%
		1x8	@ 90%

MAX WEIGHT TEST

TECHNICAL

A. Consistency on runway.
B. Speed for last six steps.
C. Consistency of height 8-10 jumps.

MULTI-THROWS

Meso Power (Step Throw)

FLEXIBILITY

Static Stretching

PSYCHOLOGICAL

Intensity of Power Workouts—
Concentration on Consistency

LEGEND OF WORK-REST RATIOS							
WEEK	Monday	Tuesday	Wednesday	Thursday	Friday	Saturday	Sunday
I	T	T	A.R.	P.P.	T	R	P.P.
2	T	A.R.	A.R.	P.P.	T	R	P.P.
3	T	A.R.	A.R.	P.P.	T	R	

T = Train; A.R. = Active Rest; R = Rest; P.P. = Warmup and Power Train

INDOOR OR OUTDOOR COMPETITION PREPARATION PHASE
(FOUR WEEKS)

Activities

RUNNING
   A. Sprint—Hurdle Drills (Daily)
   B. Power-Bound-Power-Sprint
   C. 20-40-20 Speed—20M Acceleration—40 Steady—20 Deceleration
   D. 80's curve or straight   90-100%
   E. Power Sprints   100%
   F. 100-150's   90-100%

STRENGTH

1/2 Meso
Absolute strength maintenance—Specific Strength
Power: Tuesday & Sunday 2 Sessions/Week

A.	Snatch	1 x 6	@ 80%			
B.	Helf-Squats	1 x 6	@ 70%,	1 x 5 @ 80%,	1 x 4	@ 85%
C.	Hamstrings	1 x 6	@ 70%,	1 x 5 @ 80%,	1 x 4	@ 85%
D.	Lateral Bench Hops	1 x 20 seconds				
E.	Cleans	1 x 6	@ 70%,	1 x 5 @ 80%,	1 x 4	@ 85%

1/2 Meso—Max or Near-Max Lift: 1 every 14 days or less.

STRENGTH—3 SPEED
   A. Full approach or skill drills.
   B. Speed bounding.
   C. Depth jump low variety.
   D. Short jumps.
   E. Light weight implement throwing

TECHNICAL   Full Jumps—Film Evaluation—Problem Solving

FLEXIBILITY   Static Stretching—PNF Drills

PSYCHOLOGICAL   Confidence—Concentration

LEGEND OF WORK-REST RATIOS							
WEEK	Monday	Tuesday	Wednesday	Thursday	Friday	Saturday	Sunday
1	T	T	R	S	T	c	R
2	T	T	R	T	R	c	R
3	T	T	R	T	R	R/C	R
4	T	T	R	R	C	C	R

T = Train; S = Skill; R = Rest; C = Competition

percentages range from 70-85 per cent, but with smaller repetitions.

The bounding activities have changed from power to speed. Basically, the jumper's emphasis has now moved from strength development to maintenance, and the real priority now is moving toward competition.

The Competition Phase is perhaps the most complex for the coach to prescribe to individual athletes because they must understand the activity preceding competition. Some respond well to rest and some do not. Too many times we move towards an activity and this is detrimental to the nerve recruitment properties which are necessary for high performance.

The idea, however, is to maintain strength levels, but provide sufficient recoveries. All activity is done at a moderate load with very few repetitions,

Ten days prior to a major competition we want to complete the final strength work at moderate intensity or with a single maximum-type activity.

Everything performed is at nearly top speed,

COMPETITION PHASE
(THREE TO SIX WEEKS)

Activities					
RUNNING		Speed—Special Endurance			
STRENGTH		1/2 Meso—2 Sessions/Week			

	DAY 1	Snatches	1 x 6 @ 70%,	1 x 4 @ 80%	
		Hamstrings	1 x 6 @ 70%,	1 x 5 @ 80%,	1 x 4 @ 85%
		Lateral Bench	1 x 12 seconds		
		Hops w/ Dumbells			
		Cleans	1 x 6 @ 70	1 x 5 @ 80%,	1 x 4 @ 85%
	DAY 2	Quarter-Squats	1 x 6 @ 70	1 x 4 @ 85%	
		Low Step-Ups	1 x 8 @ 70	1 x 6 @ 75%,	1 x 6 @ 80%
		Hamstrings	1 x 5 @ 75	1 x 4 @ 85%,	
		Lateral Bench	1 x15		
		Hops (Light)			
		Cleans	1 x 6 @ 75	1 x 4 @ 85 %	

	1/2 Meso—1 Session/Week				
		Cleans	1 x 6 @ 70%,	1 x 5 @ 80%,	1 x 4 @ 85%
		Quarter-Squats	1 x 6 @ 70%,	1 x 5 @ 80%,	1 x 4 @ 85%
		Hamstrings	1 x 8 @ 70%,	1 x 6 @ 75%,	1 x 6 @ 80%
		Lateral Bench	1 x 12 @ 100%		
		Hops (Light)			

	10 Days Prior to Major Competition				
		Quarter-Squat—Cleans	1 x 4 @ 70%,	1 x 2 @ 85%,	1 x 1 @ 90-100%

STRENGTH-SPEED   A. Jumps specific to event.
                                    B. High Intensity/Low Volume

TECHNICAL   Competitive Analysis

FLEXIBILITY   Some Static, Mostly Dynamic

PSYCHOLOGICAL   Confidence

LEGEND OF WORK-REST RATIOS							
WEEK	**Monday**	**Tuesday**	**Wednesday**	**Thursday**	**Friday**	**Saturday**	**Sunday**
1	S/T	T	R	A.R.	R	C	R
2	S/T	T	T	A.R.	R	T	R
3	S/T	A.R.	R	C	R	C	R

T = Train; S = Skill; R = Rest; C = Competition; A.R. = Active Rest

and with maximum recovery periods. The only concern is high performance achievement. There should be no technical changes. Confidence is the key—the athlete is ready to perform well, and he/ she knows it.

Specificity Of Strength Development For Improving The Takeoff In Jumping Events

By Warren Young, Australia

An examination of specific speed-strength qualities in all four jumping events with sound practical guidelines for assessment of these qualities and suggestions as to how improvement can be achieved in training.

The need for strength training for the jumping events is well accepted. However the specific strength qualities, or forms of strength, that are important are probably not so well known. The purpose of this article is to examine these qualities and to provide implications for the training and assessment of jumpers.

The greatest strength requirement in jumping events is in relation to the takeoff phase. Although there are some distinct differences between the jumping events, there are also some common features relating to the takeoff. Firstly, the duration of the takeoff is always less than 200ms (15). Secondly, the types of muscular contractions produced during the takeoff are common to all jumps.

In the high and long jumps the center of gravity of the body is usually lowered prior to the takeoff and rises immediately after the foot plant. Despite this, there is flexion or bending at the hip, knee and ankle joint (16). This results in lengthening or stretching of the leg extensor muscles (quadriceps, gluteal hamstrings and calves), i.e., eccentric contractions. The leg then begins to extend or straighten as a result of a shortening of the leg extensors (concentric contractions). Therefore in all jumping events the takeoff consists of an eccentric-concentric contraction sequence or a stretch-shortening cycle (SSC).

LONG JUMP

In the long jump, better athletes achieve faster runups and produce greater takeoff forces in less time than less qualified athletes (12). Generally the greater the runup speed, the greater the tendency for the takeoff leg to bend on impact as a result of the high eccentric or stretch loads imposed on the leg extensor muscles.

Better athletes are able to tolerate these loads and avoid collapsing of the leg (2, 12), which could result in a loss of horizontal velocity and poor elevation.

A recent biomechanical analysis of elite male long jumpers provided extra insight into the takeoff mechanism (11). A low body position prior to foot plant allowed the body to pivot over the takeoff leg, thereby generating vertical velocity as soon as the takeoff commenced. At the end of the eccentric phase, when the knee angle was reduced to 144 degrees, as much as two thirds of the final vertical velocity had already been generated.

It was concluded that "to ensure the pivot mechanism can operate there is a clear requirement for the body to resist flexion at touchdown. . . As approach speed increases, leg strength must also increase to be able to control the higher forces at impact" (11, p. 77).

TRIPLE JUMP

When landing from the hop and step, the impact forces are even greater than those encountered in the long jump, and can be over 20 times the body weight of the athlete (9). This is not surprising because the triple jumper has to absorb a large downward velocity before the upward concentric phase can begin. The athlete does not have the luxury of absorbing the impact forces by bending the knee and prolonging the takeoff time. If this were done, a large loss of horizontal velocity and a poor takeoff would follow.

The athlete could reduce the length and height of the hop to decrease the following impact loads, but this would obviously affect the total distance jumped. A better strategy would be to improve the ability to tolerate the high impact or stretch loads imposed on the leg muscles. This would enable the jumper to hop further with less risk of the takeoff leg collapsing at landing. In fact, the ability to tolerate the impact forces on landings may be a limiting factor to triple jump performance (17).

HIGH JUMP

Using a faster runup is potentially advantageous for a high jumper because it provides improved potential to apply greater vertical takeoff forces (4). Sotomayor and Kostadinova are examples of jumpers who successfully employ relatively fast runups (5). However, for a given athlete, increasing the runup speed would only improve performance up to an optimum speed, and then jump height would deteriorate at greater

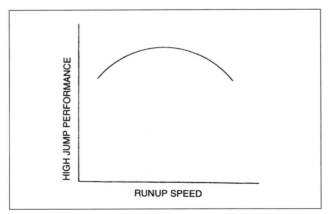

Figure 1: Simplified diagram illustrating the expected relationship between runup speed and high jump performance.

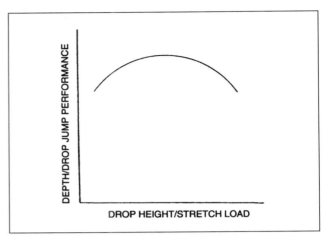

Figure 2: Simplified diagram illustrating the relationship between drop height and DJ performance.

speeds (Figure 1).

The decrease in performance at very high runup speeds could be related to technical factors, e.g., poor body positioning. However, it might also be explained by neuromuscular factors. For example, consider the performance of depth or drop jumps (DJ) which involves falling from a predetermined height and then immediately jumping vertically. The higher the fall or drop height, the greater the downward velocity of the body on landing and the greater the stretch loads imposed on the leg extension. Often, as the stretch load increases with increasing drop height, the jump increases, but then falls of with very high stretch loads (3, 16) (Figure 2). This reduced jumping may be associated with a neuromuscular inhibition (8).

With reference to a fast runup in the high jump, Dapena (5, p. 3310) states: "If the takeoff leg is not strong enough, it will be forced to flex excessively during the takeoff phase, and then it may not be able to make a forceful extension in the final part of the takeoff phase. In other words, the takeoff leg may 'buckle' under the stress. . ." The solution according to Dapenda is to use some "extra strengthening" of the takeoff leg to withstand the impact loads.

POLE VAULT

The takeoff in the pole vault cannot be considered in the same way as the other events. In the high jump the vertical propulsion is totally generated by the muscular forces during the takeoff. In the pole vault a greater runup speed is used to transfer energy to the pole which is later released to propel the athlete vertically. Therefore even though a vaulter may use a "pre-jump" takeoff technique (10), the strength qualities required for successful performance may be expected to differ from the qualities required for a "true" jumping action.

STRENGTH QUALITIES

The previous discussion reveals that for the long, triple and high jump takeoffs there are some common features:
- Large takeoff forces must be applied in a short time, therefore generating a high power output.
- Takeoff power is produced by SSC muscular contractions.
- Athletes must prevent excessive knee flexion during the eccentric phase. To achieve this, jumpers must be able to tolerate high stretch loads.

The ability to quickly switch from the eccentric to concentric phase in a SSC is described as reactive or elastic strength, According to Schmidtbleicher (14). This is a relatively independent strength quality. This means that an athlete may possess good general strength and power but will not necessarily display good power capabilities in a SSC.

Assessment of strength qualities of athletes at the Australian Institute of Sport (AIS) confirms this. The implication for the coach is that training methods that specifically develop reactive strength must be identified and prescribed.

Traditional weight training exercises, e.g., squats, power cleans and snatches are necessary for developing an optimum level of muscle mass, maximum strength and speed strength abilities. However, once this foundation has been established, reactive strength training methods (i.e., plyometrics) play an increasingly important role in the specific strength development of jumpers.

Due to the principle of specificity of training, care must be exercised in the selection of plyometric drills. To illustrate this, the result of a study on four jumpers is of interest (1). The athletes were analyzed while performing a high jump and a variety of plyometric exercises that they were accustomed to. These consisted of variations of hopping, stepping and depth jumping from single- and double-leg takeoffs.

While the mean contact time for the high jump takeoff was 177ms, the contact times for the plyometric exercises were generally greater than 250ms. Furthermore, none of the exercises were able to match or exceed the neuromuscular demands of the high jump takeoff. Since the takeoff times of the plyometric exercises were significantly longer than the time available for force production in the high jump takeoff, the training effects of these exercises would not have been optimum.

ASSESSMENT OF REACTIVE STRENGTH

The AIS has recently established a laboratory strength assessment system that is specific to sprinting and jumping movements. Although it can be used to measure maximum strength, speed-strength, reactive strength and strength-endurance qualities of the leg extensors to obtain athlete profiles and monitor training, the following discussion will be limited to reactive strength as it relates to jumpers.

A DJ may be thought of as an indicator of reactive strength because it requires a reversal of the downward movement into a concentric action to jump vertically. However, if an athlete is required to jump for maximum height and no other instructions regarding jump technique are provided, the contact times produced are generally long (over 400ms).

In this situation, the athlete bends the knees to about a 90-degree angle so that a long time can be used to absorb the impact forces and generate upward propulsion. This is clearly not specific to the takeoff conditions encountered in the jumping events.

A more specific measure of reactive strength that is used at the AIS takes into account both jump height and contact time. The objective is to maximize height, minimize contact time and therefore maximize the jump height/contact time ratio. The athlete receives feedback about these parameters immediately after a jump so that the optimum combination of jump height and contact time can be easily achieved. An example of a test results for a female long jumper is shown in Figure 3.

The typical range of contact times produced by this method is approximately 125-180ms, which is very similar to those used in the jumping events (15). This test also invokes a relatively small knee flexion and high stretch loads, which are similar to the jump takeoff.

Due to the specificity of this test, results obtained at the AIS have confirmed that it is a better predictor of the ability to jump for height from a

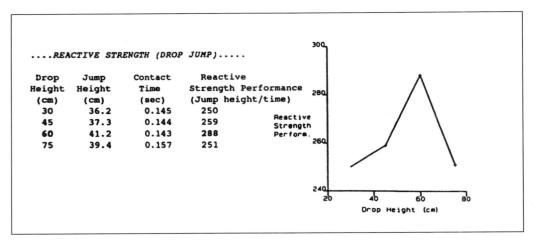

....REACTIVE STRENGTH (DROP JUMP).....

Drop Height (cm)	Jump Height (cm)	Contact Time (sec)	Reactive Strength Performance (Jump height/time)
30	36.2	0.145	250
45	37.3	0.144	259
60	41.2	0.143	288
75	39.4	0.157	251

Figure 3: An example of a reactive strength test result.

runup than a test involving a long contact time (DJ for height only or vertical jump).

AIS testing has also shown that sprinters and jumpers attain similar results on a variety of measures of power, but jumpers are generally superior in reactive strength. This makes sense because although sprinters also require fast SSC contractions, they do not have the need to tolerate very high stretch loads.

The reactive strength test is conducted with a contact mat and a portable computer which calculates and displays jump height, contact time and reactive strength performance immediately after a jump. The drop heights used are 30, 45, 60 and 75cm, and DJ is always performed with the hands placed on the hips. The results are graphed to enhance the interpretation of the test (Figures 3 and 4).

IMPLICATIONS FOR TRAINING

There are various, ways to interpret the results. Firstly, the best reactive strength performance score (e.g., 393 for the high jumper in Fig. 4) is compared to athlete norms. This gives information about an athlete's current level of reactive strength and determines the need to further train this quality. If the result is relatively poor, a greater emphasis should be placed on reactive strength training methods. Ideally, this result should be examined in conjunction with other test results of different qualities, since it is only one component that influences performance.

Secondly, the drop height yielding the best performance provides information about the ability to tolerate stretch loads. The higher the drop height, the better this ability. Untrained people, or

athletes who don't require high levels of reactive strength will generally achieve their best performances from a 30 or 45cm drop height. On the other hand, jumpers may achieve the best result from a 60 or 75cm drop height, indicating a superior tolerance to stretch loads (Fig. 4).

In addition, DJ training has been shown to reduce the neuromuscular inhibition that may be associated with high stretch loads (13). If tolerance to stretch loads can be improved, a long or high jumper may be able to utilize a faster runup without negative effects and a triple jumper may be able to hop further without collapsing on the landing going into the step phase.

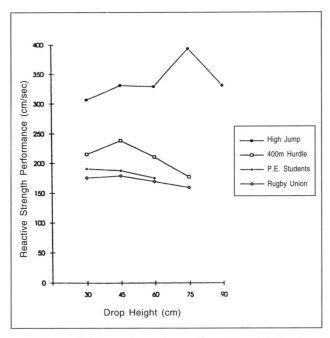

Figure 4: Examples of reactive strength test results for different athletes.

The reactive strength test can also be used to determine what drop height the athlete should use for training. In the example of the high jump (Fig. 4), drop heights of 30 to 60cm produced a sub-maximum performance. From a 75cm drop the performance was maximized, probably due to an optimum use of the stretch reflex and the storage and utilization of elastic energy by the neuromuscular system.

The most powerful contractions would most likely occur from this drop height and therefore would be expected to produce the best training stimulus.

With drop heights greater than 75cm, performance declined, presumably due to a neuromuscular inhibition. Therefore the recommended training drop height for this athlete is 75cm.

An advantage of using this test result to prescribe the training drop height is that it is individualized, which helps to ensure that athletes are not exposed to drop heights that are either too low or excessive.

It should be remembered that as the drop height increases so does the impact or stretch load. The intensity of this training method is inherently high and therefore relatively low volumes should be used, e.g., 4-5 sets of 5-8 reps, 2-3 times per week. The rest between sets should be complete (e.g., 3 minutes or more) to prevent fatigue of the nervous system and deterioration of performance from one set to the next.

Athletes with a history of injury, especially in the calf muscle, Achilles tendon and shin areas, should perform this type of DJ with caution. DJs should be performed on a firm but forgiving surface, e.g., firm grass, synthetic track, timber floor. Extremely soft surfaces (e.g., sand, gymnastics mats) absorb too much of the landing impact and may change the timing of the movements. Running shoes with good shock-absorbing qualities are preferable to running/jumping spikes for minimizing the risk of injury from intense DJ training.

Experience at the AIS has shown that for one jumper, the addition of two sessions per week of DJ training over two weeks were able to produce an improvement in reactive strength performance of over 15%. It should be noted that some of these training sessions were performed with the aid of the contact mat/computer system so that immediate feedback was provided.

This feedback may in fact be quite important for ensuring that the "correct" contact times are being performed and for motivation. The portability and low expense of this system makes it viable as a routine procedure for monitoring plyometric training as well as for testing.

DJ is only one form of plyometric training. A limitation of DJ is that it involves a double-leg takeoff. This movement pattern is not as specific to jumping events as plyometric exercises that utilize a single-leg takeoff and encourage the use of the free limbs, e.g., bounding. The advantage of the DJ training method described here is that the individual optimum stretch load and specific contact times can be used and controlled. A combination of DJ and other specific plyometric exercises would be ideal and is recommended for developing the reactive strength component of jumpers.

REFERENCES

1. Aura, 0. and J.T. Viitasalo. Biomechanical characteristics of jumping. *International Journal of Sport Biomechanics.* 5,1989: 89-98
2. Bosco, C., Luhtanen, P. and P.V. Komi. Kinetics and kinematics of the takeoff in the long jump. *Biomechanics V-B.* 1976:174-180.
3. Bosco, C., Viitasalo, J.T., Komi, P.V. and P. Luhtanen. Combined effect of elastic energy and myoelectrical potentiation during stretch-shortening cycle exercise. *Acta Physiol Scand.* 114, 1982: 557-565.
4. Dapena, J. Basic and applied research in the biomechanics of high jumping. *Med. Sport Sci.* 25, 1987:19-33
5. Dapena, J. Biomechanical analysis of the Fosbury flop. *Track Technique.* 1988: 3307-3333.
6. Dapena, J. and C.S. Chung. Vertical and radial motions of the body during the takeoff phase of high jumping. *Med. Sci. Sports and Ex.* 20(3), 1988: 290-302.
7. Enoka, R.M. The effect of different lengths of runup on the height to which a spiker in volleyball can reach. *New Zealand In. Health Phys. Ed. and Rec.* 4(3), 1971: 5- 15.
8. Gollhofer, A. and D. Schmidtbleicher. Muscle activation patterns of human leg extensors and forcetime characteristics in jumping exercises under increased stretching loads. In: G. De Groot, et al. (Eds.) *Biomechanics XI.* Free Univ. Press, Amsterdam, 1988:143-147.
9. Hay, J.G. Citius, altius, longius (faster, higher, longer): the biomechanics of jumping for distance. *Jn. Biomechanics.* 26,1993: 7-21.
10. Launder, A. The pre-jump—a revolution in the pole vault. *Modern Athlete and Coach.* 27(3), 1989: 7-9.
11. Lees, A., Graham-Smith, P. and N. Fowler. A biomechanical analysis of the last stride, touchdown, and takeoff characteristics of the men's long jump. *Journal of Applied Biomechanics.* 10, 1994: 61-78.
12. Luhtanen, P. and P.V. Komi. Mechanical power and segmental contribution to force impulses in long jump takeoff. *Eur. Jn. Appl. Physiol.* 41, 1979: 267-274.
13. Schmidtbleicher, D., Gollhofer, A. and U. Frick. Effects of a stretch-shortening typed training on the performance capability and innervation characteristics of leg extensor muscles. In: G. De Groot, et al. (Eds.) *Biomechanics XI.* Free Univ. Press, Amsterdam, 1988:185-189.
14. Schmidtbleicher, D. Training for power events. In: Komi, P.V. (Ed.) *Strength and Power in Sport.* 1992: 381- 395, Blackwell, Oxford.
15. Tidow, G. Aspects of strength training in athletics. *New Studies in Athletics.* 1, 1990: 93-110.
16. Viitasalo, J.T. and C. Bosco. Electromechanical behavior of human muscles in vertical jumps. *Eur. Jn. Appl. Physiol.* 48,1982; 253-261.
17. Young, W. The triple jump and plyometrics. *NSCA Journal.* 9(2), 1987: 22-24.

Development Of Physical And Technical Capacities In Jumping Events

By L.S. Homenkova, Russia

A summary of universally accepted training means recommended for general and specific development of physical performance capacities in jumping events with some advice on technical preparation.

TRAINING MEANS

Each jumping event in the track and field program, whether high jumping, long jumping, triple jumping or pole vaulting, has its own pattern of neuromuscular coordination and autonomous functioning. The so-called "specialization" of motor functions applies only to the final specific preparation in jumping events, as disturbing the essential relationship of physical components detracts from the athlete's technique in his event.

Specific training exercises employed by jumpers consist of one or more elements of the competition event. Specific training exercises give an athlete the experience for performing the specific exercise under varied conditions of easier, normal and harder. Such specific exercises also allow an athlete to selectively work certain muscle groups to develop the desired performance elements.

Performing specific exercises requires the athlete to pay attention to both the form and the content of the technique—and the rhythm of performance. The greater the similarity between the specific exercise and the competition jump, the faster the athlete will acquire new skills and capacities and the faster performance improvements will take place.

In performing general conditioning exercises it is important to pay attention to range of motion and freedom of movement, as well as maintaining correct posture. In order to achieve the desired maximal all-round development, each general conditioning exercise must be performed in a sufficient number of repetitions and sets to create slight muscular fatigue.

All jumping events are performed with high-speed movements against significant external resistance. Hence, their performance depends largely on speed strength. However, while a high jumper needs speed strength to generate *maximal* vertical movement, long and triple jumpers need speed strength to generate *optimal* jumping height at maximal running velocity. Pole vaulters require similar qualities as long jumpers but need, in addition, arm and trunk strength, as well as high-level coordination for the movement sequence on the pole.

To perfect physical capacities and motor skills, athletes make use of several methods. These include **repetition,** performing exercises "to exhaustion," the **variable and intermittent method,** and the **continuous method** in general endurance development. In the use of the intermittent method to develop specific endurance it is important to keep in mind the duration and intensity of the exercise (in running, the length of the segment and elapsed time), the length of recovery intervals, the type of recoveries (passive or active), and the number of repetitions.

In speed-strength development jumpers widely use what we term the **"dynamic method."** This method promotes the most rapid strength increases through the use of weight resistance exercises performed dynamically at close to maximal speed without restricting the movement range.

The variable method is useful in the development of technique, in particular when a new technique is developed. The term "variable" applies to an optimal combination of harder-than-normal, normal, and easier-than-normal exercises to exploit maximally the immediate reaction to the varied loads. The harder-than-normal conditions stimulate specific strength, while the easier-than-normal conditions promote specific speed.

The coupled effects method is used to provide a parallel development of technique and physical capacities. In this method resistances should not be so heavy that they affect technique in the performance of a part or whole of a jump.

As far as technique is concerned in the choice of different training means, it should always be kept in mind that the quality of the execution is extremely important in all performances. Self-monitoring should here include segments of the approach run, the results of jumps, memories of muscular sensations and controlling movements at different speeds. The coach's evaluation of the effectiveness of the technique is also naturally essential.

Jumpers use the following training means for general conditioning:
- **For general endurance:** long, steady runs at moderate intensity, cross country skiing, rowing, basketball, soccer and so on. All these activities are usually performed with the heart rate in the range of 140 to 160/min.
- **For musculo-skeletal system and general strength:** weight resistance exercises, gymnastics, elements of acrobatics.
- **For agility and coordination:** sports games, gymnastics and acrobatic exercises.

The commonly used general conditioning exercises include the following:
- Arm movements performed standing or walking and composed of arm flexions and extensions, handstands, rapid pushups.
- Trunk turns and twists with various arm and leg positions, circular trunk movements, back raises, reverse back raises, hip and leg lifts.
- Straight- or bent-legged swings forward, backward and sideways, circular leg movements, walking lunges, single-legged or double-legged squats and half-squats, including stops in various positions (dynamic isometrics).
- Relaxation exercises, including shaking arms and legs in different positions, such as sitting, standing, lying down or hanging. The main relaxation method is to tense selected muscles for 4 to 10 seconds and then return to a passive, fully relaxed position.

- Acrobatic exercises have a wide variety and include somersaults from a runup, backward rolls into a stand, kip-ups, back handsprings and backward somersaults.
- Partner exercises are made up from partner-assisted flexibility exercises in various positions and partner-assisted resistance exercises for different muscle groups.
- Medicine balls offer a wide variety of general conditioning exercises and include upward throws, forward throws, throws from the supine position, throws from behind the neck, single- and double-arm throws from the chest, leaps and bounds with a ball in the hands, upward and forward throws with the feet and many more.
- Weight resistance exercises (dumbbells, barbells, kettlebells, and sandbags) are not restricted to universally accepted routines but should include various types of leaps, jumps and hops with additional weight, as well as lungelike strides and running with various weight resistances.
- Exercises on gymnastics apparatus (wall bars, rings, ropes, poles, horizontal bars, parallel bars, vaulting horses and benches) include mainly simple hangs, climbs, pullups, circles, upstarts and dismounts.
- Isometric exercises are performed from varied starting positions, generally imitating certain running or jumping phases. Maximum muscle tension is held for 6 to 10 seconds. Two to three exercises are executed in sets of three to four repetitions.
- In the development of basic aerobic endurance with steady cross country runs it is beneficial to have breaks in the run to perform three to five repetitions of 150m accelerations, three to five sets of jumping exercises and 25 to 50 jumps reaching for tree branches with both arms.

SPECIFIC PHYSICAL TRAINING

Specific physical (functional) and technical preparation is composed of basic and specific exercises. These include speed-strength exercises, running and jumping exercises designed to develop and perfect motor qualities and skills directly applicable to the athlete's competition event. In the following text we will take a more detailed look at the development of speed strength and supplementary exercises recommended for preparation in different jumping events.

SPEED-STRENGTH PREPARATION

Speed-strength development includes a large number of training means and methods designed to improve an athlete's capacity to overcome significant external resistance during movements performed at maximal speed.

During a 5.0- to 5.5-second approach run jumpers must build up their maximum speed, followed within 0.11 to 0.20 sec. a 20- to 65-degree change of direction. This means overcoming and developing significant forces that average 350 to 500kg at the takeoff.

For this reason speed strength should be developed only in tandem with the movements and neuromuscular coordination that takes place during the takeoff. This is necessary to develop a running speed that corresponds to the jumper's capacity to change from horizontal to angular motion.

Jumpers use the following main exercises to develop their speed strength:

Overcoming their own body weight

Fast moving, one- and two-legged jumps in place or with a runup (various lengths and speeds), depth jumps, high jumps, long jumps, multiple jumps and bounds in various combinations. Strength exercises and exercises on gymnastics apparatus (particularly important for pole vaulters).

Different types of added weight

Running, jumping exercises, high jumps, long jumps, triple jumps and pole vaults with added weights to increase resistance (weight belts, weight vests, ankle weights, etc.).

Using natural environment

Running and jumping uphill or downhill, running up and downstairs, running on different surfaces (snow, sand, sawdust, forest trails), running with the wind and into the wind.

Overcoming external resistances

Maximal speed performances in exercises with partners, exercises with different types of resistances (0.5kg cuff weights and weight vests, 2 to 5kg medicine balls, 16 to 32kg kettlebells and dumbbells, 5 to 15kg sandbags).

SPEED-STRENGTH DEVELOPMENT

A jumper's speed strength development is meant to build speed and strength in the widest range of possible combinations. This takes place in three dimensions.

1. Speed Alone

Pure speed training develops the jumper's absolute speed in the basic exercises (running, jumping) or its parts (various body segment movements) and their combinations (starting, accelerations, runups, takeoffs, going over the bar). The conditions in which the jumper performs these exercises can be made easier to place emphasis on speed.

2. Speed and Strength Combined

Combined speed-strength exercises develop both muscular strength and speed. Jumpers perform in this method whole competition jumps, or their individual parts, either with no additional resistance or with light resistance in the form of belts, vests and cuffs.

3. Strength Alone

These exercises are designed to develop strength in the muscle groups that play an active part in the performance of the competition jump. The weight or resistance in these exercises range from 80 to 100% of the maximum and are performed at a speed of 60 to 100% of maximal speed.

We believe that an athlete's speed-strength development should follow these main recommendations:
- In performing exercises, pay particular attention to technique. This includes the rhythm of the movements, the range of movements, significant angles, and the speed of executing maximal muscular effort.
- Focus on an explosive performance of the exercise.
- In the performance of specific exercises, the work must be concentrated on specific muscle groups that serve the foot, ankle, knee, hip and abdominal movements.
- It is important in the performance of speed-strength exercises to exploit the strength and elasticity of pre-stretched muscles and constantly improve the stretch reflex by executing exercises in a regimen of spring-like action.

- In jumping exercises the focus is on explosiveness at the start of a movement and again when the direction of the movement is changed. The faster a jumper changes direction, the faster the movement is switched from flexion to extension.
- Light weight resistances of 0.25 to 1.0% of the jumper's own body weight (kettlebells, belts, vests) should be used in specific running and jumping exercises and alternated with no-resistance performances.
- The number of repetitions in a set should not exceed 20 to 25 in jumping exercises, 10 to 15 in exercises with light resistances, 3 to 5 in exercises with medium resistances and 1 to 2 in exercises with heavy resistances.
- Exercises performed in multiple repetitions must be executed in gradually increased tempo. The level of effort and the range of movement should be monitored to avoid excessive loads and muscular tension.
- A gradually increased volume (more repetitions) and intensity (heavier repetitions or faster performance) should not be overlooked in strength training. It is recommended that resistances be increased by 2 to 3% throughout a microcycle.

GOALS OF TECHNICAL PREPARATION

Jumpers aim for two interrelated goals in their technical training in attempting to master and perfect the technique of jumping and the approach run and to increase their specific performance capacities. This is expected to lead to an increased runup speed, a stabilized approach run, a more active running action in the final strides prior to the takeoff, a more effective takeoff and an efficient technique in the flight.

The improved final stages of the approach run has an active effect on the takeoff as the support phase diminishes during the planting of the takeoff foot. In the following flight phase it is neces-sary to increase the activity of the shoulder girdle and to improve the range of arm and leg movements. Long and triple jumpers should also strive to develop their landing by diminishing their body lean, holding the feet forward and level with each other.

In addition, triple jumpers should master the "pawing" movements that accompany the foot plant and the takeoff after the hop and step. Also important is improving the triple jump by combining the approach run with the different lengths and heights of the hop, step and jump phases.

High jumpers need to pay special attention to the development of the flight and bar clearance action in addition to other technical elements of the jump. Pole vaulters have the additional task of developing their approach run with the pole, while dealing with the improvement of the plant, entry into the hang and the subsequent technical elements and rhythm of the vault.

To accomplish all these tasks jumpers in training employ actual jumps from different runup lengths and various types of specific exercises. The chosen specific exercises assist in the development of motor qualities and specific skills needed to increase the power output and the effectiveness of certain technical elements.

In performing repetitions of the basic jumping technique it is recommended that the coach make the conditions for the execution of the exercise gradually harder. This can be achieved by increasing the length of the approach run, as well as the intensity at which the exercise is performed. Technique faults that crop up in the execution of basic movements are a sign that intensity has been increased too soon or by too great a magnitude. When faults occur, the jumper should reduce speed until a proper form and movement rhythm returns.

It is important for a coach to monitor all stages of a jumper's technical development. Specific exercises, designed to develop lagging muscle groups and specific physical performance capacities are critically important in the correction of many faults.

Chapter II:
The High Jump

A Closer Look At The Shape Of The High Jump Runup

By Jesús Dapena, Michiyoshi Ae, Akira Iiboshi, USA/Japan

Special video analysis is used to improve the design of the flop technique run-up by fitting a curve to the jumper's footprints to calculate the radius and the final direction for the approach run for individual athletes.

The path of the footprints in a high jump runup can be idealized as a straight line perpendicular to the bar, followed by a circular arc which ends at the takeoff (Figure 1). Such a path is defined by the position of the takeoff foot (its x and y coordinates), the angle between the bar and the final direction of the footprints' path (f), and the radius of the curve (r).

A method for drawing the path of the footprints on the ground was described in previous papers. (See Dapena, et al., 1993; Dapena, 1995a.) However, the numerical values needed for the implementation of this method were based on limited information.

Recent work by Iiboshi, et al. (1994) provides data that can help us to improve the design of the runup. They used a special video analysis technique to measure the footprint locations of the top eight men and seven of the top eight women in the high jump finals of the 1991 World Championships. The last successful jump was analyzed for each athlete, with the exception of Heike Henkel, who had to be studied in a successful jump in which the bar was set 5 cm below her winning height. The Japanese research team also collected other data, such as the final speed of the runup (v) and the final direction of motion of the center of gravity (c.g.) at the end of the runup.

FITTING A CURVE TO THE FOOTPRINTS

(NOTE: This paper will refer to athletes who take off from the left foot; to make the text appli-

cable to athletes who take off from the right foot, the words "right" and "left" should be interchanged.)

We used a computer program to fit an arc of a circle to the footprint locations reported by Iiboshi, et al. (1994). There are many ways to fit a circle to the footprints of a high jump curve; we decided to

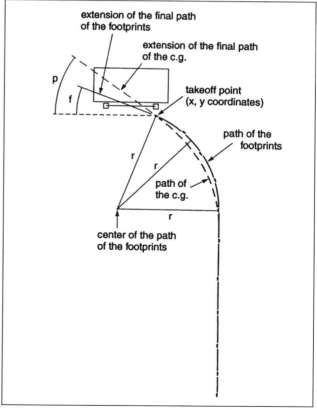

Figure 1

use the circle that passed through the takeoff footprint and made the best possible fit with the second, third and fourth footprints before the takeoff. Notice that we ignored the next to last footprint (i.e., we used footprints 0, -2, -3 and -4, skipping footprint -1). The reason for this was that many jumpers seem to plant the right foot in the next-to-last support outside the general curve, and therefore the inclusion of this footprint would have a misleading effect on the shape of the fitted curve.

Figure 2 shows the footprints of the 15 athletes analyzed at the 1991 World Championships and the circular arc that we fitted to the curve of each runup. The arc was continued backward up to the point where it was perpendicular to the bar; from there, the path was extended backward along a straight line.

The drawings show that all the jumpers in the sample followed very closely the modeled circular path in the last steps of the runup (although, as expected, in several jumps the next-to-last footprint was clearly outside the general curve). About half of the jumpers (e.g., Austin, Kovacs) used a strict "straight line plus circular arc" approach, and their footprints followed very closely not only the curved section, but also the straight section of the path modeled by the computer. The remaining jumpers (e.g., Drake, Henkel) started the straight section of the runup somewhat farther outward than predicted by the computer model, and later converged into the final circular path.

In some jumpers (e.g., Drake, Kostadinova) the second type of runup may have served to produce a more gradual transition from the straight section of the runup to the final part of the curve, which should make the transition more comfortable. The disadvantage is that this runup is obviously more complicated than the first type, and may therefore lead to more inconsistency.

In other jumpers (e.g., Grant, Kemp) the second type of runup seemed to be the result of the opposite reason: a sudden change in the direction of running at the start of the curve (essentially, a kink in the path at footprint -5) before settling into the final curvature of the runup. This does not seem advisable, because the sudden change in direction may interfere with the runup speed; it may also lead to inconsistency.

The fitted curves allowed us to calculate the radius (r) and the final direction (f) of the curve for each jumper. These values are shown in Figure 2.

RELATIONSHIP BETWEEN THE RUNNING SPEED AND THE RADIUS OF THE CURVE

The proportion between the square of the running speed and the radius of the curve used by an athlete determines how much the athlete will lean. This can be expressed by the formula $q=v^2/r$; the larger the value of q, the greater the lean. This means that an increase in v while keeping the radius constant will increase q, and the athlete will lean more; an increase in r while keeping the running speed constant will decrease q, and the athlete will lean less. If an athlete wants to achieve a given amount of lean, the ratio q between v^2 and r needs to have some particular value which will be different for each amount of lean.

If we knew the typical value of q for high jumpers, we would be able to use the running speed of any jumper to estimate the appropriate radius for the footprints of that jumper, using the equation $r=v^2/q$.

To check the value of q for each high jumper in the sample, we would need to divide the square of the average running speed of the athlete in the entire curve by the radius of the curve. Iiboshi, et al. (1994) did not measure the average running speed during the entire curve for the athletes shown in Figure 2, but they did report the final speed at the end of the runup. We used the value of this reported speed to make a rough estimate of q for each jumper, using the formula $q=v^2/r$. The value of q was 6.8 ± 0.8 m/s^2 for the men, and 4.8 ± 1.0 m/s^2 for the women.

These results indicated that the men tended to lean more than the women. A greater lean requires the athlete to make larger horizontal forces on the ground during the curve. It is possible that the greater strength of the men allowed them to run with a greater lean without excessive discomfort to interfere with the runup speed.

We can use the final runup speed of a high jumper and the average value of q to estimate an appropriate radius for the jumper's runup curve. This will not necessarily be the optimum radius for that individual, but it is useful as a rough guideline. For the men, the prediction equation is $r=v^2/6.8$; for the women, $r=v^2/4.8$. (These equations replace the one given in the previous papers, which was based on data from a single jumper.)

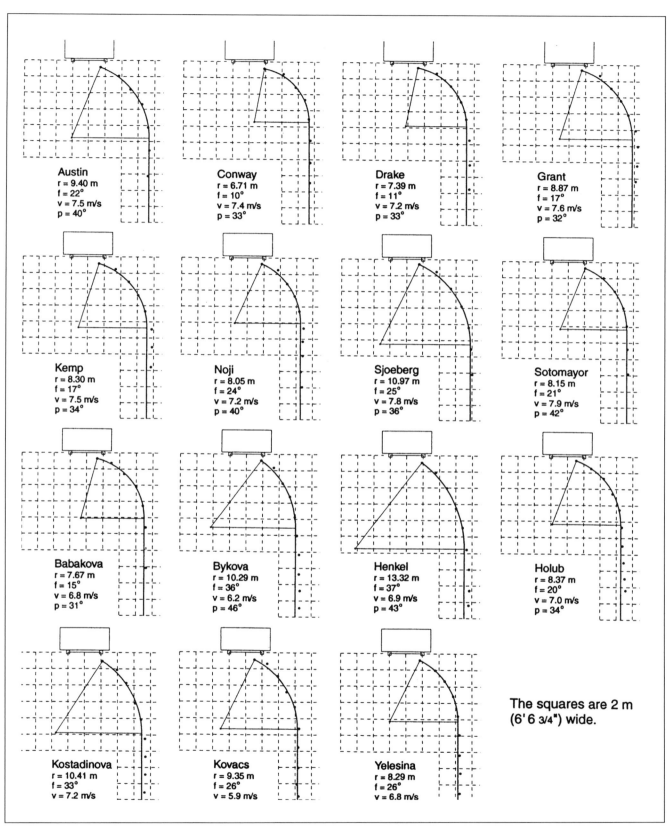

Austin
r = 9.40 m
f = 22°
v = 7.5 m/s
p = 40°

Conway
r = 6.71 m
f = 10°
v = 7.4 m/s
p = 33°

Drake
r = 7.39 m
f = 11°
v = 7.2 m/s
p = 33°

Grant
r = 8.87 m
f = 17°
v = 7.6 m/s
p = 32°

Kemp
r = 8.30 m
f = 17°
v = 7.5 m/s
p = 34°

Noji
r = 8.05 m
f = 24°
v = 7.2 m/s
p = 40°

Sjoeberg
r = 10.97 m
f = 25°
v = 7.8 m/s
p = 36°

Sotomayor
r = 8.15 m
f = 21°
v = 7.9 m/s
p = 42°

Babakova
r = 7.67 m
f = 15°
v = 6.8 m/s
p = 31°

Bykova
r = 10.29 m
f = 36°
v = 6.2 m/s
p = 46°

Henkel
r = 13.32 m
f = 37°
v = 6.9 m/s
p = 43°

Holub
r = 8.37 m
f = 20°
v = 7.0 m/s
p = 34°

Kostadinova
r = 10.41 m
f = 33°
v = 7.2 m/s

Kovacs
r = 9.35 m
f = 26°
v = 5.9 m/s

Yelesina
r = 8.29 m
f = 26°
v = 6.8 m/s

The squares are 2 m
(6' 6 3/4") wide.

Figure 2

RELATIONSHIP BETWEEN THE FINAL DIRECTIONS OF THE PATHS OF THE C.G. AND OF THE FOOTPRINTS

The sketch in Figure 1 shows that the c.g. travels directly over the footprints during the straight part of the runup. However, in the transition to the curve the body tilts toward the left. The tilt is maintained during the curve, and the c.g. follows a path that is somewhat closer to the center of the curve than the footprints. At the end of the curve, the paths of the c.g. and of the footprints converge, and this puts the c.g. more or less directly above the left foot by the end of the takeoff.

A consequence of the convergence of the two curves is that the final angle of the c.g. path (p) is always larger than the corresponding angle of the footprints' path (f). Iiboshi, et al. (1994) reported the value of angle p for each of the jumpers shown in Figure 2. Using the values of f which we computed from the fitted curves, we were able to calculate the difference between angles p and f: $15 \pm 5°$.

In the previous papers (Dapena, et al., 1993; Dapena, 1995a) the difference between angles p and f was used to produce a table that showed for several values of the final direction of the runup (angle p, which indicates the final path of the c.g.) a distance called "j". This distance is necessary for the calculation of the direction of the center of the curve relative to the takeoff point (see Figure 3), and therefore it is ultimately needed for drawing the path of the footprints on the ground. The newly calculated difference between angles p and f leads to a modified table for the calculation of j (Table 1).

PRACTICAL IMPLICATIONS

To draw the path of the footprints on the ground, we strongly advise the reader to follow the detailed instructions given in the previous paper (Dapena, 1995a), but using the new formulas to estimate the radius of the curve ($r=v^2/6.8$ for the men; $r=v^2/4.8$ for the women), and the new table to estimate the value of distance j. (If you are unable to find the previous paper, please contact *Track Coach*, 2570 El Camino Real, Suite 606, Mountain View, CA 94040, USA, for a free copy.)

OTHER CONSIDERATIONS

The jumps shown in Figure 2 used a wide range of values for the radius of the curve (between 6.71m and 13.32m). If the path of the footprints had had the same final direction (angle f) in all these jumps, the distance between the right standard and the straight part of the runup (measured outward from the standard) would have needed to have a variability of about 4 meters. This is demonstrated by the hypothetical runups shown in Figure 4a. However, Figure 2 shows that the distance from the right standard to the straight part of the runup was actually constrained between approximately 4 and 6 meters for all the jumps, a variability range of only 2 meters.

The small variability in the position of the straight part of the runup in spite of the large variability in the radius of the curve implied that the athletes in the sample tended to make systematic changes in the final angle of the footprints as they made changes in the radius.

This can be understood better with the help of Figure 4b. The straight parts of the three hypothetical runups shown in this drawing were all at the same distance from the right standard (5 meters). Each runup used a different radius, but still they all ended up at the same takeoff point.

The differences between the three runups started with differences in the starting point of the curve. By traveling deeper toward the plane of the standards before starting the curve, the athlete can use a smaller radius, and still reach the same takeoff point. However, the final angle of the footprints' curve will also be smaller (i.e., the final path of the footprints will be more parallel to the bar).

The high jumpers in the sample did not follow exactly the pattern of variation shown in Figure 4b, because the distance between the right standard and the straight part of the runup did fluctuate in the sample (see Figure 2). However, this fluctuation was rather small (about 1 meter in either direction around the 5-meter point), and therefore the basic relationships of the hypothetical

Table 1

final direction of the runup (angle p)	final direction of the footprints' path (angle f)	value of distance j
25°	10°	1.75 m
30°	15°	2.70 m
35°	20°	3.65 m
40°	25°	4.65 m
45°	30°	5.75 m
50°	35°	7.00 m

jumps of Figure 4b were present in the jumps of Figure 2: the athletes who used a large radius (e.g., Henkel, Kostadinova) tended to have large values of f, while the athletes who used a small radius (e.g., Conway, Babakova) tended to have small values of f.

In theory, a high jumper should be able to try any combination of radius (r) and final angle of the footprints' path (f): for any given value of f, the jumper should be able to try a wide variety of values of r, as shown in Figure 4a; and for any given value of r, the jumper should be able to try a wide variety of values of f, as shown in Figure 4c. However, to a great extent this did not happen; the jumpers in the sample tended to follow a pattern similar to the one shown in Figure 4b, in which there was a positive correlation between the values of r and f.

It is not clear why the jumpers linked the values of r and f in this way, but we have come up with two possible theories:

The first theory is based on the relationship between the radius of the curve and the need for the generation of angular momentum. During the bar clearance, a high jumper needs angular momentum in order to make the appropriate rotations over the bar. This rotation can be broken down into a twist rotation and a somersault rotation (Dapena, 1995b). The twist rotation serves to turn the back of the athlete toward the bar; the somersault rotation makes the shoulders go down and the knees go up during the bar clearance.

Taking into account the final direction of the runup, the somersault rotation can be broken down into a forward somersaulting component and a lateral somersaulting component. One of the main purposes of the curved runup is to favor the production of the *lateral* somersaulting component of the angular momentum. (The other one is to lower the c.g. in the last steps of the runup.)

The high jumpers who are traveling more parallel to the bar at the end of the runup will tend to need a smaller amount of forward somersaulting angular momentum and a larger amount of lateral somersaulting angular momentum in order to produce a total somersault rotation that makes the longitudinal axis of the athlete be perpendicular to the bar at the peak of the jump.

This means that, to some extent, we should expect athletes who are traveling more parallel to the bar at the end of the runup to use tighter curves (smaller radius) in order to facilitate the generation of a larger amount of lateral somersaulting angular momentum during the takeoff. This may

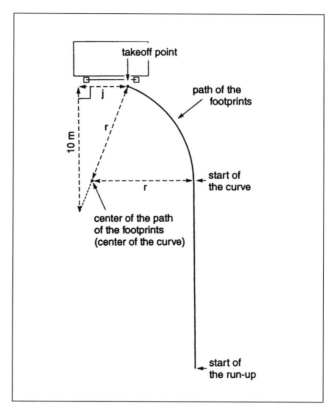

Figure 3

be part of the reason why the athletes who used smaller radius values tended to be those who were traveling more parallel to the bar at the end of the runup (Figures 2 and 4b).

The second theory is that the high jumpers in the sample may not have fully explored all the possible options for the distance between the right standard and the straight part of the runup. They may all be starting within the narrow range between 4 and 6 meters simply because the other high jumpers also start there. If this is the case, the jumpers are unnecessarily restricting the combinations of r and f that they can use.

For instance, let us assume that a jumper who is using the combination r=9m and f=23° with the straight part of the runup 5 meters out from the right standard (i.e., the middle path in Figure 4b) wishes to try a runup with a 7-meter radius, but maintaining f at 23°. If this jumper keeps the straight part of the runup at the 5-meter distance, it will be impossible to combine the 7-meter radius with a final angle of 23°; the athlete will have to change the final angle to 12° (see Figure 4b).

However, if the jumper brought the straight part of the runup to a distance of less than 4 meters from the right standard, the combination of a 7-

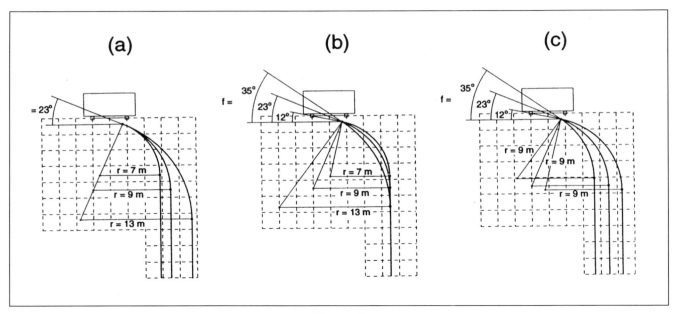

Figure 4

meter radius with a final angle of 23° would be possible (Figure 4a).

If the second theory is correct, the next question would be, what drives the athletes' decisions within Figure 4b (or within Figure 2)? Do they decide to use a certain radius, and are then forced into a final angle that may or may not be desirable? Or do they decide to use a certain final angle, and are then forced into a radius that may or may not be desirable?

At this time, we do not know for certain the reasons for the linkage found between the radius of the curve and the final direction of the footprints in the finalists from the 1991 World Championships. However, we believe that coaches should feel free to experiment with a variety of combinations of r and f, even if some of those combinations take the straight part of the runup out of the 4-6 meter range currently used by most high jumpers.

REFERENCES

Dapena, J. How to design the shape of a high jump runup. *Track Coach.* 131:4179-4181, 1995a.

Dapena, J. The rotation over the bar in the Fosbury-flop high jump. *Track Coach.* 132:4201-4210, 1995b.

Dapena, J., R.M. Angulo-Kinzler, J.M. Caubet, C. Turró, X. Balius, S.B. Kinzler, J. Escoda and J.A. Prat. Track and field: high jump (Women). *Report for 1992 Summer Olympic Games Biomechanics Projects (IOC: Medical Commission / Biomechanics Subcommission).* IOC, Lausanne, Switzerland, 261 pp, 1993.

Iiboshi, A., M. Ae, M. Yuuki, J. Takamatsu, M. Nasagawa and H.P. Tan. Biomechanical analysis of the techniques for the world's best high jumpers. *How they ran, jumped and threw: 3rd IAAF World Championships in Athletics, Tokyo '91*, Ed. H.Sasaki, K.Kobayashi, and M. Ae. Baseball Magazine Co., Ltd., Tokyo, 169-184, 1994.

Methodological Development Of High Jump Technique

By Yuri Tsherepanov, Russia

Improving high jump technique requires the use of carefully selected training means in the various stages of development. In the following text the author makes suggestions in regard to how well planned training loads, volumes and intensities can help to produce an optimal technique.

As in most track and field events, performances in the high jump can be basically improved by two factors—development of the speed-strength level and its exploitation through a rationally improved jumping technique. These two factors are inseparable because most training means used by high jumpers for the development of speed strength are at the same time also used to develop jumping technique. It should not be overlooked, however, that the development of speed strength determines the development of technique and must therefore slightly precede technique work. The improvement of technique depends largely on the athlete's functional state.

Verhoshansky claimed once that there are two conditions responsible for an effective development of high-level performances. Firstly speed-strength training means must precede deeper technical work, and secondly, it is important that the development of technique takes place in the most intensive training range. Verhoshansky recom-

mended further that it is necessary to improve the speed-strength level by employing concentrated one-directional training loads. The above statements are applicable to the choice of training loads in the development of high jump technique.

LOAD ORGANIZATION

A six-month preparation scheme in Fig. 1 represents the organization of training loads in four stages:

Stage I: Large volume, low intensity (not over 70 to 80% of maximum) loads directed to the development of the support movement system.

Stage II: Large-volume loads, not exceeding 80 to 85% of maximal intensity, reaching 90% at the end of the stage.

Stage III: High-level loads to develop speed strength and speed capacities at near-maximal and maximal intensities.

Stage IV: Competition.

The duration of each stage depends on the concrete tasks involved. For example, Stage I to III might cover two to six weeks, while Stage IV can take four to twelve weeks. The technical means in these stages are divided into three groups and distributed over the whole cycle as follows:

Group A: Introductory and imitation exercises to teach and establish the separate elements of the high jump technique.

Group B: Exercises that combine different ele-

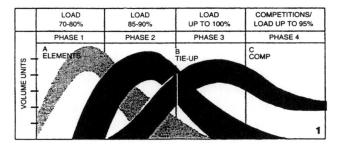

Figure 1: Duration and volume variations in the use of technical training means.

ments of the technique.

Group C: Transformation of the combined elements into high jump technique as a whole and its execution under various conditions.

The division of technique development into three groups provides an opportunity to employ in the beginning a large volume of simple and low-intensity exercises before these elements are joined together in faster and more intensive combination and finally are performed in high jumping from a full runup.

VOLUME AND DURATION

The graphs in Fig. 2 show the volumes and duration of the combined technique development means (2 to 4). A combination that is typical for beginners is shown in Graph 2. It makes use of nearly simultaneous employment of several training means. The volume is fluently increased and reduced without large concentrations in single phases. This allows the coach to discover optimal means and their combinations during the learning processes until the most rational individual technique can be established.

Variations 3 and 4 in the graph are characteristic for elite high jumpers, who make use of large volumes of concentrated training means. Elite performers have developed a constant technique stereotype as a difficult task which can be accomplished by limiting the number of general exercises at a certain stage to increase technique development intensity.

As can be see in Graph 3, emphasis is first placed on introductory and imitation exercises (Group A) and Group B and C exercises are included relatively late in order to exploit maximal volumes. This distribution of technique preparation means can be used in a six-month cycle that aims at developing jumping elements, chiefly, with a large volume of highly intensive work. It is particularly suitable prior to the winter competition phase where results are not important, as the main task is to prepare for the summer season.

Graph 4 should be regarded as an extension to Graph 2. As can be seen, the volume of Group 3 exercises is reduced to increase the volume of more intensive technical means (Group B and C). This variation appears to be the most logical in preparation for summer competition in the second half of a yearly cycle.

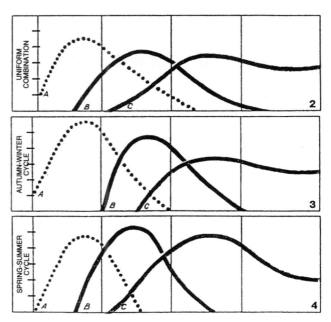

Figure 2: Organization of technique development loads in four stages.

Figure 3: A typical example of introductory imitation exercises.

TRAINING MEANS

Let us next take a closer look at each group of the training means starting with Group A. The exercises in this group are directed to the learning and and development of separate elements of the high jump, performed in a large volume during the concentrated functional preparation phases. Care must be taken in the choice and execution of the exercises because they will establish a foundation for the work that follows.

Imitation exercises are performed in a large volume not only to improve technical elements but also as conditioning exercises. Such exercises provide an opportunity to specifically strengthen muscle groups and tendons which have to tolerate

TABLE 1: Suggested percentage intensities for full runup jumps during different training stages. Percentages are based on best training results.

AUTUMN - WINTER CYCLE		SPRING - SUMMER CYCLE	
STAGE	PERCENTAGE	STAGE	PERCENTAGE
Stage 2	88-92	Stage 2	90-93
Stage 3	93-96	Stage 3	94-98
Stage 4	94-95	Stage 4	95-96

the basic load in the training stages to follow. This is the main reason why imitation exercises and functional preparation exercises are performed simultaneously.

The single technique elements are gradually combined at the end of the first training stage to form Group B exercises in the second half of a six-month cycle. At this stage Group B exercises also serve as speed-strength development exercises. Although training intensity is now increased, the use of Group A introductory and and imitation exercises is still continued. Emphasis is now placed, however, on the technically more complicated elements of the jump, because certain elements require time before they are completely mastered.

Short runup jumps over lower heights are introduced in the second training phase to be followed by Group C technical exercises. These are included only after the athlete has reached an optimal functional state and the volume of Group A and B exercises is minimal. The distribution of the training volumes of Group C exercises is shown in Graph 4.

FULL RUNUP JUMP

Jumping from a full runup deserves a close look because it is not only a technique development means but actually can be regarded as a specific preparation stage. Jumping from a full runup begins in the second training phase when the separate technique elements are joined together. However, as an athlete's functional state is not optimal at this stage, the intensity of the full runup jumps must be kept low The bar is lifted higher and the quality of the jumps improves as the functional state improves.

The intensity level of jumps from a full runup also depends on the planned tasks and the individual characteristics of an athlete. If winter competitions are regarded as unimportant, there is no sense in using close-to-maximal intensity ranges

in technical preparation. On the other hand, it would be most important to use close-to-maximal intensity ranges in the technical preparation prior to competitions where maximal results are the aim.

Under individual characteristics we look at the differences between the best training and competition results. Some athletes can have rather large, 10 to 15cm, differences, while some show only a minimal, 2 to 3cm, deviation.

This presents a dilemma in making the choice of intensities in the planning of training. Should intensities be based on the best training jumps or the best competition performances? To us it appears logical to link jumping intensity to best training results. Suggested percentage intensities related to the best training results are shown in Table 1.

It must be remembered that the suggested intensity percentages are meant to be used as a technique preparation means with the main task of improving and stabilizing all technical high jump elements as a whole. At the same time full runup jumps in the third preparation stage are also used as a basic training means to strengthen the support system.

For this purpose full runup jumps are performed under more difficult conditions. These include jumps from a faster runup, series of jumps with reduced recoveries, jumps, with light additional loads, and jumps with the bar placed higher than the athlete's personal best.

Technique development jumps and jumps under difficult conditions can be used in the following three variations:

Variation 1: First training—technique development.
Second training—jumps under difficult conditions.

Variation 2: First training—jumps under difficult conditions.
Second training—technique development.

Variation 3: In the same training unit—technique development, following by jumps under difficult conditions.

Teaching Basic High Jump Technique

By V. Taranov and V. Sergejev, Russia

There are many ways to teach and develop high jump technique. In this article the authors present their recommended step-by-step approaches in three variations in order to accommodate different types of beginners.

Although the basic teaching methods of the flop high jump are thoroughly covered in the technical literature, practical experience reveals many serious shortcomings among beginners, and even among the best juniors. Most of these are a direct result of the mistakes made in the initial learning stages and are obviously responsible for a reduced improvement rate.

Successful learning of an effective high jump technique depends largely on basic preparations in the initial stages. The basic preparation period over the first 12 to 18 months must therefore include the development of a rational running technique, strengthening of the support and movement structure and improvement of coordinative capacities. Above all, it is necessary that the coach formulates precise learning targets, decides the sequence of teaching processes and selects the most effective teaching means and methods.

The main objective at this stage is to acquire a rational structure of high jump technique as a whole, based on the evaluation of the quality of performance and the execution of imitation, as well as semi-specific and specific exercises. The coach is responsible for the beginner developing a correct image and "feel" of the target technique.

The beginner, in order to acquire the complete structure of the target technique, must have a good understanding of effective performance as a whole and solve the basic tasks of learning the takeoff, the bar clearance and landing techniques, combined with an efficient coordination of the runup with the takeoff.

The first task is solved by the formation of an image of a rational technique as a whole, using descriptions, explanations, examples and demonstrations with detailed comments. Several methods can here be employed to improve and speed up the learning process. These include slow-motion films and videos, photo sequences, drawings, adjustable models, etc.

The following tasks can be solved in a particular step-by-step sequence, or as a complex combined approach. The basic step-by-step teaching processes are described here in three variations according to individually different needs after the end of the preliminary preparations. The teaching means are only summarized, as detailed information is readily available in the coaching literature.

VARIATION I

This variation is suitable for young athletes who have an efficient coordination between the runup and lead-leg movements at takeoff. Typical evaluation can here be based on the performance of the running long jump or jumping exercises that involve a takeoff from a runup.

Sequence of the exercises:
1. Learning the structure of the running action on the straight.
2. Learning the structure of the running action on the curve.
3. Learning the structure of the running action that

changes from straight running into a symmetrical curve.

4. Performance of a runup with the aim of reaching the correct takeoff spot that is marked on the ground.

5. Performance of a runup, combined with the takeoff and an upright flight along a low crossbar.

6. As in exercise 5, but the athlete lands after the clearance in a sitting position.

7. As in exercise 6, but the athlete lands in the bar clearance position.

8. Performance of the complete jump from the runup.

VARIATION II

This variation is suitable for young athletes who can effectively combine the runup with the takeoff movements but require a more progressive approach to secure the development of an effective complete technique. Most of the listed exercises can also be successfully used in the learning process of Variation I.

Sequence of exercises:
1. Exercises that imitate arm action at the takeoff.
2. Exercises that imitate lead-leg action at the takeoff.
3. Exercises that imitate the coordinated lead-leg and arm action at the takeoff.
4. Exercises to develop a rolling heel-to-toes takeoff action.
5. The rolling heel-to-toes action combined with the curved approach run.
6. Two bounces on the takeoff leg, followed by the takeoff and landing in a sitting position.
7. As in exercise 6, but clearing a low bar.
8. A straight three-stride bounding runup, followed by the takeoff and landing in a sitting position.
9. As in exercise 8, but from a curved three-stride approach run.
10. As in exercise 9, but clearing a low bar.
11. A straight run with a takeoff performance at every third stride.
12. As in exercise 11, but on a curved path.
13. As in exercise 11, but the final takeoff is combined with a jump over a low bar and landing in a sitting position.
14. As in exercise 13, but with a proper bar clearance position.

15. A six-stride curved runup with bounding last three strides and the performance of the takeoff.
16. As in exercise 15, but clearing a low bar and landing in a sitting position.
17. As in exercise 16, but with a proper bar clearance position.
18. An extension of the six-stride runup to a length that fits individual demands. The final three strides must remain stressed.

VARIATION III

This variation is suitable for young athletes who are reluctant to clear the bar backwards and land on the back and shoulder (insufficient preparations in gymnastics and acrobatics). The listed exercises are performed prior to Variation I and Variation II drills.

Sequence of the exercises:
1. Dropping from a standing position backward onto a pile of mats. The body remains straight, arms are kept close to the body and the chin is pointing to the chest.
2. Lying on the back, the athlete imitates the bar clearance. Legs are supported by a partner or placed against a wall, while the athlete, supported by his shoulders, lifts the hips as high as possible. The exercise is completed with a backward roll.
3. Imitation bar clearance action similar to exercise 2, but the athlete executes the exercise hanging from a horizontal bar and is assisted by a partner.
4. Standing backwards, the athlete performs a high jump over a flexible training bar. It is advisable that the landing level corresponds as closely as possible to the takeoff level to allow sufficient time to perform the bar clearance action.
5. As in exercise 4, but a two-legged takeoff is performed following a short straight approach run.
6. As in exercise 4, but the two-legged takeoff is performed following a short curved approach run.
7. One-, two- and three-stride approach high jumps from an elevated takeoff (10 to 20cm), performed with the actual flop technique.
8. As in exercise 7, but the runup is extended up to seven strides.

Developing The Runup And Takeoff Position For Young High Jumpers

By Anne Stephens, New Zealand

The development of a consistent runup is an often underestimated technical area in the preparation of high jumpers. This article covers in detail how a sound runup that leads to an effective takeoff can be established and provides a series of coaching tips.

INTRODUCTION

I would like to propose looking at the high jump runup in four distinct phases:

- Initial/acceleration phase
- Rhythm phase
- The curve
- Establishment of the takeoff position.

Each of these phases builds on the other and must be performed consistently and correctly to provide the athlete with the opportunity of jumping to the best of his/her ability.

In conjunction with looking a little more specifically at the whole runup picture, I cannot emphasize strongly enough the importance of a correct running technique in the high jump. My observation is that this is a technical area that many coaches underestimate when preparing jumpers.

As well as having good running technique, it seems to me that jumpers need to do a lot of tempo running in their training, to create a rhythm mindset which will assist them in achieving a greater level of consistency in their runup. So before effective high jump training can begin, the athlete must run well and have a good understanding of tempo—remember, the high jump runup is performed at optimal speeds. If an athlete has no understanding of tempo he will be unable to establish and maintain optimal speeds.

THE INITIAL/ACCELERATION PHASE

This phase establishes the accuracy of the runup. It is important to experiment with this phase, as the more comfortable the beginning of the runup is for the athlete, the more consistent the whole runup will be.

With beginners, I feel that it is useful to use a standing start, simply for the purposes of control and consistency. This gets the athlete used to starting the runup from a marker and from a stable position.

The next step is to teach the athlete that a marker is not an immovable object and may need to be moved to accommodate such variables as how the athlete is feeling, weather conditions, track surfaces, etc.

As athletes develop a better running technique we can then begin to look at how well, technically, athletes are running off the start marker. We can also test this initial phase for consistency.

Technically, it is essential that athletes are not dropping their hips in the first few strides of the runup. We must therefore, establish the approach to the first few strides so that this does not occur.

Many jumpers use an approach (a walk-in, or a run-in), to their start maker as a way of establishing a body position to achieve correct running technique. While this is usually very effective, it must be individualized and controlled. You will see many young high jumpers changing their approach (usually they keep moving it back) as the bar gets higher. An uncontrolled approach produces a greater level of inconsistency in the runup.

There are several arguments for and against the use of bounding strides in the high jump runup. Bounding is used by some senior athletes very effectively as a form of neuromuscular stimulation prior to the takeoff.

In my experience, very few young athletes are physically strong enough to produce a consistent bound, nor are their neuromuscular systems developed enough to enable them to reproduce this type of stimulation. They simply fatigue very quickly in a competition.

However, some athletes, even from a reasonably young age exhibit a very natural bound in their runups, and while this may create some level of inconsistency, I would be reluctant to remove it, as it may be a rhythm setter for that particular athlete's runup.

Testing for consistency, you should be able to see the range of variation in the initial stage of the runup by placing a check mark on the third stride from the start marker (do not include any approach steps). Then have the athlete perform several runups, asking him not to aim for the check mark, but to run normally to assess how consistent those first three strides are. Another method of testing the consistency of various phases is to time them. This, however, is very difficult to do without extremely accurate timing equipment.

Coaching Tips:
1. Smooth acceleration off the start mark.
2. Hips high into the first running strides.
3. Consistency of the approach (walk-in, run-in).

THE RHYTHM PHASE

This phase establishes the rhythm of the runup. It's about settling into an optimal speed with a good running technique and preparing to run the curve. This is not necessarily a long section of the runup and may include the first couple of curve strides.

Establishing a rhythm to a high jump runup can be one of the most difficult things for an athlete to achieve and, as previously stated, the importance of correct running technique cannot be undervalued. Accurate tempo cannot be achieved if the athlete has no understanding of tempo and rhythm. The jumper can only develop this from doing tempo work in his running program. Tempo

Approaching the takeoff—world record holder Stefka Kostadinova of Bulgaria.

running can be defined as set pace running, usually expressed as a percentage of maximum effort over predetermined intervals.

This part of the runup is where the ability to develop an accurate tempo is critical. There are a couple of well established ideas concerning this issue, and I see no need to "reinvent the wheel."
- Counting the phases in strides, while we are looking at the four phases of the runup, the athlete may feel more comfortable using a three-phase breakdown. What we mean by this is that the athlete uses numbers as cues for the different phases and simply counts in his head while running to keep the rhythm in the runup. For example, for an athlete using a nine-stride runup, there are a number of options; 4-3-2, 3-3-2-2-, 2-3-3-2, etc.
- Putting the rhythm of the runup to a beat. Some athletes find running and counting far too complicated, and it is easier for them to get a particular beat in their heads to assist them with keeping the runup consistent.

Coaching Tip:
1. Sometimes you can learn more from listening to the runup (the athlete's footfalls) than you can from watching it.
2. Hurdle training can be a useful training tool in establishing a rhythmic pattern for the athlete.

THE CURVE

When designing a runup the most difficult thing for a coach is to decide the optimal curve position for the individual high jumper. Some points to take into consideration are:

• It is useful to have the athlete run a curve, away from their takeoff position (a backward J), at runup speed. This gives an idea of the curve angle an athlete might feel comfortable running and provides a starting point from which to develop the athlete's runup.

• The purpose of the curve is to provide the correct biomechanical conditions for the athlete to rotate in the air without twisting off the ground. To gain maximum advantage from the angle created by the curve the athlete must incorporate a "whole body lean" into the running action and not just an upper body lean into the curve.

It is advisable that the athlete's first step onto the curve, or where he begins his "whole body lean," is taken on the foot which is on the outside of the curve, i.e., left foot jumpers start the curve on a right-foot stride, and right foot jumpers start their curve on a left-foot stride. This tends to create a more balanced, smoother progression into the required running position on the curve.

Coaching Tips:
1. The analogy, "running the curve feels like riding a bicycle around a corner," can be useful in describing the feeling of running the whole body lean on the curve to the athlete.
2. Having the athlete pump the inside curve arm (left-foot takeoff, left arm) more vigorously can assist him in holding the whole body lean position.
3. The tighter the curve, the stronger the athlete needs to be. Young athletes should be running a wider curve—a gentle J—as this will produce less stress on their bodies.
4. Conversely, if the athlete cannot achieve enough whole body lean through the curve it may need to be tightened.

ESTABLISHING THE TAKEOFF POSITION

It is important when establishing the takeoff position, that the whole body lean is maintained. The athlete is required to take off from the angle created by the curve, effectively, to take off jumping "away from the bar."

The second important factor when establishing the takeoff position is the "backward body lean." The body must be in a position where, when the takeoff foot is planted, it is very slightly in front of the hips, so the body travels forward over the foot. The hips and upper body are then driven upwards into a vertical position. If the takeoff foot is behind the hips at takeoff, the body will be driven forward and the athlete will travel more horizontally than vertically.

Conversely, if the takeoff foot is too far in front of the hips, the athlete will not be strong enough to pull the body over the takeoff foot and vertical drive will be lost.

The body lean positions create optimal takeoff angles. The easiest way to think about this is to draw a bodyline from the takeoff foot to the athlete's head. The angle is created by comparing this bodyline with the position of the uprights and bar.

I have used the term "optimal takeoff angles" because I believe that these are different for each athlete. Variables you must consider are the strength of the athlete, speed of the runup and the radius of the curve.

Coaching Tips:
1. I do not believe it is useful to teach an athlete to drop the hips during the penultimate stride. This hip drop is something which occurs naturally as a part of the preparation for the takeoff.
2. It is easier to get athletes into correct takeoff positions if they maintain a tall running action on the curve.

IN SUMMARY

When athletes perform their runup well, it will look effortless, all the phases will join together as the pieces of a jigsaw puzzle interlock, and you will have created a work of art.

If the runup is consistent, in establishing a good takeoff position, then the jump will happen consistently. If the runup is inconsistent so will be the jump.

About Explosive Power In The High Jump

By Boris Kuporosov and Grigory Geratshenko, Russia

Views on the development of speed strength in the high jump, looking at the problems involved in the choice and execution of explosive power exercises, as well as finding the right training volumes and intensities.

The importance of developing high-quality speed strength in the training of high jumpers has been stressed in early publications on jumping. Several theorists and practical authorities have since the early 1960's included this specific quality under the category of jumping capacity in their lists of important basic physical capacities. As jumping capacity is based on specific explosive power, it can be defined as a high-level application of forces in the minimum of time.

The development of explosive power takes place only when the training means employed are performed at high speed. Barbell exercises in the development of specific speed strength must therefore correspond to an athlete's physical preparation level, so that the athlete is capable of executing the exercise at maximal speed. At the same time, the intensity of the exercise can be adjusted by changing the resistance level and recoveries.

It is most important to reduce the resistance, or stop the exercise in fatigued conditions, when the performance tempo drops considerably after weight has been added. However, it should be kept in mind that training at a lowered intensity level fails to effectively mobilize the neuromuscular system.

The development of fast explosive power differs from the development of other jumping capacities because it depends, above all, on the freshness of nervous processes. For this reason it is necessary to carefully use the correct number of repetitions in an exercise in order to avoid changing the direction of the exercise into development of strength endurance. The same can occur when recoveries between the exercises or sets are unnecessarily short.

VOLUME AND INTENSITY

The coach is always faced with the job of deciding how much and at what intensity to perform speed strength development exercises. No wonder that opinions range from "as much as possible to as little as possible." In our opinion the development of explosive power requires extreme care in the choice of training volumes and intensities.

It should be kept in mind that an increased intensity is responsible for further nervous energy expenditure, which means that longer recovery phases are required to restore it.

At the same time, it would be unwise to increase the number of training sessions, which will lead to an increased training volume and, in turn, inhibits the development of explosive power. In other words, the number of exercises and their total volume must be carefully calculated to provide the organism with the best possible advantages for adaptation.

Training should therefore be short and intensive, and working close to exhaustion can take place only occasionally. This is because the aim of the exercise is to activate reactions in the organism and not to suppress them. A transition to the next load level in volume, as well as in intensity, should take place only after the previous level can be performed with self-assurance and without stress.

The planning of explosive power development

programs must never become dogmatic. The concrete volumes and intensities can be inserted into a roughly outlined schedule only after the state of the organism on a particular day has been assessed and the necessary adjustments are made. Consequently it is impossible to pre-plan training loads, volumes and intensities objectively for a whole year, not to mention four-year plans.

Similarly to all physical conditioning means, training loads in the development of speed strength must take place in a wavelike and modified manner. It is necessary in the choice of exercises to employ contrasting methods in which the intensity is not allowed to reach injury danger levels. Nevertheless, it is important that the chosen exercises are executed close to maximal speed, keeping in mind that the development of explosive power requires quality rather than quantity.

Coaches should always have in reserve ways and means to change speeds, amplitudes and loads, in order to avoid monotony in the already repetitive training exercises. They also have to use their imagination in the choice of training means to avoid boredom. After all, it is nearly always possible to develop the same muscle groups by using different training means.

While this takes place, it is important not to overlook the need for sufficient recovery or reduction of the training load to allow the organism to restore its adaptation capacity for the next training cycle.

It is hard to imagine how a high jumper can successfully develop explosive power without being motivated to reach outstanding performances. The jumper must also be capable of eliminating unnecessary loads and training means from the program in order to succeed. As already stressed, quality always provides a shorter and more efficient path to success than quantity. Furthermore, variety in the use of training means and structures is always more effective than strictly following a one-sided plan.

LOAD-REST

The best indicators in a visual observation of an athlete's physical state are his movement technique and the quality of the performance of certain tasks. Further indicators include the athlete's posture, facial expressions, smiling, breathing, mood, temper, rate of recovery, etc. It is advisable to introduce an additional individual self-control system that reveals in a daily diary the functional state of the organism. This self-control system should include such recordings as sleep, feelings, appetite, mood and desire to train.

It is the responsibility of the coach to avoid situations where a jumper's organism suffers from the previously applied load and the athlete looks at the suggested training means with antipathy. These situations can be avoided by providing sufficient rest. The principle here is that you need rest *before you are tired* and not after you are very tired.

Particular attention must be directed to the load-rest combination when an athlete approaches important competitions or a series of competitions. At this stage it is important to limit speed-strength load volumes to only maintain the achieved speed-strength potential and to accumulate nervous energy.

MOVEMENT QUALITIES AND TECHNIQUE

Raising the potential quality of movements and improving technical skills should be the major aims in the training of high jumpers. It is the harmony between technique and power that determines the performance level of an athlete and the qualifications of his coach. Keep always in mind that a large volume of speed-strength exercises can demolish technique. There simply is no linear correlation between training volume and the quality of technique. Consequently, the task of improving performance can seldom be successfully solved by an arithmetical approach.

Keep also in mind also that the transition to the next intensity level in the development of bar clearance technique is possible only after a sufficient number of jumps have been performed at a previous level with complete confidence.

THE SPEED BARRIER

At some stage in the improvement of explosive power every coach is faced with the development of the so-called speed barrier at takeoff. This occurs in the transition to a new quality of speed strength and can cause problems. However, the problems can be solved by using a widely contrasting variation of training methods to allow the organism to "switch on" protection processes during high-intensity work. Nevertheless, as already stated, maximal efforts can't be avoided in the development of explosive power, as the quality of

Amy Acuff

muscle fibers will be otherwise changed.

As an athlete's performances improve, the training means employed are gradually reduced to "sharper" exercises, which include maximal effort jumps. Such exercises as depth jumps should be avoided at this point until the athlete reaches a high performance level in order to avoid traumas to joints, muscles and ligaments and, above all, to protect the nervous system.

Explosive strength development during the high performance phase requires a capacity for concentration, not only on the movement potential, but also on the formation of technique. This allows for creating a model for the forthcoming capacities at the highest performance level. An ability to increase intensity and to concentrate on the work of the explosive muscle groups at takeoff helps the athlete to prepare for future competitive performances.

Another aspect in the development of speed strength is testing. Testing can be used as a highly effective training means all year round with the exception of a period 10 to 12 days prior to major competitions. Also used as a control exercise, it can be executed in up to 15 attempts over the bar in one training session, or organized as a mini-competition. All this assists in dismantling the development-of-speed barrier, besides improving the jumper's psychological status and eliminating monotony.

Testing is an excellent addition to other training in the development of explosive power. One training session can include up to three tests, depending on the trend and tasks of a particular training phase. Naturally, the testing week should be regarded as a heavily loaded microcycle. Consequently, testing in the format of a mini-competition requires adequate recovery time to avoid nervous energy exhaustion.

IN CONCLUSION

It must be said in conclusion that this article is not meant to be an instructional text to be strictly followed but is presented as an outline to encourage thinking. It is always necessary to be aware of other ideas, while at the same time it is important to combine them with your own concepts.

Any kind of training methodology and system must be adjusted to individual characteristics of an athlete. For this reason even the most noteworthy plan should not be so dogmatic that it restricts the coach's own activity.

High-level performances are achieved only by believing your own intuitions and by drawing conclusions from failures and successes.

High Jump Drills

By Sandro Bisetto, Australia

The following text presents a series of high jump drills designed to develop the runup, takeoff and flight phases of the flop technique.

INTRODUCTION

- Drills should be performed to help develop an effective technical model. There is a vast range of drills available to help the athlete and the coach should not be afraid to experiment and try new movements or combinations if there is a specific end in mind.
- Drills for drills' sake should not be performed unless there is a specific aim that links with the technical model. When performing any drill there is also the opportunity to emphasize and focus on a particular aspect of a movement which may need to be improved.
- When the coach observes any drill or movement it is recommended that posture is considered first, as without the "trunk" being set in the correct position the limbs will therefore give different feedback to the athlete.
- Generally it is recommended that drills be learned at a slow speed and then progress to the specific timing and speed that is required. However, some drills may need to be performed at slower or even quicker tempos to try to effect tempo changes in certain movements.
- The psychology of attempting to affect changes in movement patterns must also be highlighted to athletes. The regression often experienced by trying to change movement patterns is usually met with a very negative response because it feels alien to the set pattern that has been established. It must be emphasized to the athlete that a new and hopefully more effective technical movement is "different" and not "stupid."

THE IMPORTANCE OF AN EFFICIENT RUNNING TECHNIQUE

When an athlete is introduced to specific takeoff drills it is important that he/she possess an efficient running technique. If the basic running mechanics are poor then the running rhythm, preparation for takeoff and the takeoff itself can all be compromised. It is therefore crucial that all forms of running drills are used to develop and maintain an efficient running action.

Drills can be performed in a straight line, on a J-shaped curve, following a full circle or also on the specific runup curve of each athlete. Various forms of hurdle drills are also recommended as a worthwhile form of training exercise. Examples of actual running drills and hurdle drills sessions are listed below:

RUNNING DRILLS SESSION I
a. 15m—foot walks x 2
b. 15m—ankle walks x 2
c. 15m—knee walks x 2
d. 30m—high thighs to parallel x 3
e. 30m—skip x 3
f. 30m—simulated takeoff x 2 right, x 2 left

RUNNING DRILLS SESSION II
a. 30m—high thighs x 3
b. 30m—skip with extension x 3
c. 30m—butt kicks x 3
d. 30m—straight-leg pull x 3
e. 30m—backward runs x 3

HURDLE DRILLS

a. 10 hurdles (84 cm) approx. 1.5m apart
—spider walks with skip x 4
b. 10 hurdles (84 cm) approx. 2m apart
—side-leg scissor up & back in middle of hurdle x 4
c. 10 hurdles (84 cm) approx. 2m apart
—lead-leg lift with skip of support leg
—2xR, 2xL
d. 10 hurdles (84 cm) approx. 3m apart
—trail-leg walk drill with high-thigh walks between hurdles
—3 x R leg, 3 x L leg
e. 5 hurdles (84 cm) approx. 7-8m apart
—trail-leg run drill with 3 high-thigh runs between hurdles
—3 x R leg, 3 x 1 leg

TYPES OF DRILLS

The high jump consists of different phases and different drills can be used to develop the various aspects of the jump. Drills can be loosely grouped into the following categories but there is often an overlap between the various drills.
• Runup drills
• Takeoff drills
• Flight drills.

EXAMPLES OF RUNUP DRILLS:
• Using the full or short runup:
  Run "through" the plane of the bar (no bar)
  Run "through" with a simulated takeoff
  Run "through" with a low bar
• Timed full runups for rhythm
• Scissors with no bar, low bar and then gradual increase in bar height
• Walking the runup off the short and long runup mark
• "Run pasts" off a short or full runup
• Circle runs of varying diameters
• Slalom runs of varying width and breadth.

World record holder Javier Sotomayor.

EXAMPLES OF TAKEOFF DRILLS:
The preparation for the takeoff and the takeoff itself are difficult to separate as the correct execution of one affects the other. Various takeoff drills can be performed on the grass, track or high jump curve in a straight or curved line. Both "sides" should be developed as this helps coordination as well as balancing the physical training effects of training. Caution needs to be taken with the landing action and athletes should try to "dampen" the eccentric landing forces.

- Simulated walking takeoffs on the grass every 4 or 6 steps in a straight line over 20-40m
- Simulated walking takeoffs on the grass every 4 or 6 steps in a curved line over 20-40m
- Simulated running takeoffs on the grass every 4 or 6 steps in a straight line over 30-40m
- Simulated running takeoffs on the grass every 4 or 6 steps in a curved line over 30-40m.

EXAMPLES OF TAKEOFF DRILLS (continued):

- Simulated running takeoffs on the grass every 4 or 6 steps in a straight line over low hurdles/ cones over 30-40m
- Simulated running takeoffs on the grass every 4 or 6 steps in a straight line over low hurdles/ cones over 30-40m and landing on the non-take-off leg
- Simulated running takeoffs on the grass off a measured short runup to the soccer goals or a bar above PB height
- Simulated running takeoffs into the sand pit off a straight measured short high jump approach
- Simulated running takeoffs into the sand pit off a straight measured short high jump approach and jumping over low hurdles
- Skip drills over 2 or 4 skips on the grass over 30-40m
- Skip drills over 2 or 4 skips on the high jump runup curve to a bar above PB height

EXAMPLES OF FLIGHT DRILLS:

- Backovers off a raised platform
- Backovers off the ground
- Performing short runup scissors and flop off a beat board or ramp
- Short runup flops off a mini-tramp
- Two-feet takeoff flops off 90° straight approach and turning to preferred side
- Two-feet takeoff flops off 90° straight approach and turning to non-preferred side
- Two-feet takeoff flops off 45° straight approach and turning to preferred side
- Two-feet takeoff flops off 45° straight approach and turning to non-preferred side
- Traditional gymnastics tumbling exercises.

EXAMPLES OF TECHNICAL DRILLS SESSIONS:

SESSION ONE
a) High thighs to parallel run past off 5-stride mark x 6
b) High thighs to parallel off 5-stride mark with simulated takeoff x 6
c) R/L/R/L skip with simulated takeoff x 6
d) L/R/L/R skip with simulated takeoff x 6
e) Simulated takeoffs with rubber x 8-10

SESSION TWO
a) Backovers x 6-8—ground
b) Backovers x 6-8—beat board
c) Two-feet straight flops with half turn x 3-4 each side
d) "Free" 4-5-stride scissors x 4-5, r&l sides?
e) "Free" 4-5-stride flops x 4-5
f) 5-stride r/up, flops x 6-8
g) beat board flops x 6-10 (hold takeoff position!)

SESSION THREE
a) Backovers x 6-8
b) Two-feet straight flops with half turn x 3-4 each side
c) Two-feet angled flop with quarter turn x 5-6 each side
d) "Free" 4-5-stride scissors x 6-8—r&l sides
e) "Free" 4-5 flops x 6-8
f) Beat board flops x 8-10.

LAST THOUGHTS

Drills are a necessary and useful method of developing any efficient technical model. However, the coach must be aware that drills are only effective if they affect changes in the competition performance! Some athletes respond well to drills, drills and more drills, while others are better at changing ineffective patterns while actually performing the entire jump off a short or long run.

Chapter III:
The Pole Vault

Teaching Pole Vaulting Using The Angular Pole

By Fotis Katsikas, Greece

A novel approach to teaching pole vaulting by using specially constructed single-angle and double-angle poles, made from pieces of flexible poles, which are joined together by metal angle plates, to make learning of the vault easier and safer.

FIXED METAL POLE

The fixed metal pole consists of a metal base fixed to the ground. On this base is a system that allows the pole to move freely forward and backward. To this rotating system is attached a piece of a flexible pole of a certain length (about 3m), according to the age, height and capacities of the athlete (Fig. 1).

The fixed metal pole is the simplest in the "angular pole" system. It is used at the beginning of pole vault instruction and helps the athlete to become familiar with the rhythm of the takeoff, hang, swing and other actions involved in the pole vault. The fixed metal pole is placed in front of a long jump pit or a high jump or pole vault landing area.

The athletes run freely over 10 to 15m and grip the pole at the highest point they can reach with the top arm fully extended. A takeoff, swing and penetration to the landing area follows.

ANGULAR POLE (SINGLE-ANGLE)

The single-angle pole (Fig. 2) consists of:
a) A metal base fixed to the ground.
b) On this base is a system that allows the pole to move freely forward and backward.
c) To this rotating system is attached a short piece of a flexible pole 40 to 60cm in length.
d) At the upper end of the short pole is a metal link fixed at an angle of 165°.
e) A long piece of a flexible pole is connected at this angle to the metal link. This second type of an "angular pole" helps the athlete to become

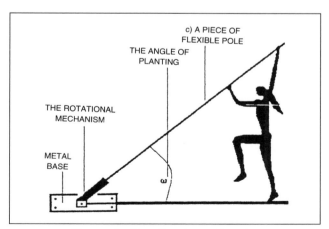

Figure 1: The fixed metal pole.
The simplest version of angular poles.

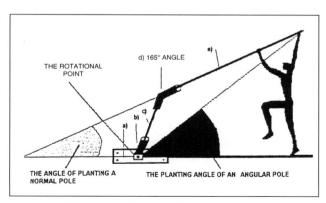

Figure 2: The single-angle pole.

more familiar with the rhythm of the takeoff, rock-back, turn and clearing of the bar.

ANGULAR POLE (DOUBLE-ANGLE)

The double-angle pole (Fig. 3) consists of:
a) A metal base fixed to the ground.
b) On this base is a system that allows the pole to move freely forward and backward.
c) To this rotating system is attached a short piece of a flexible pole 40 to 60cm in length.
d) At the upper end of the short pole is a metal link fixed at an angle of 165°.
e) A second short flexible pole piece is connected to the first-angle link.
f) At the end of this is a second 165° metal link.
g) To this is attached a long piece of a flexible pole.

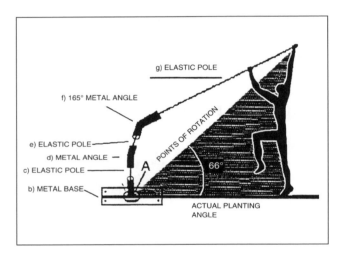

Figure 3: The double-angle pole.

The third type of an "angular pole" helps the athlete to feel the rhythm of all vaulting phases from takeoff to bar clearance. It also reproduces the feel of the bending of the pole and the recoil action. The feeling of the angular pole propelling the athlete is very similar to the real pole. Further, the angular pole can be arranged in many different ways to suit the height, age and athletic ability of the training group.

The desired inclination and pole hand-hold height can be achieved by manipulating the length of the small pieces of plastic poles. The inclination of the pole can be arranged in the desired position with a very simple device, e.g., a chain that permits the pole to incline to a certain degree.

ADVANTAGES

The angular pole helps to introduce pole vaulting to the general student body at schools and to young athletes in athletic clubs. The teaching situation is safer, easier and very close to actual vaulting. The advantages are:

- It is safe because there is control of the balance of the athlete which is very important for the first trials of a new activity.
- The height of the grip can be arranged for each individual according to the height, speed and age range.
- It makes it easier to penetrate to the landing area than with a conventional pole, particularly with the single- and double-angles poles. This is because the angle of planting the angular pole is larger than planting a conventional pole.
- The athlete can repeat the exercise many more times without getting tired because it is easier to penetrate and full speed is not necessary for each vault.
- Using a simple device (chain, string, rubber band) allows the system to return automatically to the starting position. Each attempt follows the previous one quickly, without loss of time.
- The athlete feels safe because of balance control and is free to concentrate on the main points of each exercise.
- The angular poles are made of pieces of broken poles, so they have some elasticity, giving the athlete a chance to feel the propelling action of a real pole.
- An angular pole can be constructed easily from any material. It can be used without the presence of planting boxes, specific poles and any other special equipment. It is easily movable and can be installed indoors or outdoors.
- Angular poles allow the coach to teach more actions in a training unit and more athletes can be trained in each training unit.

EXERCISES

Fixed Metal Pole

In landing in the long jump pit the pole is adjusted close to the vertical position. From this position the penetration is very easy.
- The athlete runs and grips the pole vertically with a fully extended right arm. There is a need

for a fast and energetic last stride before a left foot takeoff (for right-handed athletes). Initially, the athlete gets familiar with the rhythm of the last two strides and a takeoff from the correct foot.

- The above exercise is repeated, changing the inclination of the pole. The angle of "planting" the pole becomes smaller and the penetration more demanding. Penetration demands speed and an active foot plant. Emphasis is on the takeoff directed upward and forward (something in between the long and triple jumps). After the takeoff the athlete aims to swing as far as possible, landing in the pit without changing direction.
- The athlete penetrates in a "stride position" (as in the long jump), keeping the takeoff leg behind and the lead leg bent in the knee at a 90° angle, before gathering both legs to the chest. Landing occurs without changing direction.
- Vaulting, but changing the landing direction. As above, taking care of keeping the legs together.
- Clearing a rubber bar, placed low and brought gradually closer to the takeoff area. The height of the rubber bar is set around 80cm to 100cm. The athlete gathers the legs to the chest, tucks and at the highest point rotates to face upward. The landing is on two legs bent at the knees.

In landing on a high jump or pole vault mat:
- Legs up to the chest followed by landing either on the legs or on the back.
- Swing, legs up to the chest, followed by a rotation at the highest point and landing facing backwards.
- Clearing a rubber bar positioned relatively high with emphasis on raising the hips and rotating at the highest point above the bar.
- Complete vaulting for height.

Single-Angle Pole

- Repetition of all the exercises performed with the fixed metal pole in order to master the early movements of the vault.
- The athlete runs and grips the pole at the highest hand-hold point and penetrates to the mat in a "striding" position. The athlete hangs on the pole but does not attempt to bend it. The points to emphasize are balance and an energetic takeoff.
- Vaulting and gradually increasing grip height to develop the feeling of the hand-hold and swinging on the pole.

- With the new grip height the athlete attempts to master the rock-back, the rotation, the extension, and bar clearance actions.

The single-angle pole exercises offer the athlete an opportunity to become synchronized with a pole that offers limited elasticity. The pole compresses slightly when the athlete rocks back and recoils later to propel the athlete in a direction that corresponds to the position of the center of gravity of the body. This is a very important point for every future pole vaulter.

Double-Angle Pole

Athletes will have now become familiar with the rhythm of vaulting in performing exercises on the fixed metal and single-angle poles. Linking the second angle to the system makes the situation more demanding but still easier in comparison to the flexible pole. The grip is higher and the time an athlete hangs and swings on the pole is extended. The elasticity of the pole is more perceptible due to the two angles and pieces of flexible poles.

Generally speaking, the double-angle pole allows the athlete to exactly duplicate the takeoff performed with a flexible pole. The only difference is that the penetration effort is less demanding. This is because the rotation of the pole begins at a plant angle that corresponds with the chord of the angular pole.
- All previously outlined exercises are appropriate in using the double-angle pole.
- The athlete takes a 10 to 15m runup, grips the pole at high hand-hold height and penetrates in a "stride" position to the landing mat. The athlete hangs from the pole as in the metal pole technique and does not keep the body away from the pole as in the flexible pole action. Emphasis is on an active takeoff forward and upward and balance in the air.
- Vaulting and gradually increasing the grip to develop the feeling of hanging and swinging on the pole.
- With the new grip height the athlete tries to become familiar with the rock-back phase and attempts to rotate at the highest point.
- The clearance of the bar with good technique.

The athlete can experience the bending of the pole in the double-angle pole exercises. When he is in the rock-back phase with his back parallel to the ground, the pole is fully stressed and some kind of elasticity is apparent.

BENDING THE POLE

In using the double-angle pole the athlete is very close to the bending technique of a flexible pole. Consequently all the exercises intended to teach the bending technique must aim at allowing the athlete to master the technique of keeping his body away from the pole.

Suggested Exercises

The athlete takes a runup, grips the pole at high hand-hold height with a vertically extended right arm and extends the left arm horizontally. The left arm is nearly straight, the elbow at a fixed angle. The left hand is positioned 60 to 80cm below the top hand.

- The athlete learns to penetrate into a "striding" position, keeping the takeoff leg deliberately behind the body.
- At first staying behind the pole is attempted in a "striding" position. In the next phase the athlete joins the legs, tucks and then drives them to the front as far as possible.
- As above, but the athlete drives the legs upwards, leaving his shoulders and head back in an effort to lift the hips and attain an inverted position. He now tries to extend the legs and hips and at the same time turns to face the bar. Finally he tries to rotate over the bar.
- Finally the athlete attempts to pull, turn and push himself as high as possible to complete the total vault.

CONCLUSIONS

Using the fixed metal and angular poles gives a wide variety of youngsters an opportunity to meet the demands of pole vaulting. It provides the first and most important step which could eventually lead an athlete to the Olympic dais or to a world record.

However, among the many kids who are going to try the above exercises only a few are going to be inspired. The majority are going to cope only with the simplest of the exercises. Many are going to try them but at the end they will find them not worth further effort. Some are not going to penetrate into the pit, while others may even fail to jump and grip the pole. This allows the coach to make the first selection by eliminating:

- All those who are not excited by pole vaulting
- Those who have difficulties even with the simplest exercises.

By continuing to introduce more and more difficult exercises, we finally find kids who have the capacity to perform complex exercises and obviously possess the basic qualities for pole vaulting. They will now have to join athletic centers for pole vaulting in order to develop all the qualities that are necessary for this complicated event. The way to the top for these gifted youngsters is now determined by the policies of the country concerned.

Women Become Pole Vaulters

By Igor Nikonov, Russia

Performances in the women's pole vault have improved rapidly over the last couple of years, although female vaulters have by no means reached their potential in this event. In the following discussion the author outlines the basic aspects of pole vault technique and looks at the problems female vaulters face in their physical preparation and technique development.

SELECTION

A correct selection of potential female pole vaulters plays a considerably important part in the development of this new event. However, it takes two or three years of systematic multifaceted training before a decision about an athlete's potential to succeed in the pole vault can be made. According to physiologists and experienced coaches the first reliable signs become apparent in the 13 to 14 yrs. age range. It is the age when there is little difference between the physical development of girls and boys.

The selection process begins with the fundamental selection of track and field as the sport of choice and is followed by two to three years of diverse development that includes pole vault elements. The diverse development during this basic phase is essential for faster improvement at the next stage when specialization in the pole vault takes place. In general, girls who have taken part in gymnastics and acrobatics and show good results in the long and high jumps appear to be suitable for the pole vaulters group.

Well known pole vault coach V. Jagodin claims that gymnasts usually make rapid progress in vaulting and reach heights in the range of 3.40 to 3.60m in a short time. However, he also claims that this could sometimes be followed by a period of stagnation. In the opinion of this author, attention in the selection of potential female vaulters should be directed to girls with a good development in sprinting speed and jumping power.

PHYSICAL PREPARATION

Pole vault technique studies have shown that the loads created during a vault exceed the athletes own body weight several times. A resistance that corresponds to 150 to 250kg is created when the pole is planted in the box. This is increased up to 400kg during the transfer of the horizontal speed into the vertical, when centrifugal force reaches 150 to 250kg. All this gives a clear indication of a close correlation between pole vault technique and physical capacities.

Consequently, in the physical preparation of female vaulters we should keep in mind the differences in muscular strength between men and women athletes. Studies indicate that the strength level of the lower extremities exceeds the development of upper extremities in women. It is a fact that makes the learning of vaulting technique more difficult and has a considerable influence on the work capacity on the pole.

Based on previous studies and practical experience, we would like to recommend a sequence in the physical preparation of female vaulters that begins with an evaluation and development of the weak links in performance capacities. This is then followed by a harmonious and multifaceted development of physical capacities according to the specific demands of the pole vault until the desired physical parameters have been achieved. The solution of this task can be assisted by the use of regular control tests that are adjusted to an athlete's current pole vault result. (Fig. 1)

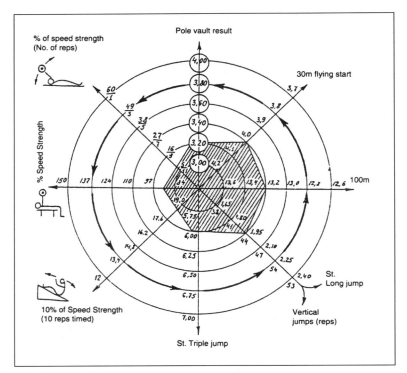

**Figure 1: Recommended control tests.
The circularly based tests are calculated to correspond to
certain pole vault performances.**

As can be seen in Fig. 1, the circularly based tests are calculated to correspond to a certain pole vault performance. At the same time it should be kept in mind that the tests are only a rough guide because there are no universal training means that can solve all preparation problems. Further, as the organism adapts rapidly to a constantly used stimulus, it would be ineffective to attempt to transfer one-sided development to the demands of the pole vault technique.

It is important in the planning of strength development to keep constantly in mind that the lower part of the female vaulter should be lighter than her upper part. This applies both to initial selection and to the development of physical capacities.

Heavy weight training is responsible for increased pelvis and hip muscle hypertrophy and therefore upsets the desired balance between the lower and upper body. This can be avoided by emphasizing the development of lower extremities with exercises directed to improve running speed and speed-strength.

The recommended distribution of speed, speed strength and strength development exercises is 30%-30%-30%. The remaining 10% is set aside to improve any other weak links in the performance capacity.

TECHNIQUE DEVELOPMENT

The technique development of female pole vaulters has a lot in common with that of male vaulters with some specific differences. Both are briefly summed up in the following analysis of the different pole vault phases.

The approach run is one of the fundamental elements of the pole vault, because all the subsequent phases after the takeoff depend upon an effective transfer and maintenance of the runup speed. We can arbitrarily divide the length of the approach run into three categories:
1. Short—10 to 12 strides (15 to 18m)
2. Medium—14 to 16 strides (21 to 24m)
3. Long—18 to 20 strides (27 to 30m).

Each of the three variations presents a stage in the development of pole vault technique during the preparation process and allows the athlete, with certain limitations, to achieve maximal controllable speed. Each of the variations corresponds to a physical development phase of female vaulters reflected in their technique level at certain stages.

In general, it can be said that a 100m performance in the 13.4 to 13.6 sec. range corresponds to the short runup, 13.0 to 13.2 sec. to the medium runup and times below 12.8 sec. to a long runup. All female vaulters are warned not to lengthen their approaches before they have established the required sprinting preparation base.

The Pole Carry

The height and the width in holding the pole is an important technique element with a considerable influence on the effectiveness of the vault. A high grip on the pole is justified because the result depends about 50% on the grip height. However, a high grip requires a well developed shoulder girdle and a powerful takeoff, not to mention good runup velocity. Further, it must be kept in mind that a 10cm raise in the grip height requires changes to the pole carry, planting action and changes to the check marks of the approach run. Even more important, it requires a higher level of specific physical preparation.

A wrongly selected grip height can be responsible for several faults including:

- An inclined trunk position during the runup to avoid a premature drop of the front end of the pole.
- A delayed planting action, caused by a backward move of the hands behind the projection of the body.
- An excessive pole bend during the penetration, leading to stalling before the pole reaches the vertical.

In the choice of the width of the grip (distance between the hands), it should be kept in mind that a wide grip makes pole carry during the runup easier, but the planting action and the rotation on the pole more difficult. On the other hand, a narrow grip makes the pole carry in the runup harder and can lead to an unbalanced takeoff. But it makes the rotation on the pole easier to control. The best solution is to place the hands a shoulder-width apart which corresponds to a distance of 30 to 40cm.

Taking into consideration that female vaulters have a lower grip height than men and use lighter poles, they can at least in the beginning stages employ the now outdated variation of a hand shift of the ridged poles era. This of course, requires a reasonably clean left hand to make its upward slide possible.

The Plant

Female athletes perform the plant during the last two strides. The right arm with the pole is raised so that the right hand is above the shoulder at the moment the right foot contacts the surface. Both hands lift the pole during the last stride so that it is as high as possible when the takeoff foot lands. This action is well performed by Abramova in Fig. 2a.

The Takeoff

The only difference between men and women vaulters is the slight left arm bend of female vaulters in the final phase of the takeoff. This can be

Stacy Dragila

explained by the fact that women grip the pole about one meter lower than men and it is impossible to bend the pole initially with a straight left arm when the grip height hasn't reached at least 4.00m. As the grip height is increased, so does the left arm straighten (Fig. 2b).

The Hang.

The hang begins with an active swing that follows the takeoff. This creates the force that rotates

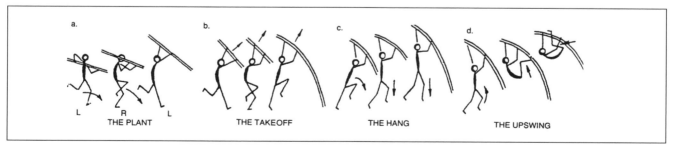

Figure 2: The major phases of pole vault technique.
a=S. Abramova (plant); b=M. Andrejeva (takeoff); c=E. Bell (hang); d=M. Andrejeva (upswing)

the female vaulter about the vertical axis from the athlete's top hand through her center of gravity. To avoid an early rotation on the pole, some male and many female vaulters attempt to drop the lead leg to stop the rotation about the vertical axis. How much the lead leg is dropped and straightened is individual and is developed from experience. (Fig. 2c). This "penetration" position is necessary to exploit the takeoff impulse before the upswing movement commences.

The Upswing

This element of the pole vault technique involves the transition from the hang by the grouping of all body parts close to the grip on the pole through an upwards roll and a rock-back. The higher the hips and legs are raised, the faster and more efficient is the turn on the pole. While this upward rolling movement, created by a rotation about the shoulder axis, bends the pole further, it happens at a stage when a fast straightening of the pole is about to begin. It is therefore necessary to complete the turn on the pole before it straightens to exploit its catapulting effect. The upswing element is well demonstrated in Fig. 2d.

In order to exploit the catapulting impulse of the straightening pole and to gain advantage from the extension, the vaulter extends her virtually straight body directly in line with the pole. This is followed by an upward pull with the arms that is completed with a turn. The arm pull must coincide with the recoil of the pole and the turn should be initiated from the feet. A correctly executed pull and turn into a handstand takes place in the vertical plane along the pole. It is responsible for a smooth transfer from a hang into a support position of a bent-arm handstand.

There are many faults that crop up in this phase among female vaulters, starting from an inefficient grouping of body parts followed by an attempt to simply extend the legs forward towards the crossbar.

The Bar Clearance

In the bent-arm support, with elevated legs on the pole that moves slowly towards the vertical, the upper body is forced directly below the legs to assure that the athlete's center of gravity is kept above the handgrip. A slight drop of the elevated legs that follows helps to release the left hand from the pole to move into a right-arm support position.

The final pushoff with the right arm is smooth and should not be hurried. The longer the vaulter has contact with the pole, the longer she can guide her actions. Once the pole is released the fly-away follows a predetermined path.

IN SUMMARY

To sum it up, it can be said that women pole vaulters have, in the short time since the event was accepted, made good progress in the development of technique. It has reached the stage where they are capable of producing performances similar to the results of male vaulters during the era of bamboo poles. At the same time it is obvious that women vaulters still have several technical shortcomings and are nowhere near their performance potential. That appears to apply in particular to physical preparation which is an aspect that considerably influences technical development.

Considerations For A Revision Of The Model Pole Vault Technique In Germany

By Dieter and Helmut Kruber and Horst Adamczevski, Germany

Suggested changes to the German model technique of the pole vault based on observations of the former Soviet Union's vaulters at the World Championships in Stuttgart and information available from Russian coaches.

INTRODUCTION

The results of the World Championships in Stuttgart (1993) showed the superiority of the vaulters from the former Soviet Union. Seven (58%) of the 12 finalists came from this region and six (75%!) of the first eight were athletes from the former USSR.

Our following considerations for a revision of the technical pole vault model are therefore based, above all, on the observation of the athletes from the former Soviet Union. We also developed a questionnaire which was forwarded to different Russian coaches for a clarification of some open questions.

Further insight into the work of former Soviet coaches was gained from Vladimir Ryshih, a coach of the Volkov School, who worked a year in the Zweibrücken training center in Germany and Moscow coaches Kostelev and Parnov, who also spent some time in Zweibrücken. A coaching course conducted in Germany by Bubka's former coach, Vitaly Petrov, provided further insight into the Russian technique and training concepts. In addition, the authors attended three Soviet training camps in Moscow and Saproshe.

MODEL TECHNIQUE RUNUP

The vaults of the world's elite, as could be seen at the World Championships in Stuttgart, essen- tially followed the same model technique. This model technique of the former Soviet vaulters deviates partly from the technique used up to now by the majority of German coaches.

Pole Carriage

The views of the German and former Soviet coaches are essentially similar on this topic. The pole must be carried with an uncramped finger and arm support to make a relaxed and tall sprint runup possible. A tight grip on the pole by either the front or the rear hand is therefore not appro- priate. The front arm's elbow should be placed under the pole.

Particularly favorable, according to Petrov, is to keep the rear hand close to the hip so that the pole can be brought as straight as possible forward for the plant. The German coaches allow here for more liberal variations that sometimes have a nega- tive influence on the speed of the planting move- ments.

Recommendation: The pole should be carried still, without any interfering movements, relatively steep, with the rear hand close to the hip. The fingers are kept open during the runup and the lead arm's elbow is low.

Runup Rhythm

At the World Championships, hardly any ath- lete began his runup with preliminary strides. Nearly all vaulters used a standing start and accel-

Figure 1: The model pole vault Technique.

erated with powerful dynamic strides.

It was further striking to discover a great majority of the world's best vaulters shortened not only their last stride, but also the third last stride. This meant that their rear leg was not fully extended in the last three strides. Apparently the world's elite prefers stride frequency over the driving action.. Measurements in Stuttgart indicated clearly no velocity losses occurring from this approach. As a rule, the athletes were significantly faster over the last five meters of the runup (an exception was Tradenkov).

THE PLANT-TAKEOFF COMPLEX

The world's elite, in particular the former Soviet vaulters, prefer a two-contact plant that several Germany coaches have been experimenting with. The comparison between the two-contact and three-contact plants is shown in Fig. 2a/b.

The two-contact plant is for leading vaulters with a high grip, better suited for the development of velocity over the last few meters of the runup than the three-contact plant. However, more experiments are needed to find out the suitability of this planting action for children and young athletes.

The Impulse Plant

The impulse plant taught in the pole vault schools of the former Soviet Union does not opti-

cally differ from the planting action recommended in Germany. The morphological characteristics of this plant are a fully extended top arm, a takeoff with a high knee lift (as vertical as possible under the top hand), an upward extension of the lower arm and a fixed narrow angle of the lead-leg knee joint after the takeoff (Fig. 3).

Figure 2a: The two-contact plant.

Figure 2b: The three-contact plant.

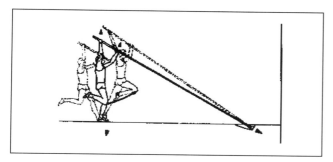

Figure 3: The impulse plant.

In the impulse planting processes preferred by the Russians, the athlete attempts to execute the plant explosively and synchronize the final extension of both arms, the extension of the takeoff leg and hips, the fixation of the lead-leg knee angle and the contact of the pole end with the back of the box.

The total impulse achieved by the pole vaulter system leads to the release of enormous forces that allow athletes to use poles designed for 20kg heavier vaulters. However, it should be kept in mind that this synchronized plant-takeoff impulse is attainable only after very extensive practice.

THE TAKEOFF AND LONG PENDULUM

The takeoff should take place from a shortened last stride with a high knee lift. This occurs simultaneously with a total extension of the body under the top hand. A completely accurate takeoff is rare, even among the elite vaulters. At the same time, "running under" is also seldom seen.

"Penetration" is regarded as an extension of the takeoff. This term has been lately criticized by Russian coaches because it appears to suggest an active bending of the pole by the vaulter. Such an active bending, expecially when it takes place with the help of the lower arm, leads nearly always to a takeoff in front of the vertical line from the top hand because a position under the lower hand allows the lower arm to develop more force. Naturally this extends the duration of the takeoff phase.

The misunderstandings about penetration are based on the wrong notion that penetration is a specific activity. Actually, penetration is not an activity but rather a position that is created as a result of a good planting movement and a dynamic takeoff (Fig. 4, center picture). Instead of penetration it is therefore more appropriate to talk

about the forward movement of the pole or the need to accelerate the pole. This acceleration begins with the planting action and ceases when the vaulter has left the ground.

An intensive forward-upward directed impulse from a takeoff that takes place vertically under the top hand, or 5 to 10cm in front of it, leads to an automatic pole bending. In the vaulting action that follows, the takeoff leg is, after its intensive driving action, left well behind the vaulters body. This stretches the hip flexors to create pretension, which is extremely important for the subsequent forward whip of the takeoff leg. The lower arm is first bent in the elbow to allow the forward movement of the chest to continue. The body of the vaulter hangs in this phase exclusively from the top arm. The lower arm follows the bending of the pole and reaches a passively extended position. We talk about a disengagement of the lower arm (Fig. 4).

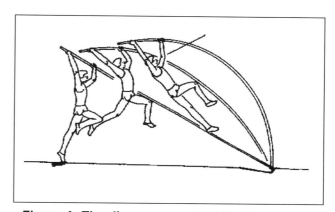

Figure 4: The disengagement of the lower arm.

The question about fixing the lead leg, or dropping it, remains open. Both variations have biomechanical advantages and disadvantages. The world's best vaulters demonstrate both variations in about equal numbers. However, it appears to be increasingly important after the takeoff to rapidly reach the I-position when very hard and fast poles are used. This is likely to be possible only when the long pendulum swing is executed with an active forward whip of the takeoff leg.

The term "pendulum" is here actually misleading because it suggests a passive movement. It should be replaced with the term "takeoff leg whip." This takeoff leg whip is initiated with an active kicking movement of the lower leg. The completely stretched takeoff leg now swings upward-forward (pivoting around the hip axis) and should bend after the crossing of the pole axis.

THE FIRST AND SECOND UPSWINGS AND HIP EXTENSION INTO THE I-POSITION

The upswing phase of world-class athletes continues from the long pendulum with a disengaged lower arm. The extension of the lower arm in this phase is a passive movement and should never be considered to be a pushing action. An efficient upswing is possible only when the lower arm is completely relaxed.. However, after the lower hand has passed the hip, it is necessary for the lower arm to again seek contact with the pole (Fig. 5). Many world-class athletes consider this movement as a lower hand pull to the chest

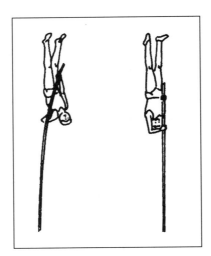

Figure 5: The I-position. Left: Bubka's successful contact with the lower arm. Right: Tarasov's unsuccessful contact.

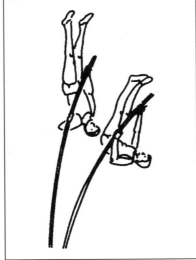

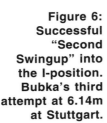

Figure 6: Successful "Second Swingup" into the I-position. Bubka's third attempt at 6.14m at Stuttgart.

The action that the former Soviet Union's coaches distinguish as the second upswing takes place when the lower arm makes contact with the pole. This is a new concept for us. It refers to the dropping of the shoulder axis when the hips have passed the lower hand (Fig. 6). It is a movement absent in beginners because the lower hand presses against the pole changing the rotation from the shoulder axis to a pivot around the lower hand.

An extension of the hips into the I-position begins in the final phase of the second upswing. An attempt to avoid the pull to the chest in this phase swings the vaulter past the pole (see the faulty performance by Tarasov in Fig. 5).

THE PULL-TURN FOR BAR CLEARANCE

It's still not clear whether the pull-turn movement is executed actively or passively. Hopefully an explanation will become available from a biomechanical analysis conducted with the help of high-speed cameras at the World Championships in Stuttgart. We presume that this phase is a passive guidance of the pole when an athlete has reached an ideal I-position at the right time and uses a pole at least 20kg over his body weight. A less than ideal, or delayed, I-position, as well as the use of soft poles, leads to an active pull-turn phase.

IN SUMMARY

The following points in the model technique for the pole vault should be revised or taken into consideration:

- A pole carriage with rear hand close to the hip.
- A shortening of the final strides, particularly the last stride.
- A two-contact plant for athletes with a high grip and a fast runup.
- A plant that is synchronized with the takeoff, arms extension, fixed lead-leg knee angle and the contact of the pole end with the back of the box.
- No bending of the pole with the lower arm.
- A disengagement of the lower arm during the long pendulum and the first upswing.
- An introduction of a "second upswing" as a term that describes the dropping of the shoulders with an extension of the hips.

The Pre-Jump Takeoff In The Pole Vault Revisited

By Alan Launder and John Gormley, Australia

Do elite pole vaulters, at least on some occasions, leave the ground before the tip of the pole actually touches the back of the box? The authors of this article are prepared to conclude that this is the case and explain why.

This article was stimulated by a paper by two British authors, Young and Yeadon, whose article "Optimum Takeoff Position in the Vault" was printed in the last issue of the now defunct British Athletic Federation journal *Athletics Coach.* In reporting "research" of doubtful objectivity and validity they have contributed little to scientific knowledge concerning the takeoff in the pole vault.

Young and Yeadon merely repeat what has been common knowledge among coaches for many years, namely that the farther ahead the takeoff foot is of the top hand at takeoff, the greater will be the velocity losses.

Consider for example the paper "The Runup Speed in the Pole Vault" by Ulrich Steinacher, originally published in *Die Lehre der Leichtathletik* in October 1989 in which he states ". . .an optimal vault performance can be achieved only when the vaulter/pole system executes a precise and correct planting movement with minimal velocity losses in the last three strides. Coaches must pay a lot of attention to the development of a smooth planting procedure in training."

He then goes on to state "considerable velocity losses can occur at the takeoff by running under. If the dynamic takeoff spot from a full run up is more than 60 to 70cm ahead of the top hand, the velocity can be reduced by as much as 3.5m/sec and the support phase will last 0.14 to 0.16 seconds. A takeoff point 30 to 35cm ahead of the top hand will reduce velocity losses to 1.4 to 1.8m/sec and the support phase to 0.12 to 0.14 sec."

The paper by Young and Yeadon reveals little or no understanding of the target technique for modern elite vaulters. Even worse, some of the comments made may mislead coaches who put trust in statements delivered with the imprimatur of science. This is disappointing considering Young's reputation and experience as a coach and that of Yeadon as a sports scientist.

They have ignored the possibility that the pre-jump concept might have merit and have therefore failed to use their considerable computer modelling skills to establish the validity, or otherwise, of this concept of the takeoff. Even more surprising is that they appear to have missed or chosen to ignore a large number of empirically based observations, some of which used photographic and mechanical methods, concerning both the free takeoff and the pre-jump, some of which are summarized below.

To appreciate the potential of a pre-jump takeoff it is vital to have a clear understanding of the technical model developed by the coaches from the former USSR. The key elements of this model, which was driven by the search for ways to employ ever-increasing grip heights and stiffer poles, were all indicated by Petrov in his original presentation in 1985.

Unfortunately the problems caused when translating complex technical concepts from one language to another and the even greater problem of converting revolutionary ideas into concrete technical models in the minds of listeners or readers, especially those who are convinced that they already know all they need to know, has meant that Petrov's words passed almost unnoticed.

That few if any reputable sports biomechanists and coaches appear to have attempted to seriously examine, or scientifically test, what he said even 13 years on is surprising given the dominance of Russian vaulters during this period.

Pole Flex
10 degrees

Pole is straight

Foot Clearly Off
The Ground

The Russian target technique stresses:

- A high-angle initial pole carry intended to minimize the problems of accelerating to sprint speed while carrying a long pole with a relatively narrow grip.
- A relatively narrow grip, which is necessary for the completion of an explosive plant and subsequent fast inversion!
- A very specific runup structure in which cadence is emphasized over the final 6 to 8 strides to prevent the stride length from continuing to increase.
- A very specific point at which the lowering of the pole begins, designed to meld the speed of the dropping pole with the speed the athlete is running.
- A "free takeoff" and the "pre-jump," for the reasons indicated below.
- The lowering of the shoulders simultaneously with the legs swinging up in the inversion. This is the second major innovation that has passed almost unnoticed, despite the extreme vertical positions Bubka invariably demonstrates.

However, it is the concept of the "free" takeoff and its extension the "pre-jump" that have proved to be the most controversial. This is somewhat surprising, given the evidence provided by the

photograph of Bubka's takeoff for the first ever 6-meter jump (in Paris in 1985). He is clearly off the ground as the gap between his toe and the shadow of that toe show.

While recognizing the limitations of the photograph and the uncertainty associated with calculations based on simple measurements taken from it, it is possible using the bar height (of precisely six meters) to use simple geometric principles to estimate other critical distances. Using this method our calculations show that Bubka's takeoff toe was approximately 5 to 8 centimeters above the runway and approximately 8 to 10 centimeters behind the perpendicular from the top hand at the instant the photograph was taken. Naturally we recognize that such measures will not be precise due to both the camera position and perspective error from a two-dimensional image.

Accepting the limitations in the method employed, the pole does flex about 10 degrees, but this appears to us to be localized around the grip position of the left hand. We believe that the incipient bend here is caused by the vicious upward punch of both arms (Petrov's instructions are "move the pole always") at this point and not by the pole contacting the back of the box.

Additional evidence that the pole has not touched the back of the box is provided by the position of Bubka's right arm which has clearly not been driven backwards by the forces which we would expect to be initiated at the instant the pole tip touches the back of the box.

However, readers are also referred to:

1. A report of two German coaches (Thomas Kurschilgen and Franc Pejic) after a two-week visit to the Donetsk pole vault center in 1988. As part of a 12-page report they state "that the takeoff must be 'free', similar to a long jumper with both arms held high. Only immediately after leaving the ground is the resistance in the box noticeable. Only a free takeoff enables maximum acceleration of the pole and jumper and creates a high takeoff speed for an effective transmission of energy."

2. Stefanie Grabner's "Kinematic Analysis of the Women's Pole Vault" in *New Studies in Athletics*, 1997. On page 60 she quotes Keller, "During the takeoff the vaulter must on the one hand try to create a vertical impulse to straighten the pole without a reduction of the horizontal velocity and on the other hand must try to achieve a favorable takeoff position to transmit their energy to the pole," and Petrov, "To fulfil this demand, the athlete should strive for a free takeoff with only a small loss of energy and ensure that the pole plant does not take place before they have broken contact with the ground."

3. Klaus Bartonietz and Jochen Wetter "Analysis of the International Situation in the Women's Pole Vault" in *New Studies in Athletics*, 1997. One of the three major elements of their "target technique" on page 19 is "at the finish of the takeoff the pole is not yet bent ("free take off"), only when the takeoff foot leaves the ground has the pole full contact with the back of the box and starts bending." Note that Bartonietz is arguably the leading track and field biomechanist in the world.

4. Dr. Jean Claude Perrin, French national pole vault coach at a clinic in Toronto. Reported in *Modern Athlete and Coach* (Vol. 27, No. 2) "European vaulters are actually jumping into the takeoff in much the same fashion as long jumpers. They are also taking off about 30cm further back than what has been regarded as the ideal spot vertically below the top hand. As a result of the changed takeoff action the vaulters are actually in the air, or off the ground, before the pole hits the back of the box."

5. Gros, Asamizewski, Wolf (1994) in their analysis of the 4th IAAF World Championships noted that "currently a trend can be observed to minimize the time between pole plant and takeoff."

Even without such anecdotal evidence the theoretical case for the free takeoff is simple to make. No matter how a pole is planted, the instant the pole touches the back of the box the vaulter/pole system must begin to decelerate as kinetic energy from that system becomes potential energy in the rapidly bending pole. With a free takeoff, i.e., a simultaneous pole tip touch and toe tip takeoff, the pole is not loaded until the instant of takeoff, takes no energy from the system and consequently the work of pole bending is accomplished with minimal losses of kinetic and potential energy while retaining optimal rotational kinetic energy for the vaulter/pole system. As Petrov says: "And only on concluding the takeoff should the pole smoothly transfer into support. . . During the plant the pole becomes straight but it bends under the effect of the vaulter's speed and body mass."

The pre-jump, which we believe is a logical extension of the free takeoff, is also easy to justify on theoretical grounds. Apart from the obvious advantages of encouraging an aggressive plant, which melds the horizontal runup seamlessly into a "long jumping" takeoff, there is another major benefit.

As modern elite male vaulters use ever greater grip heights above 5.00, the pole/ground angle at takeoff is markedly reduced. Since this angle is crucial to the ease with which a pole will bend at takeoff, it is vital to optimize it.

Our calculations based on the photograph of Bubka suggest that he has increased the pole/ground angle by up to five degrees, compared to a toe tip takeoff. Clearly a pre-jump takeoff could optimize the pole ground angle. It would also enable the vaulter to drive the long pole towards the vertical more effectively. Even an attempt to pre-jump would tend to produce similar results, except that the pole/ground angle would not be optimized, so that in a sense the free takeoff is a missed pre-jump.

Clearly this is an interesting and important topic. To date there has been little attempt by sports biomechanists to seriously study the question: "Do elite vaulters—at least on some occasions in competition—leave the ground before the pole tip touches the back of the box. We are prepared to hypothesize that this is the case and believe it is the responsibility of those with the resources to do such studies to accept the challenge and give coaches the sound scientific information they need. Unless this happens, innovation in our sport will continue to be driven by thoughtful athletes and coaches relying on empirical observations.

Eight Elements Of An Effective Takeoff

By Peter M. McGinnis, USA

Dr. McGinnis is a noted biomechanist at State University of New York, College at Cortland, and a masters vaulter himself. This is a presentation he made at Pole Vault Summit 2000, Reno, Nevada, in January 2000.

The takeoff is the most important phase of the pole vault. The takeoff phase begins when the vaulter's takeoff foot strikes the runway at the end of his last step, and it ends at the instant of takeoff, the instant when the takeoff foot is no longer in contact with the runway. The vaulter's actions during the takeoff greatly affect the vaulter's actions during subsequent phases of the vault and ultimately affect the height achieved by the vaulter.

The importance of the takeoff phase may be best illustrated by examining the factors that determine pole vault performance. Mechanically, work and energy principles can be used to derive an equation for the maximum height achieved by a vaulter

$$PE_{apex} = TE_{to} + U_{to\text{-}rel} - E_{lost} - KE_{excess}$$

where,

PE_{apex} = potential energy of vaulter at the apex of the vault

TE_{to} = total mechanical energy of vaulter and pole at takeoff

$U_{to\text{-}rel}$ = mechanical work done by the vaulter from takeoff to pole release

E_{lost} = mechanical energy lost from takeoff to pole release

KE_{excess} = excess kinetic energy at apex of the vault.

This equation essentially states that the maximum height achieved by a pole vaulter (PE_{apex}) is determined by:

- how high his center of gravity is and how fast he is moving at takeoff (TE_{to});

- how much he pulls, pushes, and swings himself upward on the pole during the vault ($U_{to\text{-}rel}$);
- how much energy is lost or not converted to potential energy during the vault (E_{lost} and KE_{excess}).

An effective takeoff is one in which the vaulter maintains or increases the energy developed during the approach run while minimizing energy losses during this and subsequent phases of the vault. Additionally, at the end of an effective takeoff, the vaulter is in a position which improves his ability to do work on the pole during the subsequent pole support phase. Four criteria thus determine whether an action contributes to an effective takeoff. Does the action help to. . .

... increase energy coming into the takeoff?
... decrease energy lost during the takeoff?
... increase work done (and thus increase energy) during the takeoff?
... increase the ability to do work following the takeoff?

The eight elements listed below each meet one or more of these criteria. The first two elements are really not part of the takeoff phase but are included in the list since they greatly influence the effectiveness of the takeoff.

1. RUN FAST.

A fast approach run increases the energy the vaulter has to build on at the start of the takeoff phase. Elite male vaulters run faster than 9.0 m/s during the last five meters of their approach runs. There is a strong correlation between crossbar height cleared and approach run velocity.

2. TAKE A LONGER SECOND-TO-LAST STEP AND A SHORTER, QUICKER LAST STEP.

The longer second-to-last step lowers the center of gravity slightly to set up for a jumping takeoff. The shorter and quicker last step reduces the downward velocity of the center of gravity when the takeoff foot touches down at the start of the takeoff phase. This in turn reduces the braking force which acts on the takeoff foot as it first hits the runway.

3. MOVE THE HANDS UPWARD THROUGHOUT THE TAKEOFF PHASE.

This movement contributes to the vertical velocity of the vaulter at takeoff. It also increases the height of the vaulter's center of gravity. A faster velocity and higher center of gravity increase the total energy of the vaulter at takeoff. Finally, higher hands result in a higher plant and greater pole angle both of which are beneficial for getting the pole to rotate forward. Look at the positions of Jeff Hartwig's right hand in pictures 2, 3, 4 and 5. Throughout the takeoff his right hand is moving upward.

4. DON'T LET THE POLE STRIKE THE BACK OF THE BOX UNTIL YOU ARE ON YOUR TOES.

Delay the pole strike (the instant the pole hits the back of the box) until just before the instant of takeoff. If the pole strikes the back of the box earlier you may be yanked off the ground by the pole before you have finished your jumping action off the ground. The work you are able to do by pushing against the ground during the takeoff phase is reduced and you will not have as much energy at the instant of takeoff.

Look at pictures 2 through 6. The instant just before the takeoff foot hits the ground is shown in picture 2. An upward but backward (braking) re-

action force acts on the takeoff foot when it first touches down in picture 3. In picture 4 the reaction force, acting on the foot is primarily upward. In picture 5, the reaction force on the foot is an upward and forward propulsive force and Jeff is now up on his toes. Pole strike occurs at or just before this instant.

5. PLANT THE POLE WITH YOUR TOP HAND DIRECTLY ABOVE THE TOES OF YOUR TAKEOFF FOOT.

At the instant of pole strike, the top hand should be directly above the toes of the takeoff foot. This relates to the previous element. It allows you to maintain an upright posture throughout the takeoff phase and it will enable you to be on your toes when pole strike occurs. Look at picture 5.

6. START THE POLE BEND BY PUSHING AGAINST THE POLE AT A RIGHT ANGLE WITH YOUR LOWER HAND.

This action occurs at pole strike and is just a continuation of the forward and upward movement of the hands which takes place throughout the takeoff phase. The force exerted by the lower hand greatly reduces the compressive force required to buckle the pole to initiate its bending. This buckling force is supplied by the top hand (it's the force exerted by the top hand and directed through the butt end of the pole towards the box). If the buckling force is too great energy will be lost. The lower hand only pushes against the pole for a short period following the takeoff. Do not prolong the pushing action of the left arm for too long.

7. MAINTAIN A TALL UPRIGHT POSITION THROUGHOUT THE TAKEOFF PHASE.

The upright posture of the trunk helps to increase the height of the center of gravity and it increases the height of the pole at the instants of pole strike and takeoff. An upright position of the trunk at takeoff sets up the vaulter to do more

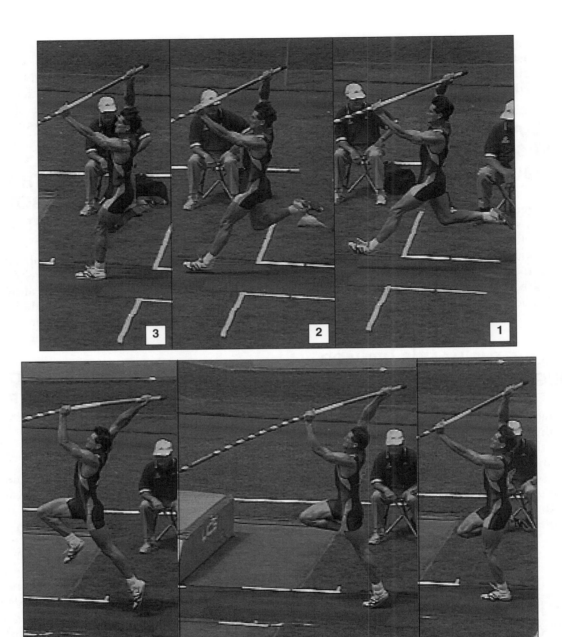

work on the pole during the pole support phase following takeoff by enabling the trunk to swing through a greater range of motion during the vault. If the vaulter is leaning backward at takeoff, this range of motion (and thus the potential to do work and increase energy) is reduced.

8. JUMP OFF THE GROUND.

Pole vaulting is a jumping event. The average takeoff angle of elite male pole vaulters is about 18°. This is slightly higher than the takeoff angle of elite male triple jumpers (~15°) and slightly lower than the takeoff angle of elite male long jumpers (~20°). Look at pictures 5 and 6. Jeff is not just running off the ground, he is jumping off the ground.

To jump off the ground effectively, the body must move through a large distance while it is on the ground during the takeoff phase. Look at pictures 2 and 6 and see how far Jeff's body has moved forward (and upward) relative to his takeoff foot (or relative to the guy sitting in the chair behind him).

1996 Olympic champion Jean Galfione

Groundwork For The Pole Vault

By Brian Risk, Canada

A sound technical piece, pinpointing critical factors of the approach and plant, by one of the world's top vault authorities. Some good sensible guidelines here, including information on pole selection and penetration problems.

It would appear to the casual observer that pole vaulting is based on acrobatics. There is some merit to this observation but, like most endeavours, the success is based on the groundwork. The skill execution while on the ground is a critical prerequisite to the acrobatics.

THREE ESSENTIAL FACTORS OF THE RUNUP

The groundwork begins with an approach run. The approach run comes in a variety of lengths and techniques but all athletes must reach a common goal. They must provide precision in execution, consistency in delivery, and maximum controllable speed.

The **precision** relates to an ability to hit an exact takeoff mark. This must occur with a stride pattern which supports maximum controllable speed and an ability to jump off the ground. For example, as one runs down a hallway and prepares to bound up a flight of stairs, it is not difficult to adjust your stride pattern to take off with the preferred leg. On the vault runway, to hit a takeoff mark precisely and without adjustments in stride length is a challenging task.

Consistency ensures that the precise movement patterns can be repeated with minimal deviation from the norm. Vaulters must be able to step onto the runway and deliver. A consistent stride pattern allows the athlete to run the full runup with minimal steering over the final six steps and hit the takeoff point exactly.

Simply hitting the takeoff mark is not difficult. Hitting it without reaching or crowding in the final six steps is the challenge.

These adjustments or steering mechanisms which alter the stride length over the final six steps have a tremendous impact on runway velocity. A mid-mark placed six steps out helps considerably with consistency and precision.

The third important variable of the approach run is the achievement of **maximum controllable speed.** This is influenced by fitness, run mechanics and approach length. A short approach will not allow a comfortable acceleration while too long a run may result in deceleration. A too-long runup may also generate undue fatigue limiting the total number of jumps available in practice or competition.

THE PLANT

The groundwork is intended to allow the vaulter to transfer runup energy to the pole. A critical part of this process is the plant. The plant occurs over the final two or three steps and should be a graceful transition of energy and position. Various terms and processes lead to the common objective of having the top arm fully extended up just prior to the final foot strike. Anything else leads to an inefficient takeoff. The goal is a high speed and high plant.

POLE SELECTION

Once the runup and plant are in place, the vaulter must have the correct pole in hand. The pole used should reflect the performance of the vaulter on that particular attempt. The pole selec-

"A driving and blocking right knee."
Pat Manson demonstrates.

PENETRATION AND DEPTH

The groundwork also has a significant impact on penetration and, subsequently, selection of depth. Numerous factors can influence the level of penetration. The exact positioning of the standards is another prediction of how the vaulter will perform.

Depth selection is a decision based on a series of factors including previous attempts, fatigue, pole selection, consistency of technique, environmental conditions and mental preparation. All of these components have a major impact on penetration.

It is best to take a positive approach to depth selection. For example, if an athlete fails to penetrate on a first attempt due to an error in technique, the temptation might be to jump the same way on a smaller pole.

Changing poles, however, plays an interesting mind game. A small pole may result in less mental

tion is based on a prediction of how the vaulter will perform. Precision and consistency developed through hundreds of rehearsals will aid this process.

The exact pole is influenced by the basic factors of runway speed, takeoff technique, angle of takeoff and angular velocity. The coach/athlete must learn or confirm something with every trip down the runway to aid in pole selection.

In addition, fatigue, psychological readiness, and previous success levels should influence the prediction. It is important that once the pole has been selected, the athlete should step onto the runway with confidence and perform at 100%. Use of the wrong pole may lead to failure and/or personal injury.

COMMON PENETRATION FAULTS AND PROBLEMS

- using a pole which is too heavy for the athlete's technique/fitness
- the soft side of the pole is positioned incorrectly
- upper arm not fully extended up at takeoff
- lack of runway speed
- takeoff point too close/far from box
- shoulders not square at takeoff
- lack of knee drive at takeoff
- left arm too passive at takeoff
- hips too low at takeoff
- failure to push up with the lower hand at takeoff
- head wind
- fatigue
- injury
- psychological duress
- premature rock-back
- insufficient left-leg swing
- throwing the head back at takeoff

CRITICAL FACTORS TO KEEP IN MIND

Runway Speed—Grip height is determined by pole speed. This is the speed at which the pole moves from the takeoff angle to vertical. A greater runway speed will foster higher grips. Runway speed is often lost due to overstriding in the final six steps to hit a takeoff mark, head wind, fatigue and injury.

Takeoff Technique—If the takeoff technique reflects an efficient transfer of energy, a longer and stiffer pole may be used. The common factors found in good technique (assuming a right-handed athlete) include a tall plant hitting its final position just prior to the final foot strike, a driving and blocking right knee, and a body posture allowing the long sweeping swing of the left leg.

Angle of Takeoff—The angle of takeoff influences the initial loading or transfer of energy to the pole. Too low or too high a takeoff angle impairs this energy transfer. Vaulters have a takeoff angle slightly lower than long jumpers and slightly higher than triple jumpers. A commonly accepted angle is approximately 22 degrees.

Angular Velocity—The vaulter can influence angular velocity with an aggressive swinging of the free leg and by using his/her upper body to put pressure down through the pole. This technique, employed by advanced vaulters, allows pole speed to be increased significantly.

tension and the vaulter can focus well on skill execution. A big pole brings new anxiety, especially if there is any self-doubt. This extra tension distracts from the ability to coordinate the superior effort required.

Athletes who rehearse with "tail wind spotting," do drills on large poles, and mentally prepare for changing poles will have the advantage.

In the above scenario, if the vaulter chooses a smaller pole and then jumps properly, he/she will overpenetrate and failure will result. It is generally best to base pole and depth selection on the historical patterns of the vaulter. This is the art of coaching and vaulting. Knowing what went wrong, what is fixable and then basing pole and depth selection on these factors is the best way to go.

And it all happens on the ground.

Brian Risk is the National Pole Vault Development Chair for Canada and author of the pole vault book, *Heat It Up!* For more info www-chi.nearnorth.edu.on.ca/polevault

An Athlete's View
Of Limits And Possibilities

By Sergey Bubka, Ukraine

The greatest pole vaulter in history speaks about his childhood, his career, the development of his technique, his meticulous approach to training and competition and the influence of his coach, Vitaliy Petrov.

Sergey Bubka, Ukraine, is the reigning world record holder in the pole vault with 6.14m (20-1¾). Bubka won six consecutive World Championships titles from 1983 to 1997—certainly one of the greatest accomplishments in the history of the sport. He has also set 17 world records outdoors and 10 indoors. He has cleared 6.00m or better in more than 44 competitions. He was voted Sportsman of the Year for 1997 by the influential newspaper L'Equipe *and honored as the best pole vaulter of the 20th century by* Track & Field News.

INTRODUCTION

Bubka describes his childhood and his early love for sport. His ferocious competitive spirit was channelled into many sports until, at age 10, he came under the influence of the pole vault coach Vitaliy Petrov. Bubka describes the special qualities and methods of a man he acknowledges is the best technical coach in the world and introduces the concept of The Culture of Movement. The influence of gymnastics on Bubka's technique is described, as is the importance of communication, feedback, and keeping an open mind to outside influences— especially from specialists in weight lifting, sprinting, medicine and psychology.

Bubka's meticulous approach to training and competition is described. Maintaining a distance from distractions, especially before major events, is vital. This can sometimes be misinterpreted.

Bubka describes the 18 months in which he was recovering from a serious achilles injury. An operation was eventually required. Athens 97 was a great motivation and Bubka describes how he was able to come back, and how he is still keen to make more world record attempts. Commercialism must be secondary to performance ambitions. Limits must not be part of an athlete's vocabulary. Above all must be dedication, attention to detail and love for the Spirit of Sport.

———•———

I will start this speech with a confession. I have won gold medals in six world championships but I have never felt more nervous than I do here today!

But although I am not used to speaking at this type of seminar I am happy to have the chance and I hope you will be interested in what I have to say.

First of all, I would like to talk a little about my childhood, because it is here that you will find the essence of the athlete I would become. I was born and brought up in the town of Lugansk in what was then the USSR and would become Ukraine. My father was a soldier and my mother a medical assistant. But they weren't active in sport.

My interest in sport came from playing in the streets around my home with my brother and my friends. As a boy I loved to play all sports. But what I loved the best were games like street hockey and football. When I played football, which was the most popular sport, I would play as an attacker, or in the defense or even in goal if I felt I had to save the team. I would play in five positions. I would run like crazy because I just had to win.

I wasn't very big for my age. In fact I was

Sergey Bubka

me to, at 8 am one morning, the teacher told us we had to walk to the gymnastic hall. When I asked how far it was and the teacher replied, "It is about 15 minutes walking," I decided that it was too far and so I went home!

Around the same time, when I was about 8 or 9 years old, a coach invited me and my brother to take special swimming lessons. I think I went twice. I remember being under the water, not able to breathe, and I knew it was not for me. I have such blood that I have to move fast, to be in the open air.

By the age of 10, I had taken part in most sports at school and outside. In the USSR at that time you did not normally start athletics at such a young age. But a friend of mine from the neighborhood recommended me to a pole vault coach named Vitaliy Petrov because he knew I was strong for my age. I remember going for a test with Petrov. He timed us running 30 meters and also made us do pull-ups. I managed to do 15. That was a big result and impressed Petrov because I wasn't just using my arms but was swinging my whole body. So he could see I had good movement.

I was the youngest in the training group which moved to the city of Donetsk because it had one of the few specialist pole vault centers in the Soviet Union. I was very lucky to have met Petrov because he was to be the greatest influence on my life as an athlete.

I was with him for 16 years and I can say that he is a very smart guy. No one in the world knows more about pole vault technique than Petrov.

As I will now explain, it is the work of a team of motivated people that has helped me develop my full potential as an athlete. The talent and determination may have always been in my blood but I will always be grateful to those people who have been with me all the time: when I lose, as well as when I win.

Petrov was a very clever coach because he was not in a rush to get results. Many coaches find talented athletes and want them to win medals immediately. But Petrov wanted me to have a long career. He always used to say: "Sergey, I want you to have your best results in senior sport."

So, for example, I did no weight training at all until I was 16: just exercises with my body. Every exercise was designed to make me stronger, but slowly, without putting too much stress on my joints and muscles as I was growing.

It is dangerous to overload the body at this age. What we were doing at times was not really pleasant or fulfilling: just very specific exercises to strengthen muscles and to make tendons looser,

probably the smallest. I played with my brother who was three years older and other guys who were even four or five years older. That was how I grew to love sport. From the age of eight I began physical education classes in school and took part in sporting competitions between schools and also between the different classes. I could really run until I was dead on the sports field because I had to win.

As long as I can remember, what I call the Spirit of Sport—the competitive spirit—was in my blood. I realized that sport was something fantastic. When I do sport, or anything else in my life, it must be 100 per cent or 1000 per cent. I must give everything I have. This is part of my character.

In my first class, because I had good speed and coordination, I was selected for special coaching in gymnastics. But when I showed up, as they asked but there was a good reason for them as they prepared the muscles for heavier loads. This is why I have had relatively few injuries in my career.

I was not really happy with my training until I was about 16. The first five or six years I could not "feel" the right movement. But when I was in competition, everything worked out well. This was because I always loved the stress of competition. Under stress I feel alive: I can concentrate and be motivated. I love to make a third attempt at a height that can win a competition or leave me in a bad place if I miss. I can compete for seven or eight hours. No problem. I don't want to leave the stadium. Because I am sensitive, I find I can use all the special things about competition to raise my performance to the next level.

Petrov planned for me to do well at the 1984 Olympic Games when I was 20. But I won my first World Championships gold a year earlier and then missed the 1984 Games because of a political boycott. Still, he was right in a way, because I broke my first world record in 1984.

Maybe the greatest thing that Petrov helped me understand was The Culture of Movement. He showed me that the pole vault was really two sports. It was athletics on the runway: during the approach run and takeoff, and it was gymnastics once you were in the air and until you cleared the bar. Petrov realized this and he began to seek out experts in gymnastics. He wanted to use their knowledge to help us. Although we knew all about speed and power as athletes, gymnastics was another world.

Since 1990 I have been helped by a gymnastics coach called Alexandr Salomakhin who lived in Donetsk. First he taught us basic gymnastic routines and then he devised special exercises for the pole vault. He helped me make really great improvements in the second phase of the vault. I would say that my ability in this phase is what helped me break world records.

He helped us to discover many things: our position in the air; our sense of where the bar is; the angles of our limbs when we are in the air. The thing is, many pole vault coaches think they know everything, but they are too focused on their speciality.

Petrov was excellent because he was interested in every detail. Even when we were jogging he would be looking at where the shoulders were, how the hips were aligned, the position of the feet.

It was important to Petrov that everything we did was technically correct. Even our strength training. Because he wanted us not to have to waste

"It's gymnastics once you are in the air."

time when we came to the fine technical work before a competition. He wanted us to be technically efficient even during the physical conditioning period.

But one of the biggest lessons I learned from Petrov is the importance of communication, not just between coach and athlete, but in the form of communication between the brain and body during competition. I try very hard to concentrate during competition—I "feel" and think about every little art of every little phase; from the start of my runup to the moment I land on the mat.

I have a picture of what I have done. I have to analyze everything, and then to make any adjustments I think are necessary. It is very important for an athlete to do this because the coach cannot be with you. When you compete you are on your own. You must learn to think and act fast. To adjust. When I compete my brain becomes a computer. Athletes must analyze, and make a picture of what they have done, of what is wrong and how to make it perfect. That is why I have confidence when I am competing. I do not have to look for my coach for explanations.

I arrive at the stadium two hours before a competition. Because I want to look at every possible

"I try very hard to concentrate during competition."

thing that could influence my result: how is the vault area, where are the stands located, what are the weather conditions? I need to be prepared for everything. I need to think about technique, about running, about my warmup—what I was doing wrong.

I also do visualization exercises, what we call in Russian "training for the brain." I also need to soak up the atmosphere: to raise my spirit and adrenaline for the competition. Finding motivation is something that you must work harder at as you get older and become more successful.

As an athlete I have also had to learn to be reserved. To waste no energy that could be used in competition. I will give you an example. By the time I was 15, I had left my family and was staying with my brother at the sport school in Donetsk. Once, I went to the grocery to buy 100 grams of cheese. But the woman behind the counter tried to give me just 90 grams. She wanted to cheat me. Now I lost my temper. I felt outraged and argued with the woman because I had been brought up to be honest with people.

But later I was told: "Don't explode. Don't waste your nervous energy on these things. You must learn to focus that energy into competition. Give it a good channel." As I got older I began to avoid anything that was too much of a distraction. I realized that I was sensitive by nature and that sometimes I let things affect me. For example, I try not to spend too much time with journalists, or even making speeches like this one!

Back in 1986, I began to get a lot of requests to make appearances. And I always accepted the invitations. I was actually happy to meet people and to speak. But when I got to The European Championships, I found that I had no nerves, no adrenaline. I was shocked. I won, but it was difficult.

So when the competition was over I spoke with a psychologist, Rudolf Zaginoff—who had been recommended by Petrov. He told me: "You were talking too much before; you spent too much time thinking and discussing the competition before it happened. By the time the competition began you were empty."

Since then, he has advised me to stay quiet in the two months before the major competitions. To be reserved, to stay calm. I am careful not to empty my psychological battery. Now, during a major competition I relax with a book, or I go to a park or other quiet places, or make conversation with my coach, family and very close friends. But I avoid stress.

This is also, a little bit, the method of the former Soviet system. In the West, athletes and the coaches talk more. They are more closely involved with promotions and publicity and other commercial activity. But in the end, the result comes first. If you don't win, then nobody will ask you for an interview or to take part in promotions.

That is the reason that sometimes I appear to be cold—arrogant—with my fellow competitors and with the media. But there is a reason. It is not part of my nature. In fact, I enjoy very much meeting people and exchanging opinions with them. But people must understand that to be successful I must be left alone.

When I am speaking about my life, and my mentality as an athlete I realize that the last year and a half have been very important. On the bright side, I made discoveries about weight lifting (by taking the advice of a specialist weight lifting coach), which have been incredible. Making some changes to this important part of my training has helped me very much, especially during the period when I was injured.

This injury to my right achilles tendon stopped me from taking part in the Atlanta Olympic Games. The worst thing about it was that I was in great shape, especially psychologically. But I consulted specialists, one from the USA and another from Finland who was also a surgeon, and it was clear that I had a tear in my tendon of almost 25%. Had I competed it might have torn 100%. This was in August 1996.

Although I tried to avoid surgery, in the end the injury did not go away. In fact it got worse, with the inflammation going to the bone, so I agreed to have an operation. This was carried out on December 23, 1996, in Helsinki. The surgeon said the injury was worse than it had appeared on the scans: they had to cut even the bone. Not until April 1997 was I able to jog.

And I will be honest with you: all my training and competitions this year (1997) have been very, very difficult. When I tried to increase the loads there would be a reaction. The cycle was up and down, up and down. Normally I would train, take anti-inflammatories, train, take anti-inflammatories, and go on like this. I had to work always with pain. This is very tiring mentally too, when you can feel an injury but still want to achieve your best results.

Sometimes after training the pain was so bad that I didn't see how I could continue. But I knew that 1997, with the World Championships, was a very important year. I wanted very much to keep my tradition going in Athens and to win six in a row. Once I was there, I had to deal with the fact that every day I was in pain.

I finished my heavy training at the end of July but still wasn't sure if I could compete in Athens. I had to make many small modifications to my training as I began to get faster and sharper. I stopped weight training and began to polish my technique. Even during the qualification on August 3 I felt pain. It was only in the final, when I was running with better technique, that the pain eased.

When I first got injured I never felt like it was the end of my career. That was because I knew what was wrong. I was injured. Injuries heal. I was still in great shape, I loved to compete and I still wanted to improve. My motivation was to take part in my 6th World Championships and to win again.

Before I competed my psychologist said: "Sergey: just remember you have never lost at the World Championships and during this competition, think of your best jumps. Put a picture in your mind." Before the final I decided on my strategy: to jump at 5.70, 5.90 and 6 meters, because I felt 6 meters would win. It was a calculated risk.

My winning jump was 6.01 and it was quite good technically. But I was a little bit too far back when I took off, because I was running faster. But because I was a little behind I was able to achieve very good penetration during the catapult phase.

I also discovered some new ways to motivate myself. One was to scream just before I began my runup because this helped me concentrate and to raise my fighting spirit. My physiotherapist Arkadij Shkvira, who used to train with me in Donetsk, also showed me some acupuncture points which, when pressed, help boost energy. After the competition I found that I had been pressing these points so hard that they were bleeding.

Many have asked what motivates me when it comes to record breaking. After all, I have set 17 outdoor world records and over 30 in all, indoors and outdoors. The main factor is that I have such a character that I want to improve. To be perfect.

Many people have said that I go for so many records because of money. But they forget that I grew up in a Socialist society: there was no money at all then. Remember, I had already set nine world records outdoors before the fall of the Berlin Wall in 1989.

I have always wanted to achieve good results in sport. Petrov said to me: "Concentrate on the results, and the money will come as a result." I think it is sad when sports people put money first. That is the ugly way. Sport then becomes like any other job. But sport should be special. It should be about emotion and desire. You must want to be the best. The business should come second always.

It is important also to be realistic. You must set goals you can achieve and then continue to work hard and improve. When I set world records I was already thinking of the next one. But it is not easy. I am not a robot. If I vault 6.13 for a world record and then later 6.14, some people think: "he has improved a record by one centimeter; he is playing games." But I don't see a world record as just an improvement but as something brand new. Each record is special in its own way. Each takes place on a different day, under different conditions, with different emotions. You must find the psychological and physical keys.

I have never recognized the concept of limits. Never. I think an athlete who accepts limits is dead. Even now, when I am almost 34 years old, I believe in new levels. I still think about clearing 6.20 next season, even though I have missed training because of injury.

It is important to plan every detail carefully, and to work together as a team. My results are due not only to my character and preparation but to the contribution of my first coach, my current pole vault coach, my running coach, my weight lifting coach, my psychologist, my doctor, my physiotherapist, my masseur. We must combine all our knowledge to improve the final result.

To conclude, I hope you have all come to realize that, above all, I love the sport. I have already been in athletics for 24 years but don't want to stop. Why should I stop if I enjoy it so much? I don't agree with the view that you should finish at the top, something which was also the philosophy in the Soviet Union. Maybe I can accept being second, or third or fifth because I still love what I do. I have always felt that a sportsman's life is the best, most beautiful life you can have.

Thank you for your attention.

Chapter IV:
The Long Jump

Development Of Basic Long Jump Technique

By Dr. Wolfgang Lohmann, Germany

There is no doubt that the stride long jump provides an excellent base for further technique developments in this event because it is easy to learn and combines all essential elements that lead to the hitchkick action. The following text outlines the development of the stride long jump and presents a series of teaching exercises.

INTRODUCTION

It must be stressed right from the start that learning the hitchkick action of the long jump is a virtually impossible task for most students because they are unable to reach the distance required to complete the movements. As the sail jump is not acceptable, it is advisable for beginners to start long jumping by developing the stride technique. This technique is relatively simple to learn and assists in creating a base for changing later to the hitchkick.

The stride long jump provides an excellent foundation for the development of the most important coordination of the approach run with the takeoff, one of the decisive tasks to be mastered in the basic training phase. Further, the stride long jump technique has a relatively simple movement sequence and therefore sets only limited demands on coordination. This allows students to concentrate on the takeoff action without having to worry much about flight movements.

DEVELOPMENT PHASES

In the development of the stride long jump it is necessary to pay particular attention to the following aspects:
- A relaxed 11-to-15-strides runup with a fluent acceleration up to an optimal speed.
- A rhythmical (unconscious) preparation for the takeoff without speed losses and without lengthening or shortening of the running strides.
- An energetic takeoff with an active foot placement, a full extension of the takeoff leg, a stressed lead-leg action and a well coordinated arm action.

Figure 1: The stride long jump technique. An excellent and simple foundation for the development of any long jump technique. Strongly recommended for young athletes and beginners.

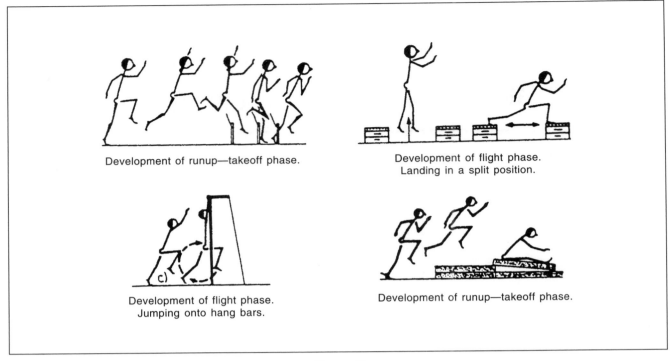

Development of runup—takeoff phase.

Development of flight phase.
Landing in a split position.

Development of flight phase.
Jumping onto hang bars.

Development of runup—takeoff phase.

Figure 2

- An attempt to maintain the stride position with an erect upper body as long as possible. The lead leg holds a horizontal position to the ground and the takeoff leg trails behind the body.
- An economical landing procedure in which the takeoff leg is brought forward level to the lead leg only shortly before landing.

Keeping the above factors in mind the actual development of the stride long jump takes place in three major phases:

1. Development of the runup-takeoff complex: this is the main task because the runup-takeoff combination is without exception the most critical phase of the long jump. This phase is refined and stabilized after the basic actions have been established.
2. Development of the flight phase: the learning of the flight phase in the stride technique takes place as a whole. It can be made easier by using in the beginning conditions that allow lengthening the flight curve.
3. Perfection of the total jump: this takes place by lengthening the runup and the improvement of the flight and landing phases. Any specific attempts to improve landing should always take place within the whole performance of the jump.

EXERCISE COMPLEXES

TASK 1: Development of the runup-takeoff phases.

Aim: Mastery of the takeoff from a fast runup with an optimal conversion of the runup velocity into the jump.

Preliminary exercises:
- Hop-ups from a short runup over several wide obstacles, hop-ups on an elevated landing area,
- Bounding, multiple jumps, bounding over low obstacles.

Basic exercises:
- Hop-ups from a medium (6 to 8 strides) runup over or on a wide obstacle, observing the main takeoff elements (foot placement, takeoff leg extension, lead-leg action, arm action).

Advanced exercises:

Long jumps stressing the takeoff in:
- jumps with landing on an elevated area,
- jumps over a rubber cord, wall of sand, high jump bar,
- jumps from a downsloping takeoff plane,
- jumps from a lowered takeoff area.

Long jumper par excellence—the young Carl Lewis at the 1983 National Championships.

Exercises stressing the accuracy and rhythm of the runup:
- controlled full-length runups with a takeoff,
- full-length runup with a check mark.

The following points should be observed in all the exercises:
- Relaxed running on the balls of the feet with a high knee lift,
- A fluent transfer from the runup into the takeoff,
- An accelerating approach run up to the take-off,
- An active foot plant at takeoff,
- A complete extension of the takeoff leg,
- An upright upper body position,
- Correct arm action.

Organization references:
- In order to develop precision the runup should always be started from a standing start.
- The use of short runups should be limited because they create a different stride rhythm in the preparation of the takeoff.

- The development of the takeoff should have variety in the use of elevated and normal takeoff areas.
- The use of a 40 to 100cm takeoff zone helps in the early stages to develop an individual running rhythm.

TASK 2: Development of the flight and landing phase

Aim: Mastery of a simple long jump technique that can be easily converted later to the hitchkick.

Preliminary exercises
- Imitation flight movements on the spot (forward leg splits with a bent front knee).
- Simplified jumps into a split position.
- Horizontal jumps with a landing in a split position.

Basic exercises:
- Stride long jumps from a 6- to 8-stride runup (later 10-14 strides) over obstacles.
- Stride long jumps from a short runup and wide takeoff zone over a distant obstacle (rubber cord, high jump bar).

Advanced exercises
- Stride long jumps with emphasis on the flight phase from a gymnastic beat board or into a lowered landing area,
- Stride long jumps with emphasis on the landing phase to a level or slightly elevated landing area.

The following points should be observed in all the exercises:
- A wide stride position with the lead leg's thigh horizontal to the ground and the takeoff leg trailing behind the body,
- An upright upper body and head,
- Alternate arm action.

Organizational references:
- The use of a marker (rubber cord) to guide the spot where the stride position is is to be abandoned.
- Although the flight phase is observed, attention should still be given to a correct execution of the takeoff.
- Use picture sequences and videos to explain the expected performance.
- Acoustic signals should be used to assist with the performance in calling out "flying."
- Vary the distances of the assisting obstacles.

TASK 3: Perfection of the total jump.

Aim: To increase the length of the runup and to solve specific aspects of the total movement sequence.

Preliminary exercises:
- Pop-ups from a full runup into the landing pit.

Basic exercises:
- Stride long jumps from a full (10 to 14 strides) runup concentrating on specific aspects of the technique,
- Stride long jumps from a full runup aiming for distance (competitive conditions).

The following points should be observed in all the exercises:
- Runup speed, individually suitable runup length,
- An explosive takeoff with a stressed lead-leg action and correct movement of the arms,

- An efficient landing performance.

Organizational references:
- A technically correct performance must always remain in the forefront.
- Sufficient recoveries between the jumps are essential.
- The focus of every jump is on the takeoff.
- Faults are to be corrected individually.

MAIN FAULTS AND POSSIBLE CORRECTIONS

Fault: The runup fails to reach optimal speed prior to the takeoff.

Correction: Controlled timed runups with a takeoff.

Fault: Chopping or stretching the last strides before the takeoff.

Correction: Controlled runups with a takeoff.

Fault: Insufficient extension of the takeoff leg.

Correction: Long jumps aiming for height over a high jump bar, jumps aiming to reach a high object, long jumps from a shortened runup.

Fault: Incorrect (forward or backward) lean of the trunk at the takeoff.

Correction: Long jumps from a medium runup, stressing an upright upper body and looking straight ahead. Failure to hit the takeoff board is ignored.

Fault: Forward rotation of the upper body in the flight.

Correction: Jumps from a beat board or springboard, one-stride jumps from a gymnastics box.

Fault: Legs fail to reach an elevated position prior to landing and hit sand too early.

Correction: Jumps with an emphasized active forward movement of the lead leg, jumps over a rubber cord or wall of sand placed near the landing area, strengthening of abdominal muscles.

Fault: Falling back after landing.

Correction: Imitation landing drills, short runup jumps aiming at landing with elevated legs.

Elements Of The Long Jump

By Kyle Tellez, USA

An overview of the most important factors in teaching the elements of the hitch-kick technique of the long jump, covering the objectives and coaching points of the four major performance phases.

In all the jumping events in track and field, there is a strong relation between the execution of the approach run and takeoff and the performance of a jump. The more consistent and more technically correct the approach run and takeoff, the better the jump performance.

Most world record performances in the jumping events in track and field have been a direct result of a successful approach run and takeoff. When a long jumper breaks contact with the ground, the center of gravity forms a parabolic curve. Once in the air, there is nothing that can done to change this predetermined flight path. Therefore, the majority of coaching time in the long jump should be spent developing a technically sound approach run and takeoff.

The purpose of this article is to highlight the most important factors in teaching the elements of the long jump. The long jump can be broken down into four components:

1. The Approach Run
2. The Last Two Strides
3. The Takeoff
4. The Action in the Air and Landing

The technical information and diagrams will be explained and illustrated using a right-footed takeoff jumper who is starting the approach run with the left foot, taking an odd number of strides (19 strides), and using the hitch-kick.

1. THE APPROACH RUN

Objective: To develop a consistent approach run that allows for gradual acceleration, beginning with the first stride and ending with maximum controlled speed at the takeoff.

A. Length—The length of the approach run should be between 12 and 19 strides (Diagram A-2, 3). The approach run should be as long as possible depending on the jumper's experience, sprinting techniques and conditioning level. The length of the approach run will determine the amount of speed that is developed. The longer the approach run, however, the more difficult it is to develop a consistent stride pattern. Thus, inexperienced jumpers should begin by using a shorter approach run of 12 strides (Diagram A-

Diagram A: Approach run and check marks.

#1		#2		#3		#4	
18 L		19	R	12 L		8 L	
	R	18 L			R		R
16 L			R	10 L		6 L	
	R	16 L			R		R
14 L			R	8 L		4 L	
	R	14 L			R		R
12 L			R	6 L		2 L	
	R	12 L			R		R
10 L			R	4 L		0 L	
	R	10 L			R		
8 L			R	2 L			
	R	8 L			R		
6 L			R	0 L			
	R	6 L					
4 L			R				
	R	4 L					
2 L			R				
	R	2 L					
0 L							
	R	0 L					

3). As jumpers gain experience, improve sprinting technique, and get stronger through a conditioning program, the approach run can be lenghtened to 14 strides and eventually 18 strides (Diagram A-1).

B. Speed—The approach run should allow for the maximum speed enabling jumpers to complete a successful takeoff.

C. Acceleration—A consistent, fast approach run will depend on a gradual acceleration. Using a 19-stride approach run, the jumper begins the run by pushing down and against the ground with the left foot to set the body in motion (Diagram B-1). In addition, there is a slight inclination of the whole body from the ground at the beginning of the run. As the jumper accelerates, the body begins a gradual straightening up into a upright position by the end of the fourth or sixth stride (Diagram B-1,2,3). Once in a full sprinting position, the jumper continues to accelerate.

Coaching Points for the Approach Run:
- A successful approach run depends on the consistency of the first two or three strides. It is here that the rhythm of the run is developed. If the run is inconsistent, it is usually because of the inconsistency in the first two or three strides of the approach.
- When establishing an approach run for beginning jumpers, it is best to work on the approach run without jumping. This way the jumpers can isolate the approach by itself and develop a consistent acceleration, stride pattern, and rhythm of the run through repetition. In addition, even with experienced jumpers, it is beneficial to practice the approach run without jumping to maintain the consistency and rhythm of the run.
- To help develop the consistency of a jumper's approach run, a check mark should be placed four strides out from the takeoff board (Diagram A-1, 2). The checkmark should measure

between 26 to 31 feet away from the takeoff board. The distance for the four-stride check mark will vary depending on the jumper's height, speed on the runway, and distance of the approach run. Experienced jumpers, who are tall, fast, and have 18- or 19-stride runs, should be closer to 31 feet to the check mark. More inexperienced jumpers who are shorter, not as fast, and have 12- or 13-stride runs, should be closer to 26 feet at the check mark. Thus, if during a competition, a long jumper's check mark is hitting at 27 feet but is supposed to be hitting at 31 feet, the jumper is probably too close to the takeoff board and is fouling or shortening the last four strides to get on the board.

- The approach run should be one of gradual acceleration. Many inexperienced jumpers make the mistake of accelerating too fast, too soon. This causes them to decelerate towards the end of the approach run. Thus, speed is lost going into the takeoff, resulting in reduced distance.
- Sprinting is a pushing action against the ground. Jumpers should not try to pull against the ground. The formation of the leg is ill-suited to exert a pulling force. In addition, a pulling action when sprinting is a direct cause of hamstring damage.

2. THE LAST TWO STRIDES

Objective: To prepare or "set up" for the takeoff while maintaining as much speed as possible.

A. The Penultimate Stride—The penultimate stride is the next to the last stride (left foot) from the takeoff where there is a lowering of the jumper's center of gravity. It is the longer of the last two strides due to the lowering of the center of gravity and the flexion of the knee and ankle of the supporting leg. There is a noticeable "gathering" of the jumper's body during the penultimate stride. In addition, the foot is placed flat on the ground.

B. The Last Stride—The last stride (right foot) is shorter than the penultimate stride due to the raising of the jumper's center of gravity. As the takeoff foot makes contact with the ground, the foot is placed flat and in front of the jumper's body. In addition, there is a slight flexion of the joints of the takeoff leg. During this slight flexion, the muscles of the takeoff leg are forced into an active stretching phase or eccentric contraction. Immediately following this active stretch-

Diagram B: The start of the aproach run.

ing phase there is a shortening or concentric contraction of the muscles of the takeoff leg. When a concentric contraction is preceded by an active stretching in the muscles of the takeoff leg, elastic energy is stored and the takeoff leg is "loaded up."

Coaching Points for the Last Two Strides:
- It is critical that jumpers stay relaxed and maintain approach speed through the last two strides.
- It is important that jumpers continue to stroke their arms through the last two strides. Stopping the movement of the arms will result in a decrease in approach speed into the takeoff.
- Jumpers must feel the lowering or "gathering" of the body during the penultimate stride. The penultimate stride is different from a normal running stride, thus jumpers should not just "run" through the penultimate. It is essential that they prepare the body during the penultimate.
- Jumpers must avoid reaching on the last stride causing the last two strides to be "long - long." Reaching or placing the takeoff foot too far in front of the body will result in a breaking or stopping effect and poor jump performance.

3. THE TAKEOFF

Objective: "Load-up" the takeoff leg to create a vertical impulse through the jumper's center of gravity.

A. Contact with the Ground—As the jumper's take-off foot makes contact with the ground and the leg is "loaded-up" with the elastic energy, a vertical impulse or lift is created through the center of gravity. This vertical impulse created from the takeoff leg projects the jumper's body up and out into the air.

B. Foot Placement—The takeoff foot is placed flat and directly in front of the jumper's body to allow for maximum vertical lift. As the body moves through the takeoff and up into the air, the jumper continues to run up and out off the ground.

C. Body Position—The position of the jumper's body is upright to the ground allowing for an optimal position at takeoff.

Coaching Points for the Takeoff:
- Coaches should encourage jumpers to think about jumping first and then running up and

out off the ground. Focusing only on running up and out off the ground tends to cause the jumpers to not "load up" the takeoff leg, thus bypassing the vertical impulse.
- Jumpers should focus their eyes up and out when leaving the ground. They should not be looking down into the sand or at the takeoff board.
- Establish a short approach run of eight strides for working on the technique of the last two strides and the takeoff (Diagram A-4). Short-run jumping allows the jumper to isolate and emphasize the proper technique. In addition, jumpers can make more jumps from a short run, thereby reducing the fatigue factor during training.
- The takeoff foot must be placed flat on the board. If the jumper places the foot heel first, it will cause a braking or stopping effect at the takeoff. If the jumper places the takeoff foot high up on the toes, there will be little stabilization on impact causing the leg to buckle or collapse.
- Jumpers should not overemphasize jumping high at the takeoff. A high angle of takeoff usually results in jumpers slowing down considerably to achieve the height, thus losing critical speed needed at the takeoff. Jump for distance, not for height.

4. THE ACTION IN THE AIR AND LANDING

Objective: Rotate the body into an efficient landing position that maximizes jump distance.

A. Center of Gravity—Once contact with the ground is broken, the jumper can do nothing to alter the flight path of the center of gravity. However, the jumper moves the arms and legs about the center of gravity to counteract forward rotation and assume an optimal position for landing.

B. Body Position—The hitch-kick technique allows the jumper to counteract forward rotation developed at the takeoff. By bicycling the legs and arms through the air, the jumper is able to maintain an upright body position and set up for an efficient landing position. If the jumper did not counteract forward rotation by cycling the arms and legs, the body would continue to rotate forward into a face-down position in the sand.

   Other techniques for long jumpers in the air are the hang and the sail. Each of these styles accomplishes the same task as the hitch-kick by counteracting forward rotation in the air in order to achieve an efficient landing position.

C. The Landing—For an efficient landing, the jumper extends and sweeps the arms down towards the ground. The action of the arms raises the legs up towards the torso and closer to the jumper's center of gravity. Thus, the action of the arms causes an equal and opposite reaction with the legs.

As the jumper makes contact with the sand, the knees bend and flex to cushion the impact. In addition, the arms are brought forward to assist the jumper's forward momentum and avoid falling back.

Coaching Points for the Action in the Air and Landing:

- Remember, the best jumps are the direct result of a well executed approach run and takeoff. Thus, if a jumper is having a problem with undesirable rotation in the air and an inefficient landing, always look to the approach run and takeoff as the source of the problem.
- Watch and review videotape. Videotaped jumps are an important tool for jumpers and coaches. Thus, have workouts and competitions videotaped so that they may be viewed. In addition, watch video of world class jumpers and compare techniques.

Erick Walder

Effect Of Muscular Strength On Long Jump Performance

By Henrik Sørensen, Erik B. Simonsen and Anton J. van den Bogert, Denmark

A study investigating how strength gains combined with corresponding body mass gains influence long jump performances, coming to the conclusion that after an initial increase in jumping distance, further strength and body mass increases do not improve performance.

INTRODUCTION

Athletes engaged in power-based activities such as the long jump often complement activity-specific training with strength training. While the objective is increased strength, this will often be accompanied by increased body mass. There is general agreement in the literature that approach velocity is the single most important determinant for success the in long jump (e.g., Hay, 1993). However, increasing the approach velocity decreases the time on the takeoff board (t); for an athlete with a certain body mass (m), capable of exerting a certain vertical force (F) during takeoff, the vertical takeoff velocity (v) will be determined by the impulse-momentum relationship

$$F \cdot t = m \cdot v \quad (1)$$

Thus, while increased approach velocity increases the horizontal takeoff velocity, which is beneficial for performance, the effect of decreased takeoff time will lessen vertical takeoff velocity and hence takeoff angle. This is detrimental to performance, as demonstrated by Sorensen, et al. (1999a).

Aside from the influence of increased strength on approach velocity, it might have a beneficial effect during the actual takeoff. However, as increases in muscular strength, above what can be attained due to neural adaptation, must be assumed to require increased muscle mass, the application of (1) becomes complex.

We speculate whether a jumper can get "strong enough," i.e., if there is a limit above which further increases in strength followed by the inevitable corresponding body mass gains, performance will cease to improve. A deeper understanding of these relationships might assist in deciding where athletes should focus their training.

The purpose of this study was to utilize a computer simulation model to investigate the relationship between strength, body mass and jump length and specifically to test the hypothesized existence of an upper strength limit.

METHOD

We developed a two-dimensional, sagittal plane, musculo-skeletal model with six rigid segments: trunk, thighs, shanks and right foot. Frictionless hinge joints connected the segments. Eight major muscles/muscle groups were included in the model: tibialis anterior, soleus, gastrocnemius, vasti, rectus femoris, hamstrings, iliopsoas and glutei.

Each muscle group was represented by a three-component Hill model from van Soest and Bobbert (1993), and mathematically formulated as an ordinary differential equation (ODE). Muscle activation dynamics was modelled as an additional ODE according to He, et al. (1991).

The model was a bang-bang simulation driven with turn-on and turn-off time for each muscle group as control parameters. Each simulation spanned the entire stance phase.

The model was implemented on an Octane R10000 workstation (Silicon Graphics, Inc.) using the DADS multi-body simulation software (version 8.5, CADSI, Coralville, IA), with modules added for muscle modelling.

Optimization of the control parameters was conducted by iterative simulations according to an algorithm from Bremermann (1970), implemented in Matlab (MathWorks Inc., Natick, MA). Cost function for the optimization was jump length calculated from kinematic takeoff parameters.

Initial kinematic data were obtained from high-speed film of an international-level long jumper. Segment lengths and inertial parameters were obtained from Winter (1990) using height and body mass from this same long jumper. Vertical and horizontal ground reaction forces were implemented as a spring-damper element and dry frictional force, respectively. Development and validation of the model are extensively described in Sorensen, et al. (1999b).

To investigate the relationship between muscle strength and jump length we took the model through a series of optimized jumps with strength for all eight muscles systematically varied between baseline values (0% strength increase) and 60% strength increase. Assuming constant specific tension and cylindrical muscles, a certain strength increase implies a physiological cros- sectional area increase and hence volume and mass increase of similar relative magnitude. Thus, the relationship between body mass (m_{body}) and strength was calculated as

$$M_{body} = S * M_{muscle} + M_{n.m.} \qquad (2)$$

with s taking values of 1.00, 1.05, . . .1.60 and the constant non-muscle mass $M_{n.m.}$ being 50% of initial body mass.

RESULTS

With baseline values (0% strength, increase, 0% body mass increase) the model jumped approximately 6.66m (Figure 1). When strength was increased by up to 20%, accompanied by a corresponding body mass increase up to 10%, jump length increased almost linearly to approximately 6.73m. This was accomplished by an increased takeoff angle, as resultant velocity remained nearly constant. The components of the increased takeoff angle were increased vertical and decreased horizontal velocity.

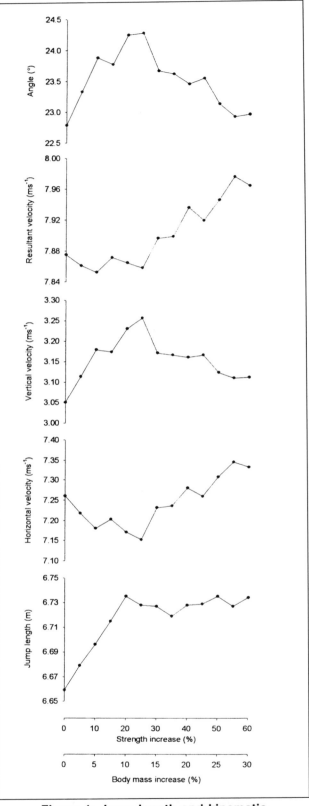

Figure 1: Jump length and kinematic takeoff parameters vs. relative strength and body mass increase.

Further increases in strength and body mass above 20% and 10%, respectively, did not result in improved jump length. The ratio between horizontal velocity increase and vertical velocity decrease resulted in a decreased takeoff angle, which counteracted the otherwise beneficial increase in resultant velocity.

DISCUSSION

The results showed that a strength increase up to 20% above baseline values allowed the model to generate more vertical velocity during takeoff. Despite a simultaneous decrease in horizontal takeoff velocity, resulting in nearly constant resultant velocity, the takeoff angle increased sufficiently to increase jump length from approximately 6.66m to 6.73m.

Strength increases above 20% were apparently counteracted by the concurrent body mass increase; vertical velocity started to decrease again, so despite increases in horizontal and resultant velocities, takeoff angle decreased and jump length remained nearly constant at approximately 6.73 m.

This renders our hypothesis about the existence of an upper strength limit probable. For our model the optimum strength-body mass relationship was obtained when the baseline muscle mass (=50% body mass) was increased 20%, i.e., when muscle mass made up approximately 55% of body mass. We will discuss the relevance of this value later.

The major advantage of using computer simulation for this type of study is its exploratory nature—the ability to answer what-if questions like "what happens if the athlete increases his strength?" (Vaughan, 1984). While such questions can be addressed via longitudinal intervention studies, the total control over input parameters as offered by a computer simulation model can never be obtained.

This said, however, the limitations of computer models should be kept in mind, most importantly that simulation experiments only tell the truth about the model that was used (van den Bogert and Nigg, 1999). Confidence in a model is acquired through proper validation, but the basic dilemma, as pointed out by Panjabi (1979), is that a model can only be validated in a number of "known situations," yet its purpose is to predict behavior in unknown situations.

The model used in this study, with baseline values for strength and body mass, was validated

Ivan Pedroso, three-time long jump World Champion.

by its ability to reproduce muscle stimulation patterns, ground reaction force profiles and kinematics from the literature and from the athlete providing data for the model (Sorensen, et al., 1999b). When we changed the model's strength and body mass in this study, we essentially used it in invalidated and unknown situations. However, the above mentioned validation parameters stayed within literature values, so we still had confidence in the model's ability to perform realistic long jumps.

Another limitation of this study was the disregard of the influence of strength on approach velocity. It can be argued that sprinters mainly benefit from extreme strength during the start, while the influence on maximal running speed is less obvious. As long jumpers are free to choose their approach so maximal speed is reached at takeoff, the strength-approach velocity relationship might be of less importance in the long jump. Nevertheless, conclusions drawn from this study only apply to the influence of strength on the jumper's actions on the takeoff board.

The model's baseline value for relative muscle mass was somewhat arbitrarily set to 50%. Values from the literature range between approximately 40% for normal, untrained individuals and 60% for individuals with extreme muscularity (e.g., Schibye and Klausen, 1992). Long jumpers are generally considerably more muscular than untrained individuals, however, not to the extreme of, say, competitive bodybuilders, so an in-between value of 50% was considered realistic.

This arbitrarily chosen baseline value had a direct influence on the 55% relative muscle mass value, which we found optimal for our model. Hence, in addition to the other limitations of computer models, this requires the upper strength limit demonstrated in this study to be considered only phenomenological.

Still, our finding rejects the perhaps naïve assumption that because strength gains are accompanied by relatively smaller body mass gains, performance gains from increased strength are essentially limitless.

While our inability to make generalizations with respect to the relative muscle mass value from model to humans detracts from the immediate usefulness for coaches/athletes, we still consider the demonstrated influence of strength and body mass on takeoff kinematics and the subsequent jump length valuable knowledge. If, for instance, an athlete after a period of strength training resulting in increased strength and body mass, is not able to increase vertical takeoff velocity and angle above pre-training values (Figure 1), it must be considered a possibility that he has reached (or passed) the optimum strength-body mass ratio.

CONCLUSION

This study investigated the relationship between strength, body mass and jump length with specific emphasis on the existence of an upper strength limit with respect to performance. The results showed that the model increased its performance until a relative muscle mass of approximately 55% body mass was obtained. Further increases in strength and body mass did not help performance. Thus, we postulate the existence of an upper strength limit. Practical implications for coaches/athletes include better reasons to determine whether strength training will benefit a particular athlete.

REFERENCES

Bremermann, H. (1970). A method of unconstrained global optimization. *Mathematical Biosciences*, 9, 1-15.

Hay, J.G. (1993). Citius, altius, longius (faster, higher, longer): the biomechanics of jumping for distance. *Journal of Biomechanics*, 26 (Suppl. 1), 7-2 1.

He, J., Levine, W.S. & Loeb, G. E. (1991). Feedback Gains for Correcting Small Perturbations to Standing Posture. *IEEE Transactions on Automatic Control*, 36, 322332.

Panjabi, M. (1979). Validation of mathematical models. *Journal of Biomechanics*, 12, 238.

van den Bogert, A.J. & Nigg, B. M. (1999). *Biomechanics of the Musculo-skeletal System*. Chichester: John Wiley & Sons Ltd.

van Soest, A.J. & Bobbert, M. F. (1993). The contribution of muscle properties in the control of explosive movements. *Biological Cybernetics*, 69, 195-204.

Schibye, B. & Klausen, K. (1992). *Menneskets fysiologi* (pp. 104-105) [in Danish]. Copenhagen, FADL.

Sørensen, H., Simonsen, E.B. & van den Bogert, A.J. (1999a). Influence of approach velocity on long jump performance. *International Society of Biomechanics XVIIth Congress*, August 8-13, Calgary, Canada (submitted).

Sørensen, H., Simonsen, E.B. & van den Bogert, A.J. (1999b). A simulation model of the long jump takeoff. *VIIth International Symposium on Computer Simulation in Biomechanics*, August 6-7, University of Calgary, Canada (submitted).

Winter, D.A. (1990). *Biomechanics and Motor Control of Human Movement* (pp. 52, 56-57). New York: John Wiley & Sons, Inc.

Vaughan, C.L. (1984). Computer simulation of human motion in sports biomechanics. *Exercise and Sport Sciences Reviews*, 12, 373-416.

ACKNOWLEDGMENT

The authors would like to thank The Danish Elite Sport Association and The Danish Research Council for Sports for financial support.

Common Long Jump Injuries

By Lee Derby, Australia

Long jumpers were surveyed to elicit information about the most commonly occurring injuries in the event. The author discusses the possible causal factors of these injuries and provides recommendations as to how to avoid acute and chronic overuse injuries.

Of the surveyed athletes, occurrence of injuries was most prevalent in the ankle, lower back, hamstrings, knee, shin and feet. These will be examined in more detail with the investigation of possible causal factors and recommendations for preventative measures for recurrence.

ANKLE INJURIES

Soft tissue injuries to the ankle are the most common long jump injuries and, according to the literature, the lateral ligament is damaged as much as five times as often as the medial ligament. The ankle joint is normally stable because of its mechanical configurations and the support given by the ligaments. However, the medial and lateral ligaments are not symmetrical in size, shape or location. The lateral ligament is mechanically weaker than the medial ligament and, together with the higher arch on the inside of the foot, stresses are directed laterally, which adds to the potential instability of the joint. Combined with the fact that there is very little muscular support on the front side of the ankle, compared to the other, it is not surprising that the lateral ligament complex of the ankle is so frequently injured in the long jump event.

Because of the anatomical and mechanical arrangement of the ankle joint, prevention of injury may be considered difficult. However, it is possible to reduce both the incidence and severity of ligament damage with adequate conditioning of the ankle joints throughout the general, specific and competitive periods. This should involve gaining strength, endurance, flexibility, power and proprioception of the ankles in a functional manner that includes stretching of the Achilles tendon.

Some medical sources also advocate the taping of ankles prior to competition or training, not to prevent normal joint mobility, but to minimize excessive mobility without interfering with the normal joint function. The tape acts as a second set of ligaments and does not weaken the joint or interfere with normal, correctly applied skills.

LOWER BACK INJURIES

The lower back may be injured in long jumping by either intrinsic (self-inflicted causes) or extrinsic (due to contact with an external object, such as a hard, unraked pit) means. In our survey 41.5% of the lower back injuries occurred during the competitive phase, with landing or takeoff actions being the primary cause.

The reasons for injury may be further categorized into:
- Traumatic (sudden trauma)—through poor landing techniques in the jump.
- Overuse (repeated trauma)—any jumper training with poor footwear on hard surfaces may be vulnerable.
- Poor technique—continually jarring the spine in an incorrect position may sustain a stress fracture of the lumbar vertebrae.
- Underlying anatomical or postural problems—e.g., leg length differences, dropped arches, one toe longer than the big toe, and poor posture can result in poor body mechanics, increasing the risk of fatigue of spinal muscles and therefore may lead to injury.
- Poor preventative training programs—e.g., lack of fitness or lack of flexibility.

Preventative measures against lower back injuries include ensuring complete flexibility of all muscles and joints associated with spinal movement (hamstrings, calves and hip flexors) and the development and maintenance of strength, power and endurance in the spine, trunk and abdominal region. Good posture in training, correct technical execution and body mechanics and a balanced training regimen, which includes a lower back program, are other methods of reducing the risk of lower back injury.

HAMSTRING INJURIES

Hamstring injuries occurred primarily in the competition period during the takeoff phase of the long jump. Causative factors have been postulated from many sources. Generally speaking, these can be divided into two categories:
1. Those directly due to lumbar spine pathology.
2. Those due to musculotendinous insufficiencies which may be contributed to by:
   • poor conditioning,
   • poor flexibility,
   • lumbar spine and/or sacroiliac pathology,
   • inefficient biomechanics, and
   • muscular imbalances.

Athletes usually sustain this particular type of injury while running at speed or jumping, with the injury occurring at or just before the foot strikes the ground. The violent extension of the foot and leg in the long jump takeoff is preceded at touchdown by a slight shock-absorbing flexion of the takeoff knee and ankle. This imposes a stretch on the extensor muscles of the propulsive leg and therefore increases the generated forces.

It is interesting to note that 23 of the 24 hamstring injuries in the survey were suffered by male athletes. Contributory factors, suggested by the number of qualified practitioners, may be due to reduced flexibility in the lower back and hamstrings compared to that of females, because of differences in the anatomical structure of the pelvic girdles and imbalance in the strength/power ratio between the quadriceps muscles and the hamstrings.

Other predisposing factors in hamstring strains include inadequate warmup, failing to gain full flexibility, fatigue, poor posture, improper skill patterns, anatomic variations and abnormal muscle contraction.

In seeking to prevent hamstring injuries, the long jump coach should fully investigate and eliminate all potential predisposing factors and ensure that the athlete undertakes a properly coordinated fitness training program with particular attention to resistance training and strong overload running to strengthen the leg adequately.

KNEE INJURIES

Though the incidence of knee injuries was highest in the general and competition periods, the specific and peak periods indicated only marginally lower occurrences. The takeoff phase was responsible for nearly 41% of the injuries, nearly double that of injuries incurred in landing.

The knee joint is a complex yet stable modified hinge joint, which functions efficiently under normal circumstances. However, the fact that weight bearing occurs upon this joint in extension, instead of flexion (which would act as a shock absorber), renders the knee joint vulnerable to stresses placed upon it by extreme actions, such as those performed in the long jump takeoff, bounding, weight training and other training components.

The stability of the knee depends on muscular support and on the action of cruciate ligaments, collateral ligaments and, to a lesser extent, the cartilages. Three major muscle groups act on the knee to add stability and to ensure its strength—the hamstrings, quadriceps and gastrocnemius. If there is any loss of muscular strength, power or endurance of these groups following a knee injury, there will be a corresponding loss of knee stability, potentially leading to further damage.

In seeking to reduce the incidence of knee injuries, emphasis should be placed on the development of strength, power and endurance of the quadriceps and hamstring muscles to ensure the maintenance of joint stability. Research indicates that knee injuries are more likely to occur when these muscles become tired and are unable to adequately control this joint.

SHIN INJURIES

Though not exclusively a long jump injury, shin splints and stress fractures were prevalent among the surveyed athletes. The greatest single factor in the development of these injuries was attributed to bounding activities, particularly in the general and, to a lesser extent, the specific preparation phases.

Shim splints are the result of a microtrauma to the muscle tendons at the attachment to the shinbone of the three muscles, which insert into various positions of the foot and toes. Overloading, particularly in the early conditioning phase, causes muscular fatigue and a loss of the shock-absorbing capacities of the feet. Continued physical activity leads to structural stress on the muscle tendon insertion with resultant pain and inflammation. Other major causal factors include a change in the running surface or footwear, poor biomechanics of running due to excessive pronation and muscular imbalances.

In order to reduce the possibility of shin splints, coaches should endeavour to:

- Begin a training program gradually. Low-to-moderate intensity and longer duration, for an athlete with a low fitness level, will allow adaptation with a reduced risk of injury.
- Gradually increase the intensity of training. Time should be spent accommodating to new surfaces, environmental changes and changes or increases in training.
- Ensure the athlete wears well fitting and well cushioned training shoes.
- Correct muscular imbalances that exist. Muscles in the front of the lower leg are frequently neglected, with greater concentration focused on the calf muscles. Dorsiflexion exercises with or without weights attached to the feet will assist in the strengthening of these muscles.
- Ensure the athlete warms up and stretches adequately prior to training or competing.
- Check for lower extremity alignment and foot structure problems.

FOOT INJURIES

Correct foot placement is extremely important for an effective long jump takeoff that, in turn, has a decisive influence on the whole jump (takeoff angle, height of the flight, rotation and the landing position). From the medical viewpoint the placement of the takeoff foot is also important in order to prevent hip, knee and ankle joint and foot injuries.

As with the majority of the most common long jump injuries, the takeoff phase proved to be most critical in injuries to the feet, particularly during the competition and general preparation periods. Dynamographic measurements have indicated that the maximal vertical ground reaction forces during the takeoff in a jump over 8m are equal to

12 to 20 times the athlete's body weight. Consequently there is a short and sudden overload on the joints, particularly during the braking phase that occurs in the foot placement.

High-speed film analysis has shown the most frequent faults in foot placement include:

- a hard, heel-first placement, responsible for braking;
- a flat, shifting placement,
- placement on the outer side of the heel and the foot, and
- an overemphasized flat and thrusting placement on the ball of the foot.

In a technically correct action the preparation for the takeoff begins in the penultimate stride. The center of gravity is slightly lowered in this stride that is often a little longer. An upward curve of the center of gravity follows with a flat, actively gripping and slightly "over-the-heel" placement of the takeoff foot. The foot placement must occur straight in the direction of the runup with the edge of the takeoff foot touching the board first. The angle between the sole of the foot and the ground should not exceed 10 to 15°.

Technical faults are only one causative factor in the incidence of foot injuries. Anatomical deviations such as a wide pelvic girdle, "knocked" knees and small mobile kneecaps, which squint inwards, cause postures which place abnormal stresses on the inside of the foot, causing excessive pronation. Pronation causes imbalance, which leads to fatigue during running and this chronic fatigue leads to abnormal running styles that will eventually develop such overuse injuries as:

- overstretching the ligaments that support the various joints of the foot;
- overworking the muscles that support the arch of the foot;
- excessive rotations of the tibia, which may lead to knee, hip and lower back injuries.

Prevention of foot injuries requires the investigation and identification of any predisposing structural faults, not only in the feet, but also the knee and hip joints. Ensuring that footwear is well fitted and supportive, with orthotic devices inserted, if necessary, to support the arch of the foot. Correction of technique, particularly in the takeoff phase, should also be considered paramount. Also important is to ensure that the training or competition surface is flat, smooth and resilient.

CONCLUSION

Having identified the most common injuries among long jumpers as those situated in the ankle, lower back, hamstrings, knee, shin and feet, it is apparent that many of these injuries are the result of overuse, in both acute and chronic forms. It is hoped that coaches will increase their awareness of causative factors that contribute to many of these types of injuries, which in turn should reduce the incidence through improved preventative measures. An understanding of training loads is the first step towards acquiring an insight into remedial techniques for avoiding overuse injuries.

In conclusion, a thorough pre-season physiological evaluation of each athlete may be one of the most effective tools in detecting any potential problem areas that may show up later in the athlete's preparation.

Kinematic–Dynamic Analysis Of The Takeoff Action In The Long Jump

By Milan Coh, Otmar Kugovnik And Alex Dolenec, Slovenia

A study attempting to identify the dynamic and kinematic parameters of the takeoff action which most affects the results of elite long jumpers, providing the means for a more objective and rational monitoring of training processes.

INTRODUCTION

The kinematic model of the long jump consists of four interdependent structural units: approach, takeoff, flight and landing. According to previous studies (Popov 1983; Hay, Miller, Canterna 1986; Brüggemann & Susanka 1987; Hay 1987; Nixdorf & Brüggemann 1990; Lees, Smith & Fowler 1994), the approach and the takeoff action are the most important factors affecting long jump results. The most basic problem is therefore an optimal transformation of the horizontal velocity the jumper develops during the approach into the takeoff velocity at takeoff.

The length of the jump is—according to the kinematic model (after Hay 1986)—defined by the height of the center of mass (CM) at takeoff, takeoff angle, takeoff velocity, takeoff distance, length of flight and the landing distance. The takeoff angle and takeoff velocity which define the flight parabola of CM depend in turn on the horizontal and vertical velocity of CM at takeoff.

The purpose of this study was to identify those dynamic and kinematic parameters of the takeoff action which most affect the results of top long jumpers.

METHODS

Subject Sample

The subject sample consisted of 24 Slovenian long jumpers who jumped at their three most important competitions in 1994. Their best attempt was used.

Measurement Procedures

For assessing the dynamic and kinematic parameters a 3-D video kinematic system was used—the CONSPORT (Consport Motion Analysis System)—and a system of photocells to measure the approach velocity from 11m to 6m and from 6m to 1m prior to the takeoff board. Two video cameras (Panasonic SVHS) were placed at an angle of 90° to the takeoff board at a distance of 17.5m (Figure 1). The coordinate system was defined by the X-axis (horizontal), Y-axis (vertical) and Z-axis (depth).

A biomechanical model of a jumper was used, defined by seventeen points. In the kinematic procedure, the parameters of the last three steps were analyzed, along with the parameters of the takeoff action (Figure 2 and 3).

In further analysis the following statistical procedures were used: basic statistic, Student t-test to assess the differences between the two groups, and correlation analysis to find the correlation between the parameters of the takeoff action and the long jump results.

RESULTS AND DISCUSSION

Besides the procedure for finding the correlations between parameters of the takeoff action and long jump results, we were also interested in seeing in which parameters the jumpers differ the most (statistically) if we divide them into two sub-

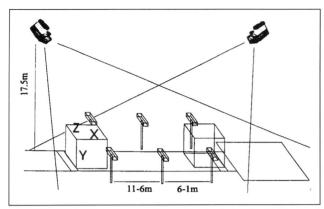

Figure 1: Position of video cameras and photo-cells.

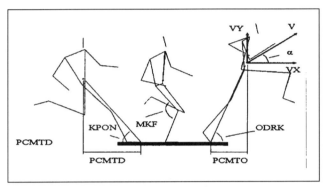

Figure 2: Kinematic-dynamic parameters of the takeoff action (touchdown, maximal amortization, takeoff).

Parameters

OFFI	official distance (cm)
EFFI	effective distance (cm)
DIF	difference between OFFI and EFFI (cm)
3L	length of 3rd last stride (cm)
2L	length of 2nd last stride (cm)
L	length of last stride (cm)
V11-6	velocity from 11m to 6m prior to takeoff board (m/s)
V6-1	velocity from 6m to 1m prior to takeoff board (m/s)
VX	horizontal velocity of CM at takeoff (m/s)
VY	vertical velocity of CM at takeoff (m/s)
V	takeoff velocity (m/s)
a	takeoff angle (degrees)
HCMTD	height of CM at touchdown (cm)
HCMTO	height of CM at takeoff (cm)
RCM	difference in height of CM from touchdown to takeoff (cm)
KPON	angle between the line joining the CM to the toe and the forward horizontal plane at the instant of touchdown (degrees)
PCMTD	projection of CM at touchdown (cm)
PCMTO	projection of CM at takeoff (cm)
ODRK	angle between the line joining the CM to the toe and the forward horizontal plane at the instant of takeoff (degrees)
MKF	maximum amortization in the knee of takeoff leg (degrees)

groups of different quality. This information is given in Table 1 where the differences between the better-jumper group (n=14) and the worse-jumper group (n=10) can be seen. Statistically significant differences (p<0.01) exist in maximal horizontal velocity (V6-1), length of second last stride (2L), projection of CM on the surface at the time of placement of the takeoff leg (PCMTD) and accuracy of the approach (DIF).

The rhythm of the last three strides of better jumpers is such that the length of the second last stride is longer than that of the last stride. For the worse-jumper group in our sample the last stride was, on the average, 34cm longer than the second last stride. This shows the inferior level of technical readiness of jumpers in this group, especially in the preparation for the takeoff action phase.

The difference between the official length of the jump (OFFI) and the effective length (EFFI) is 8cm for the better group and more than 18cm for the worse group. A significant difference between the groups was also noted in (V6-1)—1.02m. The

approach velocity obviously generates the differences in the speed of the takeoff action, resulting in vertical and horizontal velocity at takeoff (VX and VY). The values of the horizontal and vertical velocity of CM are very similar to those obtained in other studies (Popov 1983; Lees, et al., 1994).

Takeoff velocity, as one of the most important predictive parameters of successful long jumping, statistically significantly differentiates the two groups. The difference in means is more than 1.2m/s. The takeoff velocity of the better group is 9.56m/s, of the other 8.86m/s.

The position of the jumper at the moment of placement of the takeoff leg on the surface is also different between the two sub-samples. Better jumpers have statistically significantly grater PCMTD on the surface in regard to the point of contact of the takeoff leg on the surface (7cm difference), while this parameter also affects the realization of a greater VY.

Inspection of the correlation coefficients (Table 1) shows us that ten kinematic/dynamic param-

Table 1: Correlations between predictors and the criterion, differences between the groups.

X—arithmetic mean; SD—standard deviation; r—coefficient of correlation;
t—statistical significance of the difference between groups; **p<0.01; *p<0.05

Pamnrlms	N= 24					N= 14		N= 10		
	X	SD	MIN	MAX	r	X	SD	X	SD	t
OFFI	718	56.4	582	800		757	30.5	664	35.2	0.000**
EFFI	729	50.0	607	805		763	27.6	682	32.5	0.000**
DIF	13	7.4	2	25	-0.47**	8	6.1	18	5.2	0.001**
3L	213	21.9	165	249	0.43*	219	20.9	206	22.2	0.338
2L	230	23.5	183	Z76	0.39	241	19.2	213	19.4	0.002**
L	238	24.5	204	288	-0.18	231	21.2	247	26.9	0.118
V11-6	9.19	0.4	8.47	10.43	0.44*	9.49	0.5	9.00	0.3	0.050*
V6-1	9.59	0.6	8.92	10.87	0.88**	10.13	0.6	9.11	0.2	0.000**
VX	8.69	0.7	7.51	9.95	0.44*	8.95	0.6	8.32	0.5	0.022*
VY	3.20	0.4	2.21	4.14	0.59**	3.35	0.3	3.01	0.4	0.050*
V	9.27	0.6	7.98	10.51	0.58**	9.56	0.5	8.86	0.5	0.004**
α	20.1	2.7	14.0	25.7	0.37	20.6	2.8	19.4	2.6	0.341
HCMTD	0.97	0.6	0.89	1.14	0.14	0.99	0.7	0.94	0.4	0.058
HCMTO	1.18	0.8	1.03	1.36	0.43*	1.22	0.8	1.15	0.6	0.050*
RCM	22	0.5	14	32	0.11	23	0.8	21	0.4	0.358
KPON	54	6.3	59	67	0.01	55	4.6	53	8.2	0.435
PCMTD	53	0.2	27	80	0.64**	60	02	43	0.1	0.007**
PCMTO	29	0.1	12	45	0.02	27	0.1	31	0.6	0.557
ODRK	74	6.4	60	89	-0-45*	72	7.6	77	4.4	0.084
MKF	146	11.5	122	169	-0.20	145	9.8	148	13.9	0.568

eters have a statistically significant correlation with the long jump results. The highest coefficient (r=0.88) is found for V6-1 which the jumper manifests 6-1m before takeoff. A somewhat lesser correlation (r=0.69) was obtained by Nixdorf & Brüggemann (1990) on a sample of eight long jump finalists at the Olympic Games in Seoul.

A generally positive correlation between the long jump results and the maximal approach velocity for jumpers of different quality was obtained in the majority of such studies (Popov 1986; Hay, Miller & Canterna 1986; Brüggemann & Susanka 1987). Maximal approach velocity also generates adequate vertical and horizontal velocity of CM at takeoff, these being dependent on the placement of the takeoff leg on the surface, maximal flexion of the knee of the takeoff leg, compression phase and the resultant of elastic power (Lees, et al., 1994). The correlation of approach velocity and VX is 0.67; the correlation with takeoff velocity (V) is even 0.75.

A low, but statistically significant, correlation was found between the criterion and the ODRK (r=-0.45). The mean value of this parameter for our jumpers was 72°. Other studies (Popov 1983; Hay, et al., 1986) also lead us to the conclusion that this parameter does not have a very significant predictive role for long jumpers.

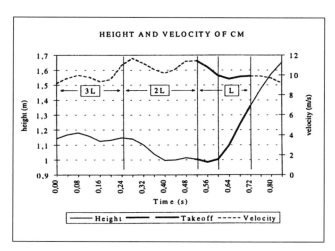

Figure 3: Trajectory and velocity of CM.

CONCLUSION

The jumpers differ most in view of the achieved results (EFFI was used as a criterion) in: maximal approach velocity, accuracy of placing the takeoff

Mike Powell

foot in relation with the takeoff board, the projection of CM at the time of placement of the takeoff leg, length of the last stride, and takeoff velocity.

From the results of correlation analysis we can conclude that success in the long jump depends mainly on: maximal approach velocity 6-1m prior to the takeoff board, the projection of CM at the time of placement of the takeoff leg, takeoff velocity of CM, horizontal and vertical velocity of CM. The research has theoretical as well as practical value, as it gives a coach the means for more objective and rational planning and monitoring of the training process of long jumpers by the use of relevant parameters.

REFERENCES

1. Bosco, C. (1985). Stretch-shortening cycle in skeletal muscle function and physiological considerations on explosive power in man. *Atleticastudi,* Fidal, Centro Studi & Ricerdche, Roma, 1.
2. Hay, J.G., Miller J.A. & Canterna, R.W. (1986). The techniques of elite male long jumpers. *Journal of Biomechanics,* 19, 855-866.
3. Hay, J.G., & Nohara, H. (1990). Techniques used by elite long jumpers in preparation for take-off. *Journal of Biomechanics,* 23, 229-239.
4. Lees, A., Smith, G., & Fowler N. (1994). A biomechanical analysis of the last stride, touchdown, and takeoff characteristics of the men's long jump. *Journal of Applied Biomechanics,* 10, 61-78.
5. Nixdorf, E., & Brüggemann, P. (1990). Biomechanical analysis of the long jump. *Scientific Research Project of the Games of the XXIVth Olympiad—Seoul 1988.* International Athletic Foundation.
6. Popov, V.B. (1983). *Long Jump.* Physical Culture and Sport, Moscow.

The Effect Of Steering On Stride Pattern And Velocity In Long Jumping

By Margy Galloway and Keith Connor, Australia

An attempt to identify whether visual control strategies (steering) in the long jump runup have an effect on the subsequent velocity or stride pattern. The results, with only a limited number of subjects, indicated that most adjustments in stride pattern take place in the last two strides and may well be responsible for velocity reductions.

INTRODUCTION

It is understood by coaches, jumpers, and sports scientists that one of the prerequisites for a good performance in the long or triple jump is the ability to take off with a high horizontal velocity. It is well documented (Hay, 1988; Hay and Koh, 1988; Hay, 1993; Hay, Miller and Cantera, 1986) that the velocity at takeoff is somewhat lower than the maximum velocity reached elsewhere during the runup. The reduction in velocity observed in the last few strides of the runup could be caused by a number of factors, including the method the athlete uses to maneuver into an optimal takeoff position, or the amount of adjustment in stride pattern required in order to hit the board accurately.

Hay (1988) and Lee, Lishman and Thomson (1982) have demonstrated that all athletes in their studies used some form of visual cueing strategies (or "steering") in the long or triple jump approach in order to hit the board accurately at takeoff. There was considerable variation in where the visual cueing strategies occurred for individual athletes (from 2.08 to 19.11m, mean = 10.71m in Hay's study). Hay suggested that it is possible to ascertain the strengths and weaknesses in an individual athlete's runups so that corrective strategies can be employed in training to overcome identified deficiencies.

The aim of the current study was to:
1. Measure the accuracy and consistency of the long jump runup of elite Australian jumpers, and to determine to what extent they use visual cueing strategies in their runups.
2. Determine the effect visual control strategies have on the velocity profile of the athlete in his/her approach to the board.
3. Use the data obtained to form the basis for training strategies aimed at overcoming identified weaknesses for individuals.

METHOD

Three Australian long jumpers were recorded on videotape at the Commonwealth Games Trials in Sydney 1998. Their best jumps in this competition were 8.14m, 7.83m, and 7.77m respectively. All six jumps for each athlete (including fouls) were analyzed. A panning camera (5OHz) was placed perpendicular to the axis of the long jump runup, at a height of approximately 20m, and 15m back.

The runup was calibrated by placing strips of alternating black and white stripes (0.5m) along the length of the runway. The camera was zoomed to a viewing width of 5m. Video frames containing each foot strike were captured, and one-meter squares and the toe of the support foot digitized. The toe-to-board distance for each foot strike was calculated from the raw data, using the method of Hay and Koh (1988). Errors were previously determined to be ±2%.

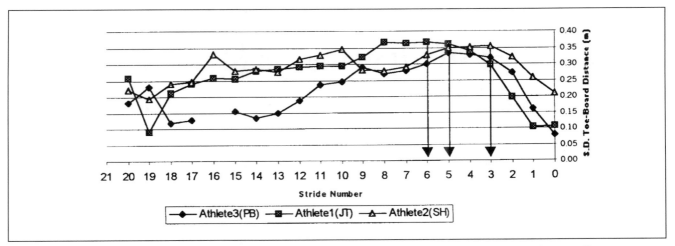

Figure 1: The standard deviation of the toe-to-board distance plotted against foot strikes. Zero on the x-axis represents the takeoff board.

A Lasergun (LAVEG) sampling at 5OHz was used to measure runup velocity. The laser was placed front on to the athlete and aimed at the mid-torso. The zero mark corresponded to the front of the takeoff board.

Velocity was calculated from the distance-time data, which had been smoothed using a 25-point moving average (IAF Biomechanics Research Project, Athens, 1997). Velocity profiles were examined and the following variables extracted: maximum velocity, velocity at steering, and velocity 1m before the board (the surface of the torso being approximately 1m before the board at the moment the foot hits the board).

Steering (or visual control strategy) was determined by the method of Hay and Koh (1988), and was defined as the point at which the standard deviation of the toe-to-board distance for each foot strike begins to decrease. This implies that the foot strikes are then becoming more reproducible as the athlete approaches the board. The six jumps for each athlete were used to determine the average toe-to-board distance for each foot strike.

RESULTS

1. Steering

All three athletes adopted steering mechanisms in their runups in order to hit the board at takeoff off as accurately as possible. Athlete 1 steered at 6 strides out, Athlete 2 at 3 strides out, and Athlete 3 at 5 strides out (see Figure 1).

2. Effect of steering on velocity profile

The velocity profiles of all athletes showed a marked drop-off immediately prior to the board. There was no evidence to suggest that the drop-off was in any way related to the point at which they began to use visual control strategies. The drop-off in velocity (mean = 0.85, ±0.24ms-1) from the point of maximum velocity to 1m before the board, occurred at a mean distance of 4.52 ± 0.70m, or two strides before the board, whereas steering occurred at 15.27m (Athlete 1), 7.35m (Athlete 2) and 11.81m (Athlete 3). Athlete 1 continued at accelerate after the steering point was reached, whereas Athletes 2 and 3 maintained a constant velocity from their steering point to approximately 4.5m before the board. A typical velocity profile is shown in Figure 2.

3. Effect of steering on stride length

Stride patterns of the three athletes showed a short-long-short pattern in the last three strides, common in the literature (Hay, 1993). Although steering occurred 3-6 strides out for these athletes, the largest adjustment in stride length occurred in the second last stride (SD=0.12 to 0.16m), followed by the last stride (SD = 0.09 to 0. 11m)—see Table 1.

DISCUSSION

With the results obtained using this methodology it is possible to determine where in the runup individuals use some sort of steering. The three athletes in this study varied in where this occurred. The effect it had on their velocity and stride pattern also varied. The results reinforce the fact that the data from different athletes cannot be grouped, and each individual must be studied in isolation in

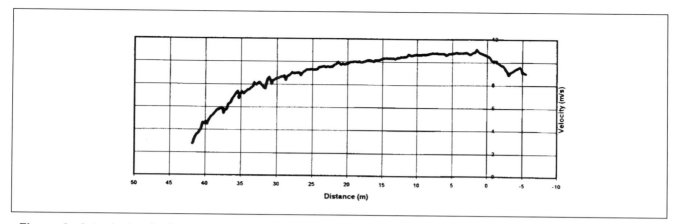

Figure 2: A typical velocity profile. The athlete steered approximately 7.31m (3 strides) before the board during this runup, whereas velocity slowed markedly in the last 3-4m.

order to determine aspects of the runup that could be improved. Once the profile of the athlete's runup has been determined, the coach, biomechanist and athlete need to develop practical strategies that address the short- and long-term goals that will influence performance.

For these athletes it was critical for them to establish a consistent first phase of the runup. This means that they should reach their steering point as consistently as possible, and would result in minimal adjustments to the final strides of the runup.

Using Hay and Koh's (1988) rating of programming ability, which attempts to rate this skill, the athletes in this study scored well below the 50th percentile. The maximum SD of toe-to-board distance was approximately 22.5cm at the 50th percentile, compared with 33.36cm in this study. It must be noted here that the wind conditions during this competition were not consistent (range 1.3-4.9ms^{-1}), and may have affected the accuracy of their runups.

The athletes need to be taught to make small adjustments to each remaining stride length after the steering point, and not to leave this until the last two strides. It was noted that two of these

athletes had abnormally long 2nd last strides compared with data collected from the World Championships 1997 (mean 2.40 ±0.09m) (IAF Biomechanics Research Project, Athens, 1997). It is believed that this overstriding may have caused the observed reduction in velocity. A systematic approach to developing a better runup rhythm was deemed essential.

Practical solutions to effecting change in runup rhythm:

1. Place mini-hurdles at varied distances causing the athlete to make constant adjustments to stride length. This is for the athlete who has problems with transition from one rhythm to another. Primary focus—the last five strides.

2. The placement of hurdles at set distances (number of stride lengths) to develop a pattern. Start at three strides, progressing to 7-9 strides. Replace the hurdles with a takeoff, with the landing continuing into the next run. Primary focus—the last nine strides,

3. Teaching the skill of the basketball lay-up, which in the case of the long jumper also mimics the takeoff preparation. Other benefits include the basics of the penultimate step and the change from horizontal movement to vertical.

Table 1: Stride length (m) for the last 6 strides (mean ±SD).
Bold stride lengths are the stride at which steering occurred.

	6L	5L	4L	3L	2L	L
Athlete 1 (JT)	2.60 (±O.06)	2.68(±0.03)	2.64(±0.07)	2.47(±0.11)	2.68(±0.16)	2.13(±0.10)
Athlete 2 (SH)	2.44(±0.06)	2.29(±0.04)	2.58(±0.05)	2.31(±0.06)	2.82(±0.12)	2.11(-+0.09)
Athlete 3 (PB)	2.48(±0.04	2.40(±0.02)	2.43(±0.04)	2.27(±0.06)	2.50(±0.12)	2.05(±0.11)

4. Acceleration runs—(generally known as Ins and Outs). Markers are placed at set distances (20m-20m-20m-20m). The athlete then runs the distances at varying paces (easy-hard-easy-hard). This method is used to develop transition running.

5. Place visual cues on the track, then later the runup, to mark the transition points, in order to establish the acceleration pattern for the runup. Note: visual cues cannot be placed closer than 5-6 strides from the takeoff board. These cues should be gradually removed, as the athlete develops a rhythm, and prior to commencing competition. The removal of obstacles and cues is essential to allow the skill to become automated and let the athlete focus on competing.

CONCLUSION

This study has shown that biomechanics can offer the coach meaningful information in relation to the performance of the athlete. The study is an example of "coach driven" research to solve the identified problem of long jumpers slowing down immediately prior to takeoff. It shows that information gathered by biomechanists can be used by coaches to develop strategies to improve performance.

REFERENCES

Hay, J.G. (1988) Approach strategies in the long jump. *International Journal of Sport Biomechanics,* 4, 114-129.

Hay, J.G, (1993) Citius, altius, longius (faster, higher, longer): the biomechanics of jumping for distance. *Journal of Biomechanics,* 26(Suppl. 1), 7-21.

Hay, J.G., Koh, T.J. (1988) Evaluating the approach in the horizontal jumps. *International Journal of Sport Biomechanics,* 4, 372-292.

Hay, J.G., Miller, J.A., & Cantera, R.W. (1986) The techniques of elite male long jumpers. *Journal of Biomechanics* 19(10), 855-866.

IAF Biomechanics Research Project Athens (1997). German Sport University Cologne, Germany.

Lee, D., Lishman, R., & Thomson, J. (1982) Regulation of gait in long jumping. *Journal of Experimental Psychology Human Perception and Performance,* 8, 448-459.

Chapter V:
The Triple Jump

Teaching The Triple Jump

By Douglas Todd, USA

A useful analysis of the triple jump and its phases combined with a series of drills to develop each phase with a focus on maintaining horizontal velocity and body position.

Important to the development of any triple jumper is an understanding of the feel or rhythm of the event. The athlete must clearly understand how the event flows from one segment to the next when done correctly. Because of this need to understand, it becomes crucial that the coach begin instruction with a whole-part-whole teaching philosophy. The novice triple jump athlete must develop the kinesthetic awareness of the whole movement before instruction progresses to the individual parts. Without knowledge of the whole, the individual parts are meaningless.

Hand in hand with developing a feel for the event is the need for the athlete to get accurate feedback from the coach and from his or her own individual feedback system (i.e., his own individual sensory perceptions of his own individual physical movements). This feedback, or knowledge of response, is vital to the learning process. Accurate knowledge of response can cut the learning curve in half.

One of the best drills that has worked for me in teaching the rhythm or feel of the triple jump is described below. I have used this teaching method with my track team athletes and with numerous physical education classes during Track and Field Activity Units. It is simple but effective. It has worked in one-on-one settings (just one athlete and me), and it has worked with a coed freshman PE class of over 50! The main thing to remember here is that technique is not the goal of this drill but timing, rhythm, and kinesthetic feel.

DRILL ONE

- Line the athletes up on the goal line of the football field. They should have as much room between them as possible. They should all be facing you. The instructor should be standing on the 10-yard line facing the group.
- Tell them that there are two possible legal triple jump combinations. They are: LEFT, LEFT, RIGHT, TOGETHER and RIGHT, RIGHT, LEFT, TOGETHER. The lefts and rights refer to foot strike patterns and the word together refers to the end of the jump when both feet are together and the athlete has landed in the sand. No one combination is better than the other, but you will have them experiment with both and find out which one they prefer. Once a preference is determined the athlete should stick with that for a while.
- Have everyone stand on the goal line facing you. Tell them to stand on their left foot with their right foot held off the ground.
- Have them hop off of their left foot and land on their left foot. When his left foot hits, the athlete should then jump off that and land on his right foot. After the right foot strikes the ground, the athlete then jumps off that foot and lands with both feet together as if landing in the sand.
- Repeat this process starting with the right foot. Do each a number of times until the athlete can determine which combination feels the best to him.
- Repeat this process, allowing each athlete to use whatever foot combination he prefers. Allow him to use a two-step runup to the line, then a five-yard runup and finally allow a ten-yard runup. The goal or emphasis in each of these drills should be the correct foot strike pattern and learning the feel and rhythm of this event. No attention should be paid to arm mechanics, length of phases, posture or any other technique variable.

BOUNDING

A triple jumper must know how to bound. This skill is crucial if the athlete hopes to be successful. There should be some type of bounding work built into practice each day, especially for the beginning athlete. Start with single-arm bounding and progress to double-arm bounding. Initially it is much more important to work on the athlete's timing and help him develop a smooth or relaxed bounding motion. Covering distance or "power" bounding can come later and will come much easier once the athlete has developed the proper timing and sequence of the movement.

Drill Two is designed to teach bounding to a large group of athletes in a relatively short period of time. It keeps everyone busy and allows even the unskilled to look good.

DRILL TWO

- For this drill you need a shopping cart. (For purposes of illustration we will assume that we have twelve athletes we are trying to teach to bound.)
- Place six of your athletes in lane four on the starting line. Place the other six athletes in lane four as well, only put them at the 50-meter mark. Each group should be in a straight line, one behind the other. Both groups should be facing each other.
- Have the first athlete in the "starting line" group put his hands on the cart handles. Start pushing the cart toward the next group. While pushing the cart and moving forward, hop from the right foot to the left foot and then back to the right. As this motion becomes more fluid, begin to take bigger or larger hops and try to bring the knee of the forward moving leg up to and at least parallel with the shopping cart handle.
- This should be repeated the entire 50 meters with the emphasis on moving from one foot to the other with the knee getting even with the shopping cart handle. Speed is not the issue for this drill but as the athlete becomes more proficient his speed will increase.
- Once the athlete has completed 50 meters, the shopping cart is "passed" to the next athlete and the process is repeated going back down the track in the opposite direction. The athlete just completing the drill moves to the end of the line and recovers before his or her next turn.
- Eventually you can remove the cart and the athletes are now bounding on their own.

This drill can be done with large groups of athletes, and it can be done on a dirt track without any problem and you can easily vary the distance. I believe this is an easy and effective way to teach athletes to bound.

PHASE OF THE JUMP

Each phase is a distinct, separate action and must be learned and practiced as such. However each of these phases must be blended together into one continuous, flowing movement when performed. This brings us back to and reinforces the whole-part-whole teaching philosophy mentioned earlier. This whole action cannot be understood and performed without an understanding and proficiency of the individual parts.

Since by now your athletes should have a good feeling or awareness of the overall movement, I believe the best course of action for the vast majority of jumpers is to then work at and drill the individual parts. Once each part is learned the task then becomes one of blending these parts back together and learning the transitions. Coaching the transitions from runway to hop, from hop to step and step to jump is where the real work is found. Smooth transitions and active landings take time to fully master. Thankfully, however, much progress and improvement can be made by improving the individual phases.

In the various phase discussions that follow I will be describing a left-left-right-together pattern. All cues and description are the same for either pattern.

HOP PHASE

The hop phase is a cyclic motion. It corresponds to the athlete's "left-left" sequence pattern that was learned in the first drill. The athlete runs down the runway, takes off or leaves the ground from his left foot, cycles this leg through and now lands on the left foot.

There are several important things to focus on in this phase. The first is being that of maintaining as much horizontal velocity as possible. To do this, the athlete's foot must strike the runway directly below the hips or center of mass.

The foot must strike the runway in a "pawing" motion. The motion is similar to that of a person trying to propel himself forward on a skateboard.

The posture of the athlete is important during this first phase as well. The body should be erect and upright at takeoff, during flight and upon landing. Any forward lean or bending at the waist can cause excessive forward rotation or inhibit necessary movement into the next phase.

It is also important that the athlete send both arms forward at takeoff in this hop phase. A double-arm takeoff is not difficult to learn and has the added advantage of getting both arms out in front at the beginning of the jump. A strong double-arm pump can increase the amount of force the athlete can apply and improve overall jump distance.

DRILL THREE

The athlete should spend time performing the hop motion. However these hops do not have to be from a full approach nor do they have to come down on the runway. One of the best ways to perform a number of practice drills is to hop into the sand. Each setup can be a little different and varied according to ability level and emphasis for that particular day.

- Line your athletes up on the runway approximately 10 meters from the sand.
- Ignoring the takeoff board, have them run to the sand and execute the left-left takeoff. Where the athlete actually jumps from is irrelevant. What is relevant is that the takeoff is more horizontal than vertical, the posture is good, the athlete has a focal point out beyond the back of the pit (he is not looking down), he lands on the same foot he took off with, and the foot strikes the sand beneath the hips and not out in front of the hips.
- Since the takeoff foot for the hop phase must move in a cyclic manner, we use the following cue. "Heel to butt, thigh high, paw." These three phrases remind our athletes that after takeoff the heel cycles up to the butt; this shortens the lever length and allows the leg to move forward quickly. "Thigh high" helps our athlete focus on a full range of motion for this leg and helps put the athlete in a good position to "paw" or strike the ground on landing. The final cue—"paw"—reminds the athlete that he is not simply landing but that he is involved in an active, aggressive, forward propelling movement.
- All of this can be done without a great deal of speed and can be done with a large group of people at once. Begin with a small runup and little speed, eventually building up to longer and longer runups and increased speeds as the skill level improves.
- Other ways to teach the hop action.
  1. Single-leg hop in place.
  2. Hop up stairs.
  3. Hop across the field with a partner following along behind and holding your non-hopping foot. (Do not allow the athlete performing the drill to wear spikes.)
  4. Hop over cones or other low obstacles. (The obstacles should break away or fall down when struck.)

STEP PHASE

The step phase is a crucial phase to the overall jump but in many ways a successful step phase is a result of a good hop phase. Knowing how to bound and performing a strong, technically sound hop will insure a good step phase. However the step phase must still be mastered and practiced. There are a number of drills that can help your athletes get the most from this part of the jump.

DRILL FOUR

- After bounding is mastered, perform a hop and then follow the hop with a split landing in the sand. (Right leg in front, left leg trailing behind.) The athlete should start back about ten meters from a takeoff area and at takeoff perform a hop. (Remember the pattern for this is left, left, right.) This time the hop must land on the runway. After the hop landing the athlete now must propel off the left foot and into a big bounding action. The right leg is in front, the thigh of the right leg is parallel to the ground, the athlete's torso is upright and he or she carries this good position into the sand, landing in this split position. Holding this position teaches the athlete to hold or ride this step position as long as possible and get as much distance out of this phase as possible.
- From this drill, the athlete can move to a hop and then step with an active landing rather than the split landing in the sand. Begin on the grass and look for the same kind of foot strike and positioning that you looked for in the hop landing. The athlete must be pawing the landing foot. The landing leg must be moving back down the runway (away from the sand), if your athlete hopes to move forward toward the sand.
- After these drills are working well, you can mix the routine up a little. Have the athlete perform

not only the hop-step drill but some hop-hop-step drills as well. It is also helpful to now have the athlete drill both sides or jump patterns. In other words, he could do hop drills on both the right and left side. This is good for strength development and by overloading the motor system with drills on both sides we can expect to see an even greater adaptation.

ARM ACTION DURING PHASES

The arm action of the triple jumper is crucial. Good arm action can significantly add to the triple jump distance and must be worked on or practiced. However, sometimes too much is made of the positioning and location of the arms at each phase, causing the athlete to forget the main reason for the arm action in the first place.

The arms are used to deliver a blow to the runway. They are used to increase the amount of force the athlete can apply to the runway, thereby increasing the amount of force returned, which translates into increased distance.

A simple arm action cue the athlete can remember is the following: "Leg back, arms forward." In other words, every time a leg is coming down toward the runway, the arms are moving forward. Each time a leg is moving back toward the runway the arms should be moving forward forcibly.

DRILL FIVE

I call this the BOOM, BANG, POW drill. Have your athlete walk with a double-arm swing and an exaggerated leg lift. Each time the athlete's leg "paws" the ground, his or her arms should be moving forward. Arms should be driven to shoulder height and then cycled back.
- This drill will help the athlete time or "sync" the very necessary arm movement with the leg action.
- Once the rhythms of the drill are learned, speed can be added and then more and more force put into the repetitions.

JUMP PHASE

This is the final phase of the triple jump action and is identical to the long jump flight into the pit. What makes this phase so difficult is the lack of horizontal velocity at this point in the jump. Another factor that can contribute to a poor jump

Kenny Harrison

phase is the athlete's body position after "landing" from the previous step phase.

Success here is dependent on what has happened before. Much time should be spent on this phase. It is possible to drill this phase off the grass into the sand, or off the grass and onto a landing pit. The important thing to remember is to drill this aspect off a bounding action with only as much speed as would be found in the actual triple jump movement itself.

It is important to spend time on this phase. Your athlete must experience the feeling of working against the forces that are attempting to negate a successful final movement. They will begin to understand the importance of effective arm action and knee drive the more they spend time trying to jump off a previous bounding movement.

DRILL SIX

- One-step jump: Use the right foot if the right foot is the one your athlete lands on from the step. Have your athlete stand with both feet together, facing the sand. Take one big step onto the takeoff foot and then perform a jump landing. Use only the speed the athlete can generate with one step. He should start close to the pit to ensure a safe sand landing.
- Bound-Bound-Bound-Jump: The athlete performs three bounds and then a jump movement into the sand. Make sure that the last foot to hit the ground before the sand is the same foot that the athlete will jump off when he performs the actual triple jump.
- Bound-Bound-Bound to low box jump: The same movement as described previously but the last jump is performed off a low plyo box. This drill requires two things to work successfully. The first is a plyo box that has a large enough surface area to provide a good target and the second is a confident athlete. Do not try to force this drill on to a new triple jumper. Bring this drill in as your athletes become more rhythmic and coordinated and are ready for a new motor challenge. Going off the box really "loads" the takeoff leg and forces the athlete to work both arm swing and free-leg drive to get any kind of distance off the jump.

Remember that most of the jump phase is covered during long jump practice. You need to work on the transition to the jump phase. Coming off of the step phase, body position is your primary concern. Correct body position prior to the jump take-off will benefit your athlete by allowing him to apply arm drive and free-leg swing (i.e., forces) in the right direction and at the right time.

FINAL

As each phase is learned you must help your athlete combine them into each other. Eventually you will make your way toward short-approach full jumps and finally full-approach full jumps. Remember to coach each phase first. Once a certain proficiency is achieved move to the transition from one phase to the next.

Focus on maintaining horizontal velocity and jump for body position between phases and NOT distance. Too much emphasis is placed on phase percentages (of the total distance), and judgements are made of an athlete's ability based upon how well their jumps fit into these "ideal" models. Distance between phases will come with strength, maturation and improved mechanics. Each jumper is different.

It is our job as coaches, to exploit what the athlete does right, to help him use these strengths to his best advantage and minimize or eliminate any weakness. The triple jump is an intricate event and takes time to master. Give your athletes time to learn and feel comfortable with the various phases and component movements. Patience will yield a consistent crop of triple jumpers for your program over the years.

Methodological Aspects Of The Women's Triple Jump

By Vitold Kreyer, Russia

An outstanding summary of technical, physiological and developmental aspects of female triple jumping, looking specifically at strength requirements and training loads, followed by a series of recommended conditoning exercises.

INTRODUCTION

It wasn't until 1993 that the first female beat the 15m barrier in the triple jump with a leap of 15.09 (5.45 + 4.08 + 5.09)—Ana Biryukova at the World Championships in Stuttgart. She was followed in 1995 by Iolanda Chen (15.03), then by Inessa Kravets and Iva Prandzheva (15.18). Kravets outstanding effort of 15.50m in 1995 stands at this stage as the world record and the "15m club" had at the end of 1998 a total of seven members.

THE TAKEOFF MECHANICS

In the takeoff performance of the three triple jump phases an athlete has to overcome resistances to muscles and tendons that exceed the body weight by five to six times (hop 300kg + step 450kg + jump 300kg). The counter-forces of inertia increase here in proportion to the runup speed (within 8.5 to 9.7 m/s) and the height of the trajectory in all three phases. A runup velocity increased by 1% would add 16cm to the distance of the jump. However, it would at the same time require up to 10% more effort in each of the three phases.

The stretching and contraction of the muscles at each takeoff occurs during the amortization phase in which the takeoff leg and the spine help to reduce the inertia forces. As soon as the resistance to the stretching muscles exceed the duress, a powerful contraction begins. The takeoff leg starts its extension when the trunk begins to straighten and the body moves forward. The shorter the amortization phase, the more efficient is the transfer of this movement. In contrast, the later the straightening begins, the shorter will be the time left to move the body forward.

The capacity of the muscles to stretch and to contract powerfully in all phases of the triple jump decides the performance. In general, the amplitude of the amortization for athletes with a well developed speed-strength level should not exceed 10 to 15° in the hip joint and 40° in the knee joint.

PHYSIOLOGICAL DIFFERENCES

The height-weight indicators of women begin to grow rapidly at the age of 19 to 20 years. Adult female triple jumpers at the 1996 Olympic Games had an index of 370 to 380 g/cm, composed of 172 to 178 cm height and 62 to 65kg weight.

The ratio of active and passive (32 to 35%) fat mass is unfavorable for women in comparison to men. The same applies to the distribution of slow- and fast-twitch muscle fibers. These factors are responsible for the differences in the neuromuscular systems (up to 30%).

It is known that slow-twitch muscle, followed by an immediate engagement of fast-twitch fibers, secure acceleration. It also is known that it is not possible to change slow-twitch fibers into fast-twitch fibers, although it is possible to change some of their qualities.

Women also differ from men in ratio of body height and leg length. They have weaker upper body, hip, back and abdominal muscles. However, all these differences are secondary to their shortcomings of instep strength, which is responsible for Achilles tendon inflammation and chronic knee pain. It should be noted here that 50% of young potential jumpers in a recent study suffered from instep abnormalities (Vorobinov).

Of further interest is the fact that the development of tendons and ligaments is considerably slower than the development of muscular strength. This creates an imbalance between muscular strength and the strength of ligaments and tendons. A balanced mechanical strength is usually not achieved before the age of 22 to 23 years, indicating the need for careful strengthening of tendons and ligaments at an early age.

Female athletes who copy strength development exercises of male triple jumpers progress quickly at first. Unfortunately this is followed, after a short stabilization phase, by a considerable drop in performance capacities, often shortening their sporting careers. The following recommendations therefore appear in order:

• The strengthening of the spine and ankle areas should gradually begin at a young age.
• Barbell exercises that involve bending and twisting movements should be avoided because they provoke spine injuries.
• Strengthening of abdominal and lower back muscles should continually take place.
• Full squats, standing presses and snatches should be avoided and replaced by similar exercises in the prone position.
• Barbell bounces do not strengthen but only condense ankle muscles. Elastic loading with dynamic and plyometric methods is by far more effective.
• Tendons and ligaments should be protected by performing exercises on soft surfaces and wearing thick-soled shoes.
• After the technique of each exercise has been

World record holder Inessa Kravets.

established, the number of repetitions is gradually increased but energy expenditure should still be under control.

WHAT ARE THE STRENGTH REQUIREMENTS OF FEMALE JUMPERS?

Only a coordinated application of different individual performance capacities make it possible

Table 1: Yearly training load for women triple jumpers.

Training sessions—230 ± 20	General strength—600 ± 50 repetitions
Competitions—15 ± 3	Speed strength—5000 ± 1000 takeoffs
Sprints (96-100%)—22 ± 3km	Explosive strength—2500 ± 300 takeoffs
Running (70%)—90 ± 10km	Reactive strength—1000 ± 100 takeoffs
Runups—250 ± 40	Specific strength—300 ± 50 takeoffs
Short runup takeoffs—1000 ± 100	Restoration activities—50 ± 10 sessions
Cross-country runs, games—50 hr	Bounding (10-15 takeoffs)—4000 ± 500

to efficiently perform the three explosive takeoffs required in the triple jump. The distance achieved in the triple jump depends on four major factors—strength, speed, psychic inspiration and technical mastery.

The strength factor has a leading role here. It can often be observed that even a small technical deviation is responsible for a considerable drop in distance among athletes who lack the necessary strength. On the other hand, jumpers with strength reserves are less influenced by technical shortcomings. Their high-level speed-strength compensates for technical deficiencies.

Unfortunately we are faced with a paradox in the development of strength. On one hand, it is obvious that strength is a decisive factor in the triple jump performance. On the other hand, over-developed strength can bring negative results in blocking the movement amplitude and therefore distorting technical elements. Overdeveloped hypertrophy can restrict movement amplitude and the road to technical perfection.

Strength has an important task in the three takeoff phases in the fast transfer from yielding to overcoming muscular work. Consequently, the choice in strength development exercises should concentrate on dynamic movements which are in character, with amplitude, tempo and rhythm closely related to the competition performance structure of the event. To avoid misunderstandings about weight training exercises it is necessary to draw attention to the following:

- Barbell exercises are only one of the many means available for strength development. Such exercises should not exceed 15 to 20% of the total development volume.
- Classic double-leg squats should be replaced by alternated single-leg squats. All snatching and pressing exercises should be executed quickly in 5 to 8 repetitions with loads of 80 to 90% of maximum.
- It is important to widen the approach to strength training by using different exercises, training means and training methods.

There is a large range of strength development exercises suitable to also improve movement coordination for rational technical elements. These exercises make up most of the conditioning training volume and include a variety of sprinting and jumping activities, such as jumps over 5 to 6 hurdles, bounding alternately on both legs, 30-40m uphill sprints, etc. All these strength development exercises are continually changed (even ev-

Table 2: A sample weekly training load for women triple jumpers during different training periods.

	TRAINING MEANS	TRAINING PERIODS			
		GENERAL	STRENGTH	TECHNICAL	COMPETITION
SPRINT PREPARATION	Runups with a takeoff and jump (number)	-	3-4	8-10	1-12
	Sprints 30-80m (96-100%) (km)	-	0.7-1.0	0.7-0.8	-.15-0.2
	Running, running exercises (km)	2.0-3.0	1.5-2.0	1.2-1.5	0.9-1.0
JUMPING PREPARATION	2-3-4-5-6 takeoffs from a 6-10 strides runup	-	50-60	80-100	30-40
	Long jumps over hurdles (takeoffs)	-	10-20	10-15	6-10
	Hops and steps repetitions (8-15 takeoffs)	100	200	150	50
STRENGTH PREPARATION	General strength (reps)	300	300	200	50
	Speed strength (takeoffs)	300	300	200	100
	Reactive strength (takeoffs)	-	100	100	30-40
	Explosive strength (takeoffs)	100	150	100	100
	Specific strength (takeoffs)	-	50	70	20

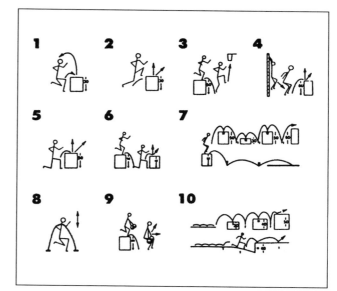

ery couple of weeks) and the choice is widened to include more event-specific exercise complexes.

For clarification we separate a series of recommended exercises according to their capacity to overcome resistance into groups:

1. General strength—selective exercises for the development of all major muscle groups with weight training equipment.
2. Speed strength—development of the capacity of fast repetitive takeoffs by overcoming the resis-

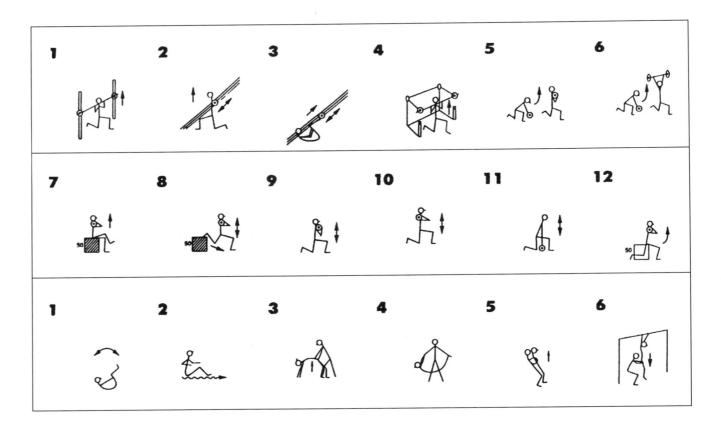

tance of the athlete's own body weight.

3. Explosive strength—development of the reactive takeoff capacity by using exercises with an additional load or resistance (30 to 50% of an athlete's own body weight).

4. Reactive strength—development of the muscular capacity to overcome resistance following the yielding phase of the takeoff.

5. Specific strength—combinations to develop the specific capacity to perform fast repetitive takeoffs under changing conditions (5 to 7kg weight belts, rubber pulleys, 1 to 2° uphill jumps, jumping over the hurdles, jumps reaching for the basketball rim, etc.).

Finally a few recommendations for the coach:
• Pay special attention in strength development of female triple jumpers to their physiological differences.
• Combine strength development exercises with stretching and mobility exercises.
• Training loads are similar to that of male triple jumpers but the percentage of maximal intensity exercises should be reduced 20-25%.
• Provide frequent variations by changing training means, methods and conditions. Avoiding monotony is particularly important for female jumpers.
• Don't forget the value of cross country running. In some cases it is an excellent way to reduce body fat.

TRAINING LOADS

The development of international-level women triple jumpers should definitely be based on a planned yearly training load (Table1). It is here necessary here to find a rational structure for the plan as a whole, as well as individual segments. The plan can be based on the hybridization principle (Matveyev), with the load distributed according to the "leaping" (Vorobjov), "contrasting" (Drosjev) or "blocks" (Verhoshansky) formation.

Practical experience over the last few years has shown that the most effective approach in preparation for major events is a combination method in which technical and physical capacities are developed in parallel. This author believes that methodical changes in work capacity phases, training means and training methods allow athletes to reach top form 4-6 times in a six-month cycle.

Differences In Some Triple Jump Rhythm Parameters

By Gregory Portnoy, Israel

The author, Coordinator of High Performance Track & Field in Israel, compares in a detailed biomechanical analysis the triple jump performances of Jonathan Edwards and Mike Conley at the 1993 Stuttgart and 1995 Göteborg World Championships and comes to the conclusion that success in this event depends on a number of rhythmic and velocity values.

INTRODUCTION

At the 1995 World Championships Jonathan Edwards (GBR) set a new world record (18.29m) in the triple jump on his second attempt. He eliminated the previous mark (17.97m) established by Willie Banks (USA) and held for over nine years. He also defeated the best triple jumpers, including Mike Conley (USA), probably the best triple jumper of the decade. Conley was often very close to the world mark, only missing the record by a 2.1m/sec. assisting wind in his triumphal 18.17m effort at the Barcelona Olympic Games.

The results of a comparative analysis of some rhythm parameters of these outstanding jumpers, Edwards and Conley, may be of interest for coaches and sport scientists.

Comparing their best results at the 1993 World Championships in Stuttgart and the 1995 World Championships in Gotheburg we find Conley to win (17.86m) in Stuttgart, Edwards being third (17.44m), while in Gotheburg, against Edwards' exceptional world record jump, Conley failed, placing seventh (16.96m) after only two fair jumps in the final. However, it seems to be more objective to analyze the rhythmical characteristics of his fouled jump (approx. 17.45m).

THE RUNUP

The runup speeds, derived from the "Biomechanical Team's Informations Bulletins" (1993 and 1995 Athletics World Championships) are summed up in Table 1, showing the changes in runup speeds developed in the last part of the runup.

As can be seen, Edwards managed to develop a fantastic speed (11.90 m/sec.) over the final 5 meters. What is surprising is the fact that he increased the speed over this last 5m section in comparison to the previous 5m by 2.10 m/sec. At the previous World Championships his velocity over the last section was slower by 0.13 m/sec. Even when assuming that there is a possible measurement error in velocity over the five-meter section, Edwards' average speed over the final 10 meters increased from 10.35 m/sec. to 10.85 m/sec.

Meanwhile Conley shows a small average speed loss over the final runup section (from 10.74 m/sec. to 10.65 m/sec.). However, the speed difference for the last two 5m sections increased (from 0.02 m/sec. to 0.45 m/sec.), which in turn resulted in a speed increase over the last section (10.87 m/sec.), although assisted by a 3.6 m/sec. wind. Nevertheless, a comparison of the runup velocity over

Table 1: Runup velocities over the last 10 meters.

VELOCITY (m/sec)	Conley		Edwards	
	1995	**1993**	**1995**	**1993**
11 to 6m	10.42	10.73	9.80	10.42
6 to 1m	10.87	10.75	11.90	10.29
difference	0.45	0.02	2.10	-0.13
11 to 1m	10.65	10.74	10.85	10.35
Wind	+3.6	+0.3	+1.3	+0.1

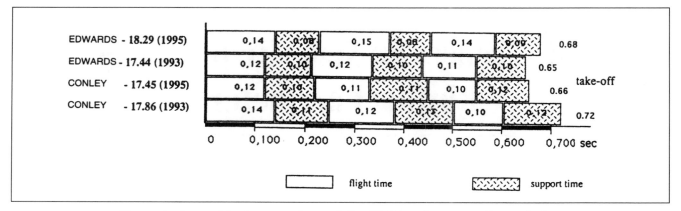

Figure 1: A graphical comparison of the flight and support times during the last three strides of the runup and takeoff.

the last two 5m sections reveals that both athletes accelerated to the board.

Let us now compare the last approach strides of both athletes in the duration and ratio of the support and flight phases (Fig. 1). It can be seen in Fig. 1 that both athletes achieved better results with an increased duration of the last three strides (Edwards: 0.65 to 0.68 sec., Conley 0.66 to 0.72 sec.).

However, they have different rhythmic structures in this section of the runup (Fig. 2). In both cases Conley demonstrates equal flight (Tf) and support (Ts) times. (Tf/Ts = 1). In his 18.17m jump this index is 0.93, somewhat lower with a longer support time.

Edwards' flight time is considerable longer than his support time and the Tf/Ts index in his record jump has essentially increased to 1.72. It should be noted that the absolute value of Edwards' support time, especially in his record jump, is considerably

shorter than that of Conley's. For example, Edwards' support time for his takeoff leg in the last stride (0.08 sec.) is 62% of Conley's time (0.13 sec.) in his 17.86m jump.

Index Kf (Table 2) determines the activity of the last runup stride in comparison with the penultimate stride. It appears that Edwards almost doesn't emphasize the last stride, keeping to an immutable rhythmic structure in the last three strides of his runup. On the other hand, Conley activates the last stride (intensification of the last stride brings better results) and in his 18.17m effort the Kf index is 0.64.

THE JUMP

The total duration of the jump or, in other words, the time from the moment of contact with the board in the hop to the moment of landing in the jump is individual and shows insignificant changes with the jumping distance. (Fig. 3).

Conley executed his 18.18m jump (1992) in 1.99 sec. The difference between the total time and the jump for both athletes is small (4-5%), but Edwards' support time for the three takeoffs (18.29m jump) is 0.34 sec. and Conley's support time (17.86m jump) is 0.43 sec., which makes a difference of approx. 20%.

Edwards shows improved performances when

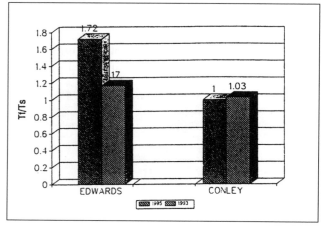

Figure 2: Ratio of the flight and suport times during the last three strides of the runup.

Table 2: Flight phases ratio in the last and penultimate runup strides (Kf).

Conley		Edwards	
1995	1993	1995	1993
0.86	0.80	0.93	0.92

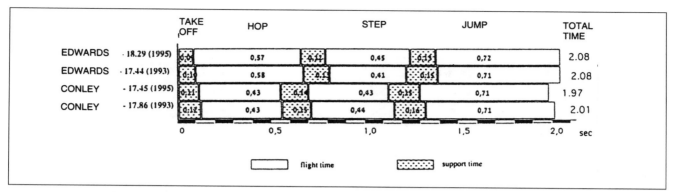

		TAKE OFF	HOP		STEP		JUMP		TOTAL TIME
EDWARDS	· 18.29 (1995)	0,0	0,57	0,11	0,45	0,15	0,72		2.08
EDWARDS	· 17.44 (1993)	0,1	0,58	0,11	0,41	0,15	0,71		2.08
CONLEY	· 17.45 (1995)	0,11	0,43	0,14	0,43	0,15	0,71		1.97
CONLEY	· 17.86 (1993)	0,12	0,43	0,15	0,44	0,16	0,71		2.01

flight time   support time

Figure 3: A graphical comparision of the flight and support times during the triple jump.

he reduced his total takeoff time of 0.38 sec. in 1993 to 0.34 sec. in 1995. Conley, on the contrary, shows poorer results as his time index is reduced from 0.43 sec. in 1992 to .40 sec. in 1995.

Figure 4 indicates that individual ratios of the support and flight phases also differ importantly.

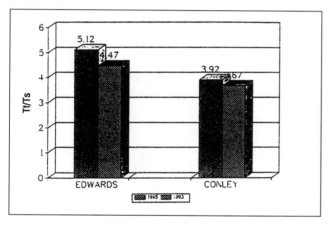

Figure 4: Ratio of the flight and support times during the triple jump.

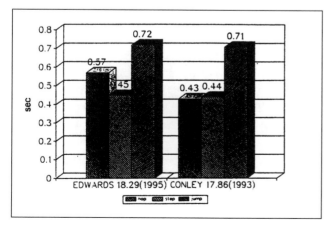

Figure 5: Flight times in the different phases of the triple jump.

Edwards' flight phases are five times longer than his support phases (Tf/Ts = 5.12). Conley's index of 3.67 is much lower. In Edwards' case the relative increases of the fight phases (Tf/Ts from 4.47 to 5.12) resulted in a better performance. On the other hand, Conley's increased flight phases (Tf/Ts from 3.67 to 3.92) were accompanied by lower triple jump results. This was further confirmed by an even lower 3.65 index in his 18.17m jump in 1992.

It should be noted that the duration of the flight phases in the step and the jump are approximately equal for both athletes, while Edwards' flight time in the hop is in 0.57 sec., much longer than Conley's 0.43 sec.

SUMMARY

1. The aim of this article was to analyze some of the temporal and velocity factors that influence the performances of the leading world-class triple jumpers (Edwards and Conley).
2. Both athletes succeeded due to their maximal acceleration over the last five meters of their runup (Conley—to 10.87 m/sec., Edwards—to 11.90 m/sec.). Both athletes accelerated to the board. Their speed over the last five meters of the approach exceeded that of the previous five meters.
3. Edwards' produces better triple jump results with a slight accentuation of the last stride. On the other hand, Conley activates the last stride in his best jumps.
4. Edwards' record jump is characterized by the reduction of the support time (Ts) and an increase of the relative flight time (Tf/Ts) in the last runup strides, as well as in the triple jump performance. At the same time, Conley demonstrates longer support and shorter relative flight times in his best flights.

Jonathan Edwards

Mike Conley

The above appears to indicate that successful triple jumps depend on a number of rhythmic and velocity values. The present analysis proves that, based on a high runup speed, both Edwards and Conley achieve their best performances in using different individual movement aims.

The Case For A Jump-Dominated Technique In the Triple Jump

By Dr. James Hay, USA

Although jump-dominated techniques have been used only rarely by elite triple jumpers recent research and careful analysis of world-class performers suggests that such techniques deserve more consideration than they have received.

The way in which an athlete distributes effort through the three phases of a triple jump is usually reckoned in terms of the *phase distances, phase percentages* and a *phase ratio*. The phase distances are defined and measured as shown in Figure 1; the phase percentages are the phase distances expressed as percentages of the actual distance; and the phase ratio is obtained by expressing the phase percentage as a ratio.

Many different (and often confusing) names have been given to triple jump techniques according to the emphasis they place on the hop and jump phases. In this article, a technique will be referred to as *hop-dominated* if the hop percentage is at least 2% greater than the next largest phase percentage; *jump-dominated* if the jump percentage is at least 2% greater than the next longest phase percentage; and *balanced* if the longest phase percentage is less than 2% greater than the next longest phase percentage (Hay, 1990).

Thus, for example, the winning jump of Kenny Harrison (USA) at the 1991 World Championships in Tokyo was made using a hop-dominated technique (Table 1); the world record jump of Willie Banks (USA) at the 1985 TAC Championships in Indianapolis was made using a jump-dominated technique (Table 2); and the second-best jump of Al Joyner (USA) at the 1984 Olympic Games in Los Angeles—no data is available on his best jump—was made using a balanced technique (Table 3).

HISTORICAL BACKGROUND

Triple jumping was dominated for much of the 50 years, 1943-1993, by athletes from Eastern Europe. These athletes were the products of two different schools of thought concerning the optimum distribution of effort. These schools, which emerged during the first two decades of the period, are the Russian school (which favored a strongly hop-dominated technique) and the Polish school (which favored a balanced technique).

There were three major exceptions to the overall domination enjoyed by Eastern European athletes with their hop-dominated and balanced techniques. In 1975, **Joao de Oliveira** (Brazil) set a world record of 17.89m using a jump-dominated

Table 1: Harrison 1991

Hop Distance (Hop %)	Step Distance (Step %)	Jump Distance (Jump %)	Actual Distance	Phase Ratio
6.89m (39%)	4.94m (28%)	6.03m (34%)	17.86m	39:28:34

Table 2: Banks 1985

Hop Distance (Hop %)	Step Distance (Step %)	Jump Distance (Jump %)	Actual Distance	Phase Ratio
6.32m (35%)	4.96m (28%)	6.69m (37%)	17.97m	35:28:37

Table 3: Joyner 1984

Hop Distance (Hop %)	Step Distance (Step %)	Jump Distance (Jump %)	Actual Ratio	Phase
6.21m (36%)	4.93m (29%)	5.98m (35%)	17.12m	36:29:35

technique of 34:30:36 (McNab, 1977; Starzynski, 1987).* This record stood until 1985 when **Willie Banks** set a world record of 17.97m, using a jump-dominated technique of 35:28:37 (Miller and Hay, 1986). Finally, 7-8 years later, **Mike Conley** (USA) used a jump-dominated technique in winning the U.S. Olympic Trials in 1992 (Hay, unpublished data) and the World Championships in 1993 (Hill, 1993). The phase ratio for his best jump at the Olympic Trials (a foul measured at 18.05m) was 32:30:39; and for his winning jump of 17.86m in the World Championships it was 32:31:37.

The phase ratios for these jumps of de Oliveira, Banks and Conley; some recent research findings; and a conspicuous lack of data or argument in favor of the hop-dominated and balanced techniques, have raised afresh the question "What is the optimum technique in the triple jump?" The purpose of this article is to make the case that a jump-dominated technique may be the optimum for most triple jumpers.

THE FORCE ARGUMENT

There have been two major studies in which the forces an athlete exerts against the ground in a triple jump (and which the ground, in reaction, exerts against the athlete) have been measured using a force platform (Amadio, 1985; Ramey and Williams, 1986). These studies showed that the greatest forces to which a triple jumper is exposed are the vertical forces produced during the initial impact of the hop landing. They also showed that these forces increase with the distance of the hop.

For two female athletes who performed hops of about 3.5m, the maximum vertical force was about 8-9 times their body weight, and for two males, who hopped about 4.5m, the maximum vertical force was about 11.5-12.5 times body weight (Ramey and Williams, 1986). And, finally, for five males, hopping about 5-5.3m, the maximum vertical forces were about 14-22 times body weight (Amadio, 1985).

It should be noted here that these large forces were recorded for hop distances that are much shorter than those recorded by elite male triple jumpers. It seems likely therefore that they greatly underestimate the forces to which the more proficient athletes are exposed.

It is intuitively obvious that there is a limit to the maximum vertical force that a given athlete can handle during the hop landing. Simple visual observation suggests that there are several possible consequences of exceeding this limit.

When triple jumpers use a high hop, the force to which they are exposed on impact is often more than they can handle effectively and the support leg buckles. This buckling prevents them from driving up strongly into the step takeoff and they either have a short step distance or, in more extreme cases, are forced to abandon the attempt.

In still more extreme cases, large impact forces lead to injury—and sometimes even to career-end-

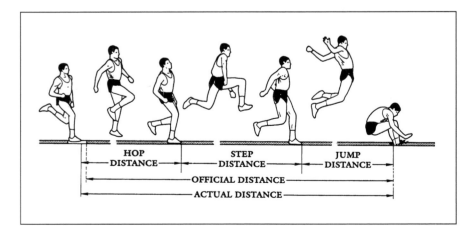

HOP DISTANCE   STEP DISTANCE   JUMP DISTANCE
OFFICIAL DISTANCE
ACTUAL DISTANCE

There is some disagreement in the literature concerning the phase ratios for Oliveira's jump (see Hay, 1992, p. 348). The figures cited here appear to be the most reliable.

Figure 1: The official, actual and phase distances in the triple jump.

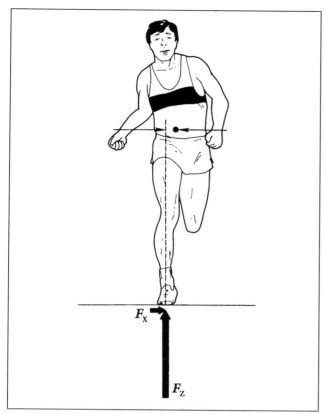

Figure 2: The vertical force exerted by the ground on the foot of the triple jumper tends to rotate him clockwise about a forward-backward axis through his center of gravity.

ing injury. Although there is no scientific evidence available that speaks to this last point, there is anecdotal evidence of serious and repeated injuries among athletes who use strongly hop-dominated technique.

Conclusion? *Seeking to increase the distance of a triple jump by progressively increasing the length of the hop is ultimately destined to produce failure in the form of weak step phases, aborted attempts and injury.*

THE BALANCE ARGUMENT

An athlete has numerous tasks to perform in the course of a triple jump. One of these is to position the body so that the forces acting upon it during each support phase produce only the rotations that are needed. Any other rotations are unwelcome because they disrupt the athlete's balance.

Consider, for example, the triple jumper shown in front view during the support phase of the hop in Figure 2. At the instant shown, the ground exerts a large upward force and a small sideways force on the sole of the athlete's shoe. The line of action of the upward force passes to the left side of the athlete's center of gravity (as seen in Figure 2) and the force tends to rotate the body in a clockwise direction. How strong this tendency is depends on the size of the force and the distance between its line of action and the center of gravity—that is, how close the line passes to the side of the center of gravity.

If the vertical forces are relatively small, small deviations from the ideal lines of action of these forces might not cause very serious problems with balance. The athlete might be able to make subtle adjustments in body position and continue into the next phase without difficulty.

But the forces are not small. In the worst instances, during the impact phase of each takeoff, they are so huge that a deviation from the ideal line of action of just a few millimeters might be sufficient to create unmanageable balance problems.

This is particularly likely during the landing at the end of the hop phase when the impact forces are generally larger than at any other time. It is not merely by chance that triple jumps are frequently aborted shortly after the hop landing because athletes are unable to maintain their balance!

Conclusion? *Use of a technique that emphasizes the length of the hop phase increases the likelihood that the athlete will have problems maintaining balance through the subsequent phases.*

THE VELOCITY ARGUMENT

It has been reported many times that elite triple jumpers arrive at the board with less horizontal velocity than elite long jumpers (Miller and Hay, 1986; Nixdorf and Brüggeman, 1987 and Susanka, et al., 1987; Nixdorf and Brüggeman, 1988 and Brüggeman, 1988; Ae, et al., 1994 and Fukashiro, et al., 1994; Hay, 1993). It has also been reported that athletes who double in the two events arrive at the board with less horizontal velocity in the triple jump than in the long jump (Hay, 1994).

These differences are probably due to triple jumpers having to limit the velocity they develop in the approach to what they can handle effectively during the takeoffs to follow. If they run too fast, they may be subject to greater forces on landing at the end of the hop than they can handle and /or they maybe unable to maintain their balance through the remaining phases.

Table 4: Average Approach Velocities for Mike Conley (USA) in Selected Meets.

Meet, Year	Average Velocity of Approach (m/s) (No. of trials over which average computed)	
	Long Jump	Triple Jump
TAC, 1983	11.1 (3)	10.5 (4)
TAC, 1985		10.6 (2)
TAC, 1986		10.8w (3)
TAC, 1987		10.4 (5)
USOT, 1992		11.1 (5)

Data for jumps made by Mike Conley over a period of several years suggest that triple jumpers do not have to limit their approach velocities in this way. In 1983, Conley competed in both the long and triple jumps at the TAC Championships. The average value for the horizontal velocity of his center of gravity at the instant of touchdown at the board (commonly referred to as the *approach velocity*) was 11.1m/s in the long jump and 10.5m/s in the triple jump (Table 4).

In the next several years, his average approach velocity in the triple jump at the same meet remained in the 10.4-10.6m/s range, with the exception of one meet in which strong tailwinds inflated it to 10.8m/s.

All this had changed by the time of the 1992

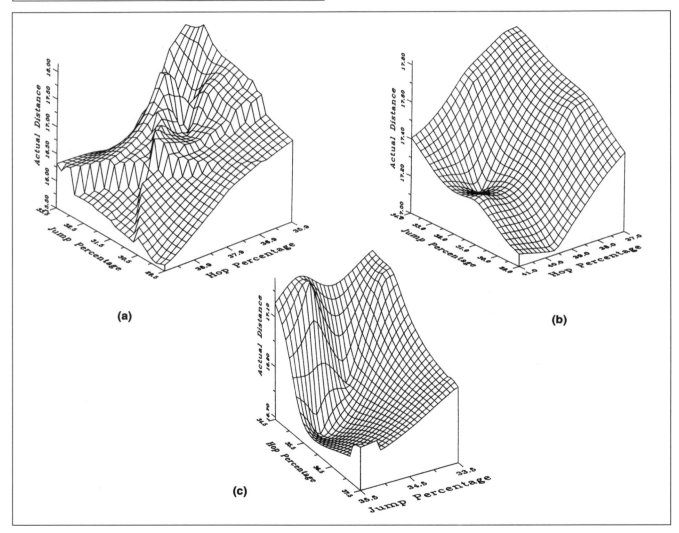

Figure 3: Three-dimensional graphs showing relationships of hop and jump percentages with the actual distance of a triple jump for (a) Charlie Simpkins, (b) Kenny Harrison and (c) John Tillman. The axes for these graphs have been rotated to provide the best view of the three-dimensional figure in each case. As a result, the axes for Tillman differ from those for Simpkins and Harrison.

U.S. Olympic Trials. In this meet, his approach velocity in the triple jump ranged from 11.0-11.3m/s, with an average of 11.1m/s.

What did he do to make this possible? He changed the way in which he distributed his effort through the three phases. After years of using a balanced technique he changed to using a jump-dominated technique. He decreased his hop distance from an average of 6.07m (computed over 14 trials from 1983-1987) to an average of 5.71m (computed over five trials in the U.S. Olympic Trials) and his hop percentage from an average of 35% to an average of 32%.

Conclusion? *Reducing the length of the hop phase appears to permit the use of significantly higher approach velocities.*

Willie Banks

THE PRACTICE ARGUMENT

As persuasive as arguments might be, the ultimate test of new ideas on athletic techniques is how these ideas work out in practice. Do athletes perform better when they use the new techniques or don't they? As is almost always the case, there is little evidence available with which to answer that question in the present instance. But there is some.

The success of de Oliveira, Banks and Conley in using jump-dominated techniques has already been mentioned. Of these, the case of Conley is the most recent and best documented. His relatively late change from using a balanced technique to using a markedly jump-dominated technique was accompanied by successes unattainable previously: gold medals at the 1992 Olympic Games and at the 1993 World Championships and triple jump distances that several times threatened the world record—notably an 18.05m foul at the U.S. Olympic Trials and a marginally wind-aided 18.17m jump at the 1992 Olympic Games.

And there is some further evidence. Figure 3(a) is a three-dimensional plot of Hop Percentage vs. Jump Percentage vs. Actual Distance of the triple jump based on data for 19 trials by Charlie Simpkins

(USA), silver medalist in the triple jump at the 1992 Olympic Games. In almost every one of these trials, Charlie's technique was hop-dominated; and yet the graph shows unmistakably that, within the range of phase percentages included (that is, from 36% to 38% for the hop, and from 30% to 34% for the jump), the shorter the hop and the longer the jump, the better was the distance of the triple jump.

Figures 3(b) and (c) show, respectively, the corresponding data for eight trials by Kenny Harrison; and for six trials by John Tillman, 1992 U.S. Olympian. In every one of these trials, the athlete's technique was hop-dominated; and, within the ranges of the phase ratios shown in each graph, the shorter the hop and the longer the jump phase, the better was the distance of the triple jump.

In short, the results show that for every one of these athletes, the more he gravitated towards a balanced or a jump-dominated technique, the farther he jumped.

Conclusion? *Although they have used hop-dominated techniques for many years, some of the world's best triple jumpers still jump farther when they use*

---

* Phase data for the medalists in the women's event at the 1992 U.S. Olympic Trials (Hay, unpublished data) and in the 1993 World Championships in Stuttgart (Kiyomi Ueya, Yamanashi University, personal communication, 1994) indicate that elite male and female athletes are alike in this regard. All of these athletes used hop-dominated or balanced techniques.

shorter hop distances and longer jump distances than is normal for them. In other words, even athletes of this caliber tend to over-hop.

A FINAL THOUGHT

In a hop-dominated technique, the jumper lands from the longest phase on one foot on the hard, synthetic surface of the runway. In a jump-dominated technique, the jumper lands from the longest phase on two feet in the sand of a landing pit. If you were a triple jumper faced with the choice, would you prefer to land from your longest phase on one foot or two? On a hard surface or a soft one?

CONCLUSION

Although jump-dominated techniques have been used only rarely by elite triple jumpers*, the arguments presented here suggest that such techniques are deserving of much more consideration than they have received. At the very least, the case for using a jump-dominated technique seems to be sufficiently persuasive to suggest that coaches and athletes should explore thoroughly the possible benefits of a jump-dominated technique.

What should an athlete do to change from a hop-dominated or balanced technique to a jump-dominated technique? Conversations with Dick Booth (coach of Mike Conley), recent research on arm actions in the triple jump (Yu, 1994) and some simple logic suggest the following:

(a) Emphasize running off the board. Avoid the pronounced lowering of the center of gravity in the penultimate support phase that is characteristic of a long jump takeoff, and emphasize maintaining velocity through the takeoff.

(b) Aim to stay low during the flight phase of the hop. Emphasize running (or driving) forward rather than upward at takeoff. Keep the angle of takeoff low.

(c) Use an alternating arm action at the hop and step takeoffs (to maintain horizontal velocity) and a double-arm action at the jump takeoff (to generate vertical velocity).

(d) Use a strongly active landing at the end of the hop phase to maintain horizontal velocity.

REFERENCES

Ae, M., Fukashiro, S., Yamanoto, E., Ito, N. and Saito, N., (1994). Biomechanical analysis of the takeoff techniques of men's triple jump, in Sasaki, H., Kobayashi, K. and Ae, M. (ed.), *Techniques of the World's Best Track and Field Athletes* (Japanese), Baseball Magazine Co. Ltd, Tokyo, 152-166.

Amadio, A.C. (1985) *Biomechanische Analyse des Dreisprungs.* Doctoral dissertation. Deutsche Sporthochschule, Köln.

Brüggeman, G-P. (1988). Biomechanical analysis of the triple jump—an approach towards a biomechanical profile of the world's best triple jumpers. *New Studies in Athletics* (Scientific Research Project at the Games of the XXIVth Olympiad—Seoul 1988), 303-362.

Fukashiro, S., Wakayama, A., Ito, N., Arai, T., Iiboshi, A., Fuchimoto, T. and Tan, H.P., (1994). Biomechanical analysis of the long jump, in Sasaki, H., Kobayashi, K. and Ae, M. (ed.) *Techniques of the World's Best Track and Field Athletes* (Japanese), Baseball Magazine Co. Ltd, Tokyo, 135-151.

Hay, J.G., (1990). The biomechanics of triple jump techniques, in *Techniques in Athletics Congress Proceedings* (ed. G-P. Brüggeman and J.K. Ruhl), Cologne, Federal Republic of Germany: Deutsche Sporthochschule Köln, 1:296-308.

Hay, J.G., (1992). The biomechanics of the triple jump: a review, *Journal of Sports Sciences*, 10:343-378.

Hay, J.G., (1993). Citius, altius, longius (faster, higher, longer): the biomechanics of jumping for distance, *Journal of Biomechanics*, 26 (S1): 7-21.

Hay, J.G., (1994). Effort distribution in the triple jump *Track Technique*, 127:4042-4048.

Hill, G., (1993). Conley's technique, *Track & Field News*, 46(11): 31.

McNab, T. (1977). *Triple Jump*, 7, British Amateur Athletic Board, London.

Miller, J.A. and Hay, J.G. (1986). Kinematics of a world record and other world-class performances in the triple jump, *International Journal of Sport Biomechanics*, 2, 272-288.

Nixdorf, E. and Brüggeman, G.P. (1987) Biomechanical analysis of the long jump, *International Athletic Foundation Scientific Report on the II World Championships in Athletics, Rome 1987.* International Athletic Foundation, London.

Nixdorf, E. and Brüggeman, G-P. (1988). Biomechanical analysis of the long jump—an approach toward a biomechanical profile of the world's best long jumpers. *New Studies in Athletics* (Scientific Research Project at the Games of the XXIVth Olympiad—Seoul 1988), 263-301.

Ramey, M.R. and Williams, K.R. (1986). Ground reaction forces in the triple jump, *International Journal of Sport Biomechanics*, 1, 233-239.

Starzynski, T. (1987). *Le Triple-saut.*, Editions VIGOT, Paris.

Susanka, P., Jurdik, M., Koukal, J., Krátky, P. and Velebil, V. (1987). Biomechanical analysis of the triple jump. *International Athletic Foundation Scientific Report on the II World Championships in Athletics, Rome 1987.* International Athletic Foundation, London.

Yu, B. (1993). *The actions of the free limbs and their relationsips with performance in the triple jump.* Ph.D. dissertation, University of Iowa.

The Keys To Jonathan Edwards' Success

By Vitold Kreyer, Russia

Former world record holder Vitold Kreyer takes a close look at the technique of Jonathan Edwards, analyzes his record-breaking performances and provides some comments on Edwards' training.

INTRODUCTORY REMARKS

Jonathan Edwards (height 181cm, weight 71kg) was born on May 10, 1966 in London. He is married with two children. Edwards began triple jumping at the age of 17 and his training has been guided since 1968 by British National Coach Carl Johnson.

Looking at Edwards' triple jump career reveals that that he failed to qualify at the 1988 Olympics in Seoul and again at the 1992 Barcelona Games. His amazing breakthrough that shocked the world came in 1995 when the British star produced 18.43 (+2.4m/s) and 18.39m (+3.4m/s) performances in Lille and followed it up with 14 competitions over 12 weeks that included six attempts over the 18m barrier.

Observing Edwards' behaviour during competitions reveals that he is virtually always in motion, sitting down only to change spikes. His preparation for the next jump begins seven to eight minutes ahead of his turn. The preparation being with a series of high-step jumps, followed by walking with emphasized arm action and a few stretching exercises. It is also interesting to note that during this short preparation Edwards never wears tracksuit pants. He walks around, concentrating mainly on the strength and direction of the wind.

COMPUTER IN THE BUSHES

We are looking and analyzing Edwards' second attempt at the World Championships in Göteburg in 1995. Although not as informative as the actual video recording, it nevertheless provides ample information on the technique of the world record holder, whose 18.29m jump at the Worlds hardly differs technique-wise from his much shorter performances.

Runup + Takeoff + Hop (18 strides, 6.33m + 10cm)

As can be seen from the frames 3 to 5 in the action sequence, Edwards approaches the takeoff board without speed losses) reaching a velocity of 10.52m/s at the takeoff stride. His last strides are active and rhythmical without any obvious preparation for the takeoff. The takeoff foot is actively placed on the board at an angle of 66° and a fast forward drive of the hip helps to produce a takeoff time of 0.112 sec.

The above movement structure (frames 5 to 7) leave no doubt that the aim is to produce a fast and long hop, projected at a low angle and made possible by the 10.52m/s velocity and a stressed hip movement of hips and arms. That hip movement, according to Coach Johnson, receives special attention in training.

Hop + Step (6.33m + 10cm, 5.22m)

Frames 6 to 10 clearly demonstrate the benefits of Edwards' hips movement that reaches 110° and his wide "reach" of 57cm from the body's center of gravity. His takeoff leg, after a 10.52m/s velocity, is rapidly catapulted forward to land rolling over the heel to toes.

The takeoff into the step (frames 20 to 23) begins with an energetic double-arm action that according to some authorities is preferred to a single-

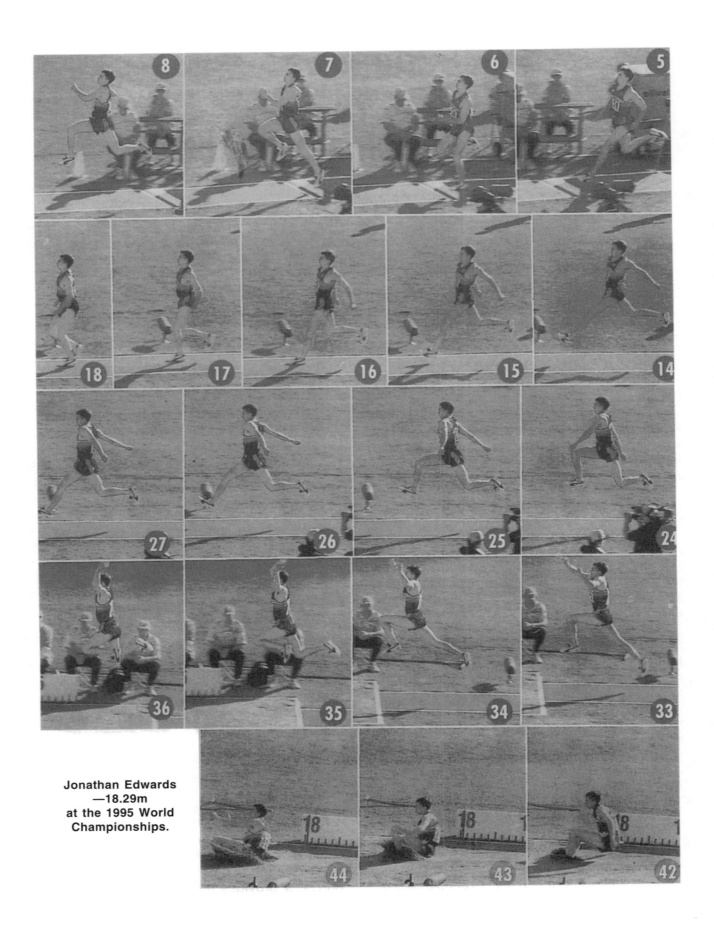

Jonathan Edwards
—18.29m
at the 1995 World
Championships.

arm movement. An excellent upright body position without a noticeable lowering of the hips allows Edwards to execute another effective takeoff, reducing the velocity only slightly to 8.5m/s. This makes it possible to reach an unbelievable 6.74m in the jump phase.

Step + Jump (5.22m, 6.74m)

Edwards makes no preparation for the execution of the last takeoff into the jump, which is reflected by the takeoff time of t = 0.132sec. It should be noted here the similarity of the three decisive moments of his takeoffs (Frames 6, 17, 29). All demonstrate only a slight drop of the hips in the amortization of the knee joint within 30 to 35°.

The jump in itself, although performed using a rather simple action, succeeds because of the remaining 8.5m/s. takeoff velocity, an active lead leg, an upright upper body and a high position of the forward stretched legs at the landing (frames 32 to 40).

ADDITIONAL ANALYSIS

In continuing our analysis it is interesting to note first that Edwards apparently doesn't believe the biomechanical data released by Leif Dahlberg's group on his 18.29m jump. The data showed a runup velocity of 9.8m/s up to 6m before the takeoff board that increased to 11.9m/s over the last 5m. Is this believable?

There is also conflicting information on the distribution of the three triple jump phases in different performances by Edwards. According to the French journal *Athletisme* his wind-assisted 18.43m effort in Lille was composed of 6.78m + 5.60m + 6.05m (37 + 30 + 33%). The corresponding measurements made in his Göteborg winning jump of 18.29m, made from toes to heel, instead of toes to toes, showed a distribution of 6.05m + 5.22m + 7.02m (33.1 + 28.5 + 38.4%)

The most reliable distribution to the author appears to be the version published by German sport scientists on Edwards' third place effort at the World Championships in Stuttgart in 1993. His fifth jump was composed of:

17.44m (+0. 1 m/s) = 6.53m + 4.93m + 5.99m
(37.5% + 28.2% + 34.3%)
- reactivity times (t): 0. 11 - 0. 12 - 0. 15 sec.
- velocity losses (Vh): 0.58 - 0.42 - 0.72m/s

All the above leaves an impression that the "computer in the bushes," responsible for the recording of Edwards' movement structures, trajectories, distribution of distances and runup velocities, can either make mistakes or the athlete himself makes changes according to conditions.

KEYS TO TRAINING

Looking at Edwards' training in 1995, published by his coach Johnson, reveals that he followed a liberally performed microcycles system. The preparation period in a traditionally periodized method appeared to be a little short, lasting 29 weeks. Fast sprinting begins in the fourth week, triple jumping from a 10-stride runup in March, increased gradually to 16 strides and finally to the full 18-stride approach. Training was basically structured so that every fourth week in a month was set aside for recovery and testing.

All this is understandable and follows universally accepted principles. However, what is rather hard to understand is how Edwards managed to produce his exceptional performances after a long virus infection late in 1994. His amazing wind-assisted 18.43m jump in Lille took place on the 170th day after the infection. It can only be assumed that Edwards somehow managed to preserve his performance capacity by a sharp general preparation after recovery. However, even if this is true, we can only wonder at the results.

Further information presented by Coach Johnson indicates that Edwards' training in April and May during his sensational year was made up of 5 to 6 workouts a week, 18 to 20 a month. While this in the pre-season training phase can be regarded as normal, far more interesting facts appear in the test results, some rather conflicting when the development of strength and speed strength is compared with the development of speed.

Here are some examples. During the general physical preparation phase in 1993 Edwards executed 60-63 repetitions of half-squats in 60 seconds. In 1995 he had improved to 72 to 73 repetitions. The same applies to leg raises in a hanging position, where he improved from 37 to 50 repetitions, and the standing long jump. It is interesting to note here that Edwards improved his maximal half-squat in 1994 to 235kg before this exercise was eliminated from his program.

In other speed strength tests Edwards' improvements included the snatch (from 85kg in 1994 to 105kg just after his 17.46m performance in 1995), in the clean (from 122.5kg in 1994 to 132.5kg in

1995), and in the overhead shot throw (14.30m to 15.30m) during the same time period. Considering that weight training was included into Edwards' program three times a week the improvements are acceptable but not exceptional.

In contrast, the improvements in speed development are far from impressive. Edwards improved in the 30m sprint from 3.68sec. in 1994 to 3.54sec. in May 1995. In the 60m sprint he was clocked 6.94sec. in training 10 days prior his 18.43m jump. In a second test on the same day he reached 6.74sec., made up of 4.00sec. plus 2.76 sec. This means that he developed a velocity of 10.86m/s in the second half of the distance.

Finally, the most specific test—the triple jump. In 1995 Edwards reached 16.10m from a 10-stride runup, 16.70m from a 14-stride runup and 16.60 from a full (18 strides) approach in testing. However, it has been mentioned that Edwards once succeeded in jumping over 17m from a 12-stride runup.

IN CONCLUSION

According to Johnson, the key that opens an athlete's performance capacity is 30% neurological. To make it possible to control and concentrate on neuromuscular effort requires:
- a simultaneous recruitment of the maximal number of muscle fibers;
- an improved nervous regulation system;
- the development of elastic strength;
- the avoidance of muscular hypertrophy.

Fine, but how can we explain what happened to Edwards in the 1996 Olympic year. It simply was not the same Edwards we had observed a year earlier. True, he still produced technically excellent jumps and enjoyed an uninterrupted preparation for the Atlanta Games. There were no health problems, but Edwards failed to reach 18m in a series of starts in May and June. His performances ranged from 17.39m to 17.80m.

Then came Atlanta where Edwards failed to reach the qualification standard but made the final with a 16.96m jump, sufficient to be placed in the first 12. He began the final with two fouls but somehow managed to produce a 17.88m effort for the silver medal, despite a rather technically poor jump.

How can we explain the differences in Edwards' performances in 1995 and 1996? It appears that his phenomenal performances in the virus-infected 1995 resulted from what is in the coaching terminology known as the "lack of training" syndrome, which occurs mainly in either early or late developed athletes. Is the last applicable to Edwards, taking into consideration that he was virtually unknown until his 17.44m performance in the 1993 world titles in Stuttgart?

The Triple Jump

By Dean Hayes, USA

An outline of the main technique factors in the performance of the triple jump, followed by recommended training programs and drills, as well as some step-by-step advice on the development of beginners.

The triple jump is a unique event requiring a combination of speed, strength, and balance. It is composed of three distinct phases (parts) that must flow into one another. They are the hop (takeoff and landing on the same foot), the step, and the jump (performed similar to the long jump). The hop and jump are relatively easy to master but the step is a difficult skill. The triple jump was formerly called the hop, step and jump but was changed to emphasize the equal importance of each phase.

Triple jump performances in the United States lagged behind the rest of the world for a number of years, until 1976 when the United States had six jumpers over 55 feet in the Olympic Trials. The European countries and Brazil have been major areas of triple jumping because soccer is a major sport in these countries and the athletes are accustomed to using the legs and feet. Our program in the United States must specially promote triple jumping in order to be competitive with the rest of the world.

Triple jumpers must possess above-average ability in sprinting and jumping, and at the same time possess powerful muscles and good motor skills. The program discussed in this chapter is both for the beginning and advanced jumper. Discussion is divided into technique, drills, weight lifting and training routines.

The 1995 World Championships in Sweden saw two barriers broken. Jonathan Edwards set the world record at over 60 feet and Inessa Kravets jumped more than 50 feet.

THE APPROACH

The triple jump approach should be long enough to allow the jumper to accelerate to nearly full speed. At the same time, the approach must be relaxed so that the athlete is under control. If the approach is too slow the jumper will lose momentum in the later phases of the event. If it is too fast the jumper will be unable to control the legs and keep them from collapsing.

The length of the run should be about 100 feet to 130 feet. The beginning jumper's approach should be approximately 100 feet. As the jumper gains experience and maturity the approach can be lengthened.

Beginning jumpers may wish to use a check mark along the latter part of the approach. As the jumper gains experience he may prefer using only the beginning mark. The jumper should practice his approach until he is consistent. Approach steps should be worked on just before the competitive season begins.

THE HOP

The first phase of the triple jump is the hop and the first part of the hop is the takeoff. The objective in the hop is to go forward and up (not up and forward as in the long jump). This is accomplished by keeping the body upright and rotating the heel of the hop leg high up under the buttocks and then extending it as far forward as possible. The idea is for the athlete to feel that he is "running off the board." Remind the jumper to stay upright and not lean forward, as the leaning makes it difficult to bring the leg up for the next phase.

There are three methods of arm action: single, double, and a combination. The combination usually is a single-arm hop and double-arm step and jump. The double arm begins in the last step before the jumper begins the action to get his arms in place for the takeoff. The athlete stops the arm that is going back. He stops it at the hip on the takeoff, and then lets it go forward with the other arm so that both arms go forward as the leg rotates under the buttocks.

Do not allow the athlete's hands to go higher than the chin. If the arms are driven too high the foot will come down too hard and too fast. A great number of jumpers draw both arms behind the back about 1½ steps before the takeoff board and this is acceptable for beginners, but after some experience it is better if the jumper can change to the previously discussed method. Pulling both arms back tends to slow down the approach just before the board and the loss of speed at this point hinders the flow of the other phases.

The selection of the method of arm use should be based upon the speed of the athlete. The fast athlete can utilize the double-arm method, the average speed jumper can use whichever method is most comfortable and the slow athlete usually can best utilize single-arm action. The coach and athlete should experiment and use the method best suited for their purpose. The rule stated above is only a guide.

The single-arm method is simply a running motion off the board as if the jumper is taking one more step, only the "running step" is a hop.

In the hop, the leg should be pulled through for extension and as the foot is about to land it should be flattened so that the jumper can "roll" over his foot into the next phase. If the jumper lands on his toes, it interrupts the speed and flow and if he lands on his heel it can cause heel bruises. Also, a "heel landing" makes it more difficult to control the forward movement. The landing should be very slightly on the heel, then a "rolling" action of the foot.

THE STEP

Just before the hop is finished the arms are pulled back again in preparation for the step phase—the second phase of the triple jump. The step is accomplished by bringing the other leg (opposite of the hop leg) forward. The jumper should strive to get the upper leg perpendicular to the body (hip area) or parallel to the ground. The arms come forward if double-arm action is utilized. If the single arm is used, the opposite arm goes forward as in running. Again the arm(s) should not go higher than the chin.

There are two methods of executing the step. One method is to keep the body upright and the upper body basically perpendicular to the ground. The upper leg is parallel to the ground and the lower leg is positioned so that the toes are just ahead of the knee. This is done so the jumper can "ride" the leg or hold it up. At the last instant, the jumper extends the leg and reaches out as far as possible. This extension is aided by pulling the arms back to prepare for double-arm action in the jump phase. Again, the foot should hit the ground almost flat-footed. The heel "barely" leads the action.

The other method for "stepping" is to let the lower leg extend ahead of the knee during the step. This requires the upper chest and head to be stooped slightly forward in a effort to hold the foot up. As the foot is extended or held forward, the arms are drawn behind the back to prepare for the jump phase.

THE JUMP

As the jump phase is initiated the arms are interchanged if the single-arm style is used. If the double-arm style is used the arms are pulled through with a punch and the jumper executes a style similar to the long jumper. Generally a hang style jump is used because there is not enough time for a hitch-kick.

The jumper should try to get as high as possible. Both arms used in the hang style as they reach up and then extend forward. The feet are extended so that the heels lead the way into the pit.

TRAINING PROGRAM

The training program used is the most important factor in the success of a triple jumper. The program that follows should be utilized in its entirety. Leaving out one segment will hinder the effectiveness of the program. A good conditioning base is important and development of the leg and arm skills is necessary. The drills must be done over and over so that they become second-nature and are automatic.

The triple jumper must develop "thinking feet." Try to put forth a special effort to develop the parts of the program where the jumper is weakest. Triple jumpers must train regularly and aggressively in order to compete successfully. A well trained jumper does not leave his jumps on the practice field.

Early Season: Utilize lots of volume running such as 8 x 300 meters, 10 x 200 meters, or 6 x 400 meters. Use a long grass run of 5 miles at least once per week. Do an abundance of hill running and stretching. The jumper must be in good physical condition before the beginning of the regular training program. The triple jump is very tough, physically.

Early Season (Fall) Weekly Training Schedule

Monday	Grass run (3-5 miles)
	100-200-300-400-200-100/jog same
	Weights
Tuesday	10 x 200 with 200 interval
	Run stadium steps with weight jacket
	Do easy takeoff drills (just to get the arm technique)
Wednesday	8 x 300 with 300 interval
	6 x 75 easy
	Weights
Thursday	Grass Run
	Run Stadium steps
	Takeoff Drill
Friday	Grass Run
	Weights.

In-Season Weekly Training Schedule

Here is the workout schedule for the remainder of the year. Variation in this routine is dictated by faults or weaknesses found in the jumper's technique. Skip one weight training session before each big meet such as the conference or state meet. The same is true for bench workouts.

Monday:
(1) Bounding: 3 x 25 to 100 meters of hopping. Use the regular hopping leg twice and the other leg once. If the athlete is having trouble making the transition from one phase to the other, use 3 x 50 meters of R-R-L-L-R-R as this incorporates the bounding and adds practice of changing from the hop to the step. Also, this drill helps to improve the capabilities of each leg.
(2) Running: 2 x 300 meters for endurance; 6 x 75 meters for speed.
(3) Weight Lifting: This will be discussed later.

Tuesday: This a "drill" day.
(1) Bench work. Do six good drills of each of the three exercises. The drills will be discussed in detail later.

(2) Run 10 x 3 low hurdles set at high hurdle spacing (10 yards between). This is for rhythm and evenness of steps on the runway. It also teaches aggressiveness.
(3) Run 6 x 100 meters or work on the actual approach.
(4) Run stadium steps 5 times. If steps are not available, use a hill.
(5) This is a good day to practice the actual triple jump takeoff. This is done at a reduced speed, but correct techniques are stressed, especially the correct arm action.

Wednesday:
The same basic program as Monday, but use running of 5 x 35 meters and 5 x 50 meters.

Thursday:
The same workout as Tuesday.

Friday:
Same as Monday except much more relaxed and easy.

BENCH DRILLS

The following three drills are the core of the triple jump training program. These drills help the jumper to learn to do each phase of the triple jump correctly. At the same time, the drills give the jumper the thrill of competing. The drills emphasize each phase and the movement from one phase to another.

In the first drill the benches are 12 inches high. The jumper "bounces up" on to the bench and then drives off. The sequence of this drill is hop-step-hop-step-hop-jump. The drill can be reversed so that both legs are developed equally.

The second drill aids in developing the step phase and encourages a "bounce" action. The step between benches is a real "jump step." The legs can be reversed in this drill, too.

In the third drill, the real jump foot is the left foot. This is a pop-up drill. It requires only a short run and therefore does not fatigue the jumper. Actually, a five-step approach can be used for all the drills.

Each of the drills ends with the jump phase into the landing pit. The heels lead the jumper into the pit.

WEIGHT TRAINING

Weight training is a major portion of the triple jumper's training routine. Proper lifting techniques should be followed. The athlete should begin with a very light weight and increase the weight gradually. Lifting weights regularly is important and should be done at least three times a week. As training progresses workouts should become more intense. Athletes should not be totally exhausted. If the weight workout is too difficult, the athlete's jumping workouts will be adversely affected.

The following is a weight routine recommended for triple jumpers:

Knee Extensions—3 sets of 10 repetitions
Leg Curls—3 sets of 10 repetitions
Incline Sit-Ups—3 sets of 15 repetitions
Leg Presses—4 sets of 10, 7, 4, 2 repetitions
Toe Raises—3 sets of 20 repetitions (using a 2" x 4" under the toes)
Half-squats—3 sets of 8 repetitions (use one-half of body weight)
Split Squats—2 sets of 10 repetitions (use one-fourth of body weight)
*Note: Half-squats and split squats are coordinated in two-week periods. Squats are done M-F-W and split squats are done W-M-F.
Knee Raises—3 sets of 15 repetitions
Step-Ups—3 sets of 10 repetitions with heavy weight.

The following guidelines should be followed in the weight lifting program for jumpers.
1. Lift every other day.
2. Alternately work the upper body and lower body during workouts.
3. Wear a weight belt for heavy lifting.
4. Lift in a group. Athletes must help each other. Besides the safety factor, this adds incentive to "lift more with less effort."
5. Do not increase the poundage too quickly.
6. Periodically schedule a testing session in which maximum lifts are utilized to test increases in strength.
7. It is best to use "free weights" in training because balance is learned and stress is put on the athlete through a greater range of motion. Weight machines are recommended for younger athletes or large groups since poundages can be easily changed.
8. It is necessary for the jumper to stretch and loosen up before the weight workout.

THE BEGINNING TRIPLE JUMPER

The triple jump is an unnatural event and should be introduced to the prospective jumper by watching films to get a quick preview of the event. Film study should be followed by a brief demonstration of a standing triple jump emphasizing the leg movements only. Instruct the prospective jumper to do a few standing triple jumps.

Jumps should be done with each leg to decide which is most comfortable. Empasize an even distance for each phase, and don't allow the athlete to go for "distance."

Instead, stress the learning of the leg movements in each of the three phases. Instruct the athlete to hop, step, and jump and land flat-footed, not on the toes. Landing on the toes causes the jumper to lose forward speed and is very hard on the legs.

Although a beginner will probably have problems with the flow of the triple jump it will "begin to come" after a few attempts. "Flow" is the bounce or rhythm that is so important to good triple jumping. It gives the jumper the exhilarating feeling of flying through the air.

If the jumper does not try to extend this reach too far he can keep the jump under control and feel encouraged about his progress. Also, this will keep him from leaning too far forward during the jump and give him time to have an active "phase leg."

The phase leg should be developed next by having the jumper stand on one leg and jump up making the standing leg rotate under the buttocks and reach out in front before landing. The athlete should alternate legs for this drill so that coordination is developed in both legs.

Of the three triple jump phases, the step is the most difficult to master. The hop is relatively easy to perform but the recovery is difficult. The athlete usually will no have problems learning the basics of the jump phase. The greatest triple jump improvement will be achieved through improvement of the step. However, one must remember that each phase is dependent on the others.

The next stage of development for the beginner comes trough bounding drills. These drills should be done for control rather than for strength in the beginning. Later, strength (endurance) can be included.

Three main drills are used in this stage. The first dill is a hopping drill. This should be done with both legs (R-R-R-R...or L-L-L-L...). As the jumper becomes stronger and more confident the distance is increased. Check to be sure that the jumper's body is upright throughout the hopping. It is recommended that beginners do two sets of 25 meters of hopping on Monday, Wednesday and Friday (3 days week).

The second drill is a step drill. This is R-L-R-L-R. . . Again, emphasize the upright body and "bounce" in the legs. The beginner just reaches out as far as he can, being careful not to lead with the toes. The landing is flat-footed, with a "pawing" action just before the foot strikes the ground.

The third drill is helpful to the jumper in changing from the hop to the step. The drill is R-R-L-L-R. . . The coach should watch the jumper perform these drills. Also, it is beneficial if two or more jumpers work together as the competition tends to make the jumpers run faster and stretch farther. The triple jumper works on the jump phase by doing pop-ups just like the long jumper. The pop-up should be performed, since the time in the air is too short for a good hitch-kick.

The next step in developing the beginner is to incorporate a short run with the jump. This can be accomplished with the use of two drills. The first drill is running over low hurdles. This is done at least twice a week. The hurdles should be spaced at high hurdle distance and "three-stepped."

Also, the athlete should attempt to jump the hurdle with a one- and a three-step approach. This gives some speed but not enough to cause a total breakdown of the step phase. Emphasize a "level flight" during each phase by keeping the body upright. If the jumper gets too high in a phase, it causes the landing leg to break down and curtail momentum for the next phase.

The next step in developing a triple jumper is deciding what type of arm action should be used. Single-arm action and double-arm action are the possibilities. In single-arm action, the jumper alternates the arms with the leg which is utilized in each phase. In the double-arm motion, both arms go forward each time a leg goes forward until the final part of the jump phase. Some jumpers use single arm in the hop to maintain speed, and use a double arm in the step and jump.

During the triple jump, the athlete should not look down toward the ground. This tends to pull the body forward and down and makes it impossible to lift the knee high during the last two phases. Stress "riding the knee" by getting the upper leg in a position of 90 degrees to the body.

At this stage, the athlete should be ready to attempt the complete triple jump. Start with a seven-step approach (under control) and stress the hop phases with an easy step and jump included. The distance of the hop should be relatively short so it does not cause the jumper to break down. The athlete should avoid getting too much height because this causes a jarring effect and can lead to a breakdown, too. The head should be level, with the eyes focused straight ahead. The athlete should attempt to go through the complete triple jump to learn extension in each of the three phases.

The final phase of instruction is to lengthen the approach. A distance of about 120 feet should be adequate. Use a controlled run to begin with and increase the speed as the athlete is able to utilize it.

TRIPLE JUMP DRILLS

Standing Triple Jump. The athlete faces the pit and places a mark 20-50 feet from the pit. From the mark, the jumper does a standing triple jump and lands in the pit. Next, mark off the hop distance, the step distance, and the jump distance. Concentrate on knee drive for the hop and step and arm action (both arms driving) for the jump. The distance should be about 8-10 feet for the hop, 11-13 feet for the step, and 12-15 feet for the jump. Anything between 30 and 38 feet is a good distance for beginners for men. Women should be proportional.

Hurdle Hopping. Place four to eight low or intermediate hurdles about five to six feet apart. The jumper, with the aid of the double-arm upswing, leaps over the hurdles with both legs together and with the knees brought up to the chest in order to clear the hurdle. As strength increases, the height and the number of hurdles can be increased. Adjustments of hurdle height and distance between the hurdles can be made for individual jumpers. Beginners will likely have difficulty with the intermediate hurdles.

Split Squat. This is a squat jump in which the legs are alternated. Disregard arm action because it is not a triple jump action. Bring front knee up close to about a 90-degree angle with a slight bend in the back leg. Then alternate legs.

Double-Leg Jumps. Drive off both legs with the use of the knees and ankles. As soon as the jumper is off the ground, the left knee is driven up as high as possible, beyond parallel. Landing is on both feet. Settle down and drive back up this time, lifting the right knee as high as possible. Keep the foot under the knee while using arms vigorously.

Hopping. Stay on the same leg with a single-arm action (unless double-arm action is used). As the jumper lifts off the jumping leg, he brings the thigh to parallel and as it returns to the ground, the opposite knee comes, from the behind (split) position, forward as it would in the step phase.

Safety and Equipment

Triple jumpers should use light, durable shoes with heel cups inserted in them. Constant pounding and landing on the heels requires the use of heel cups if bruises and injuries are to be avoided.

The Competitive Experience and Attitude

The season itself is just a means to test the progress of a jumper. If the jumper also long jumps it is probably best to take only three long jumps and three triple jumps, if both are on the same day. If the jumper gets a big personal best, it is usually better to skip the next jump so that the jumper can get his mind back together. Also, train as regularly as possible and only ease up in training two to four practice sessions before the event that is the "goal" of the year. Your aim is to do your best, not to worry about your place.

With solid practice habits you should feel confident in your ability to do your best. Pick a goal of being your best in a certain meet, not how far you jump. Remember to work on the parts of the jump that give you the most trouble. Repeating the things you can do well doesn't give you the help you need. Practice hard so you know you are ready.

This material has been made available through the courtesy of Championship Books & Video Productions, Ames, Iowa, USA.